FRIENDLY *FIRE*

OTHER BOOKS BY THE AUTHORS

Redemption: The Myth of Pet Overpopulation and the No Kill Revolution in America
Irreconcilable Differences: The Battle for the Heart and Soul of America's Animal Shelters
All American Vegan: Veganism for the Rest of Us

REDEMPTION

AWARDS
USA Book News, Best Book
Independent Book Publishers Association, Silver Medal
Cat Writers Association of America, Best Book

PRAISE
"A gripping story, told by an iconoclast determined to make a difference." —*Seth Godin*

"*Redemption* is a passionate advocacy for ending the killing of homeless dogs and cats in shelters. Telling the story of how the movement of animal sheltering in the United States was born of compassion, and lost its way... *Redemption* offers hope that America can yet change its ways. Highly recommended." — *Midwest Book Review*

"An important work." —*The Bark*

"Within its pages, readers and animal lovers can find the blueprint not so much for our failure to save the animals in our communities, but for our ability to start doing so today." —*San Francisco Chronicle*

"I cannot remember any work that has so dramatically altered my point of view on any subject— nor another book that has me so excited to think of what real reform can do to save the lives of shelter pets." —*Pet Connection*

"A unique and important book." —*Library Journal*

"For anyone who has ever loved an animal, this book, like no other non-fiction, takes you through the full spectrum of emotions: from sadness to anger, from fear to hope. But redemption? That is ultimately left up to each and every one of us." —*Air America Radio*

"[E]very former, current or future pet owner [should] read and think about this book. It will inspire you to respect and help our animal friends in a positive, supportive and loving way." —*Vacaville Reporter*

"[An] excellent, empowering new book." —*Fetchdog*

IRRECONCILABLE DIFFERENCES

AWARDS
Independent Book Publishers Association, Bronze Medal

PRAISE
"The world owes much to those rare individuals who see things differently—and who then devote themselves to vindicating their maverick conclusions." —*The Bark*

"The perfect follow-up to Winograd's outstanding first book *Redemption*." —*Animal Wise Radio*

ALL AMERICAN VEGAN

AWARDS
USA Book News, Best Book

PRAISE
"For anyone who has thoughts about switching to a vegan diet this book is compulsory reading material. Illustrated with full-color comic strip-like, very humorous drawings, and equally entertaining, sometimes hilarious text, this book is a pleasure to read." —*San Francisco Book Review*

"Fast food fans will find plenty to tempt their palates... vegan substitutes are quick, easy and irresistible." —*Contra Costa Times*

"*All American Vegan* is a guide to animal-free cooking that manages to be your standard American cooking. Just without that meat stuff. Emphasizing the power of substitution and that going vegan is easier when a meat eater can keep eating their favorite foods, the authors offer plenty of typical vegan food that is far from what is associated with the bizarre and foreign things often thumped by hippies and what comes to mind when one thinks vegan." —*Midwest Book Review*

FRIENDLY FIRE

NATHAN & JENNIFER WINOGRAD

First Edition

Cover and original interior illustrations:
Jennifer Winograd

All other interior illustrations:
iStockphoto.com

Printed in the United States of America

TO ANIMAL RESCUERS NATIONWIDE who—with small budgets but big hearts—provide our nation's homeless animals with the kindness, devotion and lifesaving that most shelters and animal protection groups refuse to.

"I hate to think what will befall this Society when I am gone."

HENRY BERGH
1813-1888
Founder, The American Society for the Prevention of Cruelty to Animals (ASPCA)

THE HUMANE SOCIETY OF THE UNITED STATES

THE AMERICAN SOCIETY FOR THE PREVENTION OF CRUELTY TO ANIMALS

THE AMERICAN HUMANE ASSOCIATION

PEOPLE FOR THE ETHICAL TREATMENT OF ANIMALS

CHAMPIONING SHELTER KILLING
THWARTING SHELTER REFORM

W H Y ?

TO THE READER

ACROSS THE UNITED STATES TODAY, 90 million cats and 75 million dogs share our homes and are cherished members of our families. We talk to them, keep their pictures in our wallets, celebrate their birthdays, travel with them and greet them upon coming home even before saying hello to the spouse and kids. We include them in holiday celebrations and take time off from work to care for them when they get sick. And when it is time to say goodbye, we grieve.

Every year, we spend more than 50 billion dollars on our animal companions. And we donate hundreds of millions of dollars more to charities that promise to help animals, with the largest of these having annual budgets in excess of 100 million dollars. In fact, giving to animal related causes is the fastest growing segment in American philanthropy. In a national poll, 96 percent of Americans—*almost every single person surveyed*—said we have a moral duty to protect animals and we should have strong laws to do so, while over half have changed their lifestyle to protect animals and their habitats.

Most Americans today hold the humane treatment of animals as a personal value, reflected in our laws, the proliferation of organizations founded for animal protection, increased per capita spending on animal care and great advancements in veterinary medicine. By contrast, the agencies that the public expects to protect animals—our local animal "shelters"*—are killing roughly four million of them annually. And for far too long, we have been told that the killing is exclusively the public's fault; that shelters are merely performing the public's dirty work, with skill, compassion and dedication.

Many people believe that animal shelters find homes for as many animals as they can, and gently "euthanize" the rest because there is no other choice. Many people believe that if there were alternatives, shelters would not kill because they are staffed with benevolent animal lovers, laboring against overwhelming odds and offering a "humane death" only when necessary.

These shelters and their large national allies—the Humane Society of the United States (HSUS), the American Society for the Prevention of Cruelty to Animals (ASPCA), the American Humane Association (AHA) and People for the Ethical Treatment of Animals (PETA)—encourage this belief. Accordingly, they claim that leadership and staff at every one of these agencies "have a passion for and are dedicated to the mutual goal of saving animals' lives" (see page 61).

It is this portrayal that has historically silenced criticism of shelters, the vast majority of which have a paltry number of adoptions and staggeringly high rates of killing. In fact, shelter killing is the leading cause of death for healthy dogs and cats in the United States. Today, an animal entering a shelter has only one chance in two of making it out alive, and in some places it is as low as one in ten, with shelters

This dog was one of the lucky ones who died in a humane shelter rather than on the streets. Here caring shelter workers administer a fatal injection

ONE OF THE LUCKY ONES?

A large national organization boldly publishes, without the slightest hint of sarcasm or irony, a picture of a puppy—a young, healthy, perfectly adoptable puppy—put to death with the accompanying caption: "This dog was one of the lucky ones who died in a humane shelter... Here caring shelter workers administer a fatal injection..."

blaming a lack of available homes as the cause of death. And yet, there are over seven times as many people looking to bring an animal into their home every year as there are animals being killed in shelters because they lack one. Half of all animals who enter our nation's shelters go out the back door in body bags

* A shelter is a refuge. Given that many U.S. animal "shelters" do little more than kill animals, it is not accurate to refer to them as shelters. Accordingly, we have set the word off in quotations. And while we continue to use it throughout the book without distracting quotations, we do so only because the term is well-known, even if it is factually inaccurate.

rather than out the front door in the loving arms of adopters despite the fact that there are plenty of homes available. And when animal lovers question the excuses used to justify this killing, shelters and their national allies respond, "We are all on the same side," "We all want the same thing," "We are all animal lovers" and insist that criticism of shelters and their staff is unfair and callous because "No one wants to kill." The facts, however, tragically and frequently tell a very different story.

The large national animal protection groups tell us repeatedly that our nation's animal shelters are staffed by animal lovers who hate to kill and would do anything in their power to protect animals and save their lives. The facts, however, tell a very different story.

SEEING THROUGH THE LABELS

Since many of the agencies contracting to perform animal control come with the name "Humane Society," "Society for the Prevention of Cruelty to Animals (SPCA)," or "Animal Care and Control," the assumption is that these shelters are operating humanely, doing the best they can and are staffed by directors and employees committed to animal protection. In reality, agencies that may have initially been founded by people with enormous dedication to animal welfare lost focus when these organizations took over the pound contracts from the cities and towns in which they reside. Instead of working to stop the killing, they *did* the killing. And while many of these organizations have since become very large

and influential, they have also become bureaucratic, lacking the dedication that characterized their early founders.

In fact, neither compassion for animals nor passion for saving their lives is required for employment as a shelter director. A director applying for work need not prove "lifesaving"* success, only experience running other shelters. The fact that a director oversaw a shelter that killed the vast majority of the animals does not end the director's career. The most important question—"How successful were you at saving lives?"—is rarely, if ever, asked.

At the same time, the large national animal protection organizations have historically assured the public that they are overseeing

---

* Throughout this book, we use the terms "lifesaving" or "saving lives" to describe when a shelter adopts out animals–or, in the case of feral cats, releases them back into their habitats–instead of killing them. But for most animals entering shelters this description is inaccurate. If an animal has been hit by a car or is suffering from a serious disease and enters a shelter which provides her with veterinary assistance that prevents death, that animal has been saved by a shelter. Likewise, when a rescue organization takes an animal from death row at a shelter, that animal has also been saved because the rescuer intervened to prevent the animal from being killed by someone else. But when the term "lifesaving" is used to describe a shelter choosing to adopt out an animal instead of killing that animal, killing is implied to be a natural outcome of animal "homelessness" that must be overcome, which it is not. Homelessness is not a fatal condition–or at least it shouldn't be. Moreover, the vast majority of animals who enter shelters are healthy and not in danger of dying but for the threat the shelter itself poses. Shelter employees cannot accurately be described as having "saved" an animal when the only threat the animal faced was the one that they themselves presented. If someone was threatening to kill you, and chose to let you live instead, you would not describe that person's actions as having "saved" you. Accordingly, we have set the word off in quotations. And while we continue to use it throughout the book without distracting quotations, we do so only because the term is well-known, even if it is factually inaccurate.

these shelters to make sure they are being operated in the most humane way possible. Yet because these organizations are staffed by the people who have risen from the ranks of killing shelters and who consider those currently running shelters to be their friends and colleagues, our national animal protection organizations are plagued by the same regressive mindset as those who run shelters. Instead of being watchdogs to our nation's shelters, they have become their cheerleaders.

As a result, not a single large national organization has truly spoken out on behalf of saving animals in shelters. There has been little accountability, little innovation and almost complete hegemony over the national discourse that argues that killing is kindness—all of which have conspired to cement a crisis of uncaring in our nation's animal shelters.

Across the United States, public and private shelters are not doing enough to save lives. They are not run compassionately, effectively, or in a manner which maximizes lifesaving. Tragically, until very recently, most animal advocates failed to demand greater lifesaving or the resignation of those directors who refused to even try. And at the core of this failure are misperceptions about the reasons why animals are being killed in shelters, the motivation of the people who carry out the killing and the role the large national groups play in legitimizing, defending and even promoting the killing. The notion that most shelter directors and their staff, as well as the staff and leadership of national animal protection groups, share the same goals and values as most animal advocates has for too long stifled criticism and, as a result, prevented needed and true reform.

Across the United States, our shelters are not doing enough to save lives. They are not run compassionately, effectively, or in a manner that maximizes lifesaving.

THE NO KILL MOVEMENT

But there is hope. Over the last decade, a growing number of shelter directors across the nation have rejected the "adopt some and kill the rest" model of animal sheltering which has dominated in the United States for the past 100 years. Instead, these directors have implemented the No Kill Equation, a bold set of programs and services which provide alternatives to killing for upwards of 95 percent and as high as 98 percent of all animals entering a shelter (see pages 56-58). And they are achieving unprecedented success. Today, No Kill communities in which no healthy or treatable animals are killed can be found throughout the United States.* Some of the communities are urban and some are rural. Some are in the North and some are in the South. Some are large, taking in roughly 23,000 animals a year, and others are small, taking in only a few hundred or a few thousand. Some are politically liberal and some are politically conservative. Some are new No Kill communities and others have been No Kill for better than a decade. And while these communities share very little demographically, they prove that despite all those things that separate us as Americans, people from all walks of life want to build a better world for animals. We now have No Kill communities in California and New York, in Kentucky and Virginia, in Nevada and Texas, in Michigan, in Indiana and elsewhere. But they remain the exception. Why?

Why are some shelters still killing in the face of alternatives, while others save all but non-rehabilitatable animals? One common excuse is that every shelter with a higher rate of lifesaving is somehow "unique." But this excuse ignores the fact that each community that has experienced lifesaving success was, at one time, as regressive as those that continue killing. Why does one shelter send thousands of animals every year into foster care, while other shelters

> When it comes to the shelters whose directors are killing large numbers of animals, those choices and priorities manifest themselves not only in their appalling kill rates, but also in the poor and oftentimes cruel treatment the animals in their facilities must endure.

do not? Indeed, in one shelter, volunteers who took motherless newborn kittens home and bottle-fed them until they were old enough to eat on their own and be adopted were fired for doing so. Why does one shelter seek out rescue groups, while other shelters kill animals these groups have offered to save? Why do some shelters neuter and release free-living, unsocial (feral**) cats, while others not only oppose such efforts, but send officers out to write citations and threaten jail time to people who care for these cats?

The answer is simple: the most important factor that determines whether communities save lives or end them is the person who runs the animal control or large private shelter in that community, and that person's commitment—or lack thereof—to implementing the No Kill Equation. That is why a national study found

---

* Some of these are individual city shelters which only service one municipality. Others are county shelters that impound animals for all the towns, cities and unincorporated areas in the community. As such, there are several dozen communities representing hundreds of cities and towns across the U.S. which have ended the killing of healthy and treatable animals.

** The term "feral" means an animal who has changed from being domesticated to being wild or untamed. This is not accurate for many free-living, unsocial cats who have been born and raised without human contact. Such cats act like wild animals and, as all cats are, are genetically identical to the African or Spanish wildcat, which is legally classified as a wild animal. The difference between wild and domestic is a mere behavioral one, based on their experiences, or lack thereof, with humans. Moreover, the term also includes the false assumption that these cats are not part of the natural environment and therefore do not belong there. Accordingly, we have set the word off in quotations. And while we continue to use it throughout the book without distracting quotations, we do so only because the term is well-known, even if it is factually inaccurate. The correct terms for these cats are "community cats," "free-living cats" or even "wild cats" (see pages 196-202).

that rates of lifesaving were not determined by rates of funding (see pages 229-231). All the money in the world won't save dogs and cats in shelters run by directors who simply refuse to implement alternatives to killing. And when it comes to the shelters whose directors are killing large numbers of animals, those choices and priorities manifest themselves not only in their appalling kill rates, but also in the poor and oftentimes cruel treatment the animals in their facilities must endure.

A CRISIS OF UNCARING

Not only are millions of animals needlessly killed in our nation's shelters every year, but

We trusted them, content to write them checks to do the job while we looked the other way because the "experts" were in charge, and in so doing, have allowed our shelters to remain virtually unsupervised and unregulated for decades, with devastating results.

they are neglected and abused in the process. As the movement to end shelter killing has grown in size and sophistication, the networking made possible through the internet and social media has allowed animal lovers to connect the dots between individual cases of animal cruelty and neglect in shelters nationwide. These incidents reveal a distinct pattern. Animal abuse at local shelters is not an isolated anomaly caused by "a few bad apples." The stunning number and severity of these cases nationwide lead to one disturbing and inescapable conclusion: *our shelters are in crisis.*

Frequently overseen by ineffective and incompetent directors who fail to hold their staff accountable to the most basic standards of humane care, animal shelters in this country are not the safe havens they should and can be. Instead, they are often poorly managed houses of horror, places where animals are denied basic medical care, food, water, socialization and are then killed, sometimes cruelly. The first time many companion animals experience neglect and abuse is when they enter the very place that is supposed to deliver them from it: the local animal shelter.

It is a tragic story true to cities and towns across this nation. And the large national animal protection organizations are as much to blame as the individual shelter directors themselves. For decades they have perpetuated the fiction that all is well in our nation's shelters. They have assured us that they are overseeing these organizations, providing guidance and assistance to make sure they are run humanely and effectively: through their shelter assessments, their national conferences and their publications for sheltering professionals. In reality, they have ignored abuse, failed to create substantive standards by which to measure success and hold directors accountable and remained deafeningly silent regarding the cases of abuse occurring at shelters nationwide. In short, they have failed us. We trusted them, content to write them checks to do the job while we looked the other way because the "experts" were in charge, and in so doing, have allowed our shelters to remain virtually unsupervised and unregulated for decades, with devastating results.

In fact, excluding laws imposed by health departments regarding the use of controlled substances, the disposition of rabid and "aggressive" animals and mandated holding periods, shelter directors in this country have essentially unlimited discretion as to how they operate their facilities. If a shelter director decides to kill each and every animal even if there are empty cages, it is legal for him to do so. In fact, many shelters routinely keep banks of cages intentionally empty so that their staff does not have to clean those cages or feed the animals inside them. If a non-profit rescue organization wants to save an animal on death row at a shelter, the shelter director has the authority in every state but two to deny the group the ability to do so, and they frequently do. Likewise, shelter directors can kill orphaned kittens and puppies rather than work with volunteers who want to provide foster care. They can ban volunteers from walking dogs and socializing cats. And they can limit the number of hours they are open to the public for adoptions, or have hours that make it difficult for working people to reclaim their lost animals or adopt new ones.

There are no checks and balances to ensure that our shelters are run in line with the most up-to-date sheltering policies and procedures. Instead, our shelters are run on the honor

Whether by coming to the defense of regressive shelter directors, working to defeat progressive shelter reform legislation, fighting new and innovative programs to save lives, or calling for the wholesale slaughter of entire groups of animals in shelters, HSUS, the ASPCA, PETA and other animal protection groups are the biggest barrier to ensuring the survival of animals in shelters today.

system, and it is a discretion shelter directors abuse time and again by failing to implement readily available lifesaving alternatives or to work cooperatively with those who want to help them save lives. And without exception, whenever animal lovers have questioned this arrangement, developed innovative and compassionate alternatives to killing or have brought the need for greater regulation to light, the large national animal protection groups have opposed them. They argue that such reforms are unnecessary, and that, paradoxically, any alternative to killing or any form of regulating shelters to ensure that animals are treated with compassion and are not needlessly killed is not only unnecessary, but will actually put animals in harm's way.

When a statewide survey found that 71 percent of rescue organizations reported that they were turned away from New York State shelters and then those shelters killed the very

The No Kill movement is working to bring standards and accountability to a field that has historically lacked it, by exposing the truth about our shelters, by calling for the replacement of poorly performing shelter directors and by seeking legislation that legally mandates common sense procedures that shelters should already be doing.

animals those groups offered to save, the ASPCA fought to maintain the status quo, defeating legislation that would have given rescue groups the right to save at private expense, the animals shelters are killing at taxpayer expense. When animal lovers in Texas tried to end the practice of gassing animals, a slow and exceedingly cruel way for animals to die, a coalition of animal control groups led by HSUS defeated the bill. Even though the Virginia Animal Control Association defeated legislation to end the statewide practice of killing animals when there are empty cages, when rescue groups are willing to save them and in the case of feral cats, when they can be neutered and released, PETA supported their cause and the National Animal Control Association (NACA) gave them an award for "Outstanding State Association." When a Louisiana shelter killed every single animal in its facility, including cats, because a handful of dogs contracted a mild illness which clears up on its own, HSUS defended them. In Hillsborough County, Florida, despite the fact

that the shelter's then-director killed animals in order to keep cages empty, the ASPCA stepped in not to encourage reform, but to buy them a new "euthanasia table" on which to kill animals. And when a shelter in Reno, Nevada, finished the year saving a higher percentage of animals than virtually every other community in the nation, AHA encouraged them to take a giant step backward and enact a punitive cat licensing scheme which could have led to the round up and killing of homeless and outdoor cats.

Whether by coming to the defense of regressive shelter directors, working to defeat progressive shelter reform legislation, fighting new and innovative programs to save lives, or calling for the wholesale slaughter of entire groups of animals in shelters, HSUS, the ASPCA, PETA and other animal protection groups are the biggest barrier to ensuring the survival of animals in shelters today.

SEEKING REFORM

The No Kill movement seeks to change this tragic reality by bringing standards and accountability to a field that has historically lacked it, by exposing the truth about our shelters, by calling for the replacement of poorly performing shelter directors and by seeking legislation that legally mandates common sense procedures that shelters should already be following.

Where laws mandating lifesaving policies and procedures have passed—California, Delaware and some local communities, for example—greater lifesaving has immediately followed. Legally requiring shelters to do what they refuse to do is the quickest and most effective means animal lovers have to reform our nation's shelters, and to orient them toward lifesaving and away from killing. Yet, whenever and wherever animal lovers mount campaigns for reform or seek legislation, the opposition of HSUS, PETA and the ASPCA hinders their efforts. Too often, animal lovers, the media and legislators become confused and cannot see beyond the names and reputations of these organizations to discern their true motives. Too often, the opposition of animal protection organizations sows seeds of doubt regarding the need or nature of common sense reform and efforts falter or fail.

We are a nation of animal lovers, and we, and the animals we love, deserve better. We deserve shelters that reflect our progressive and compassionate values, not thwart them. We now have a solution to shelter killing and it is not difficult, expensive, or beyond practical means to achieve. Only one thing stands in the way of its widespread implementation: a deeply troubled and dysfunctional animal protection movement that undermines the effort

at every turn. If we are to prevail, we need to understand the historical, sociological and financial motivations behind this paradoxical opposition so that we can neutralize its harmful and deadly effect. By explaining the nature of this opposition, we hope to inspire in others—animal lovers, public officials, legislators, the media—the confidence and courage necessary to see through, and stand up to, those who seek to delay and derail urgently needed shelter reform.

We now have a solution to shelter killing and it is not difficult, expensive, or beyond practical means to achieve. In assuring its widespread implementation, only one thing stands in our way: a deeply troubled and dysfunctional "animal protection" movement that undermines the effort at every turn.

The Story of a Little Cat

Stuck Between Two Walls and Hardened Hearts

SHELTERS ARE SUPPOSED TO RESCUE ANIMALS from cruelty and neglect. They are supposed to be a sanctuary for lost dogs and stray cats. They are supposed to be a refuge, a safe haven for animals whose people can no longer keep them or no longer want them. Unfortunately, for too many animals, they are not.

Meet a little cat who was stuck inside a wall of a U.S. animal shelter, a cat who was stuck near the employee break room, where every employee could hear his cries while they sat and drank coffee, and ate lunch and socialized. They later told a newspaper reporter that they "pleaded" with shelter supervisors to do something about the cat. But neither they nor those supervisors did what compassion dictates. Not a single one of them took action. And because of that, the cat paid the ultimate price. This is how a local newspaper, the *Dallas Observer*, described it:

Before it starved to death last May, the cat could be heard by shelter workers, crying and clawing, trying to escape the confines of the break room wall behind which it had become trapped at Dallas Animal Services. Cats do especially badly in animal shelters, naturally preferring dark, quiet repose to loud, boisterous interaction. This cat, terrified, had jumped away from staffers who were trying to clean cages, going straight for a loose ceiling tile and bolting into darkness.

But somewhere in its search for safety, the cat fell between shelter walls and landed between the walls of the employee break room and the ladies' restroom. It couldn't move. It could only yowl and scratch. For more than a week.

Imagine it. Really try to imagine it. A shelter filled with employees whose job it is to care for animals. Imagine a cat calling out in panic and fear, stuck in a wall, where the employees are eating and talking and not a single one rescues the cat. Sure, one of them calls a cruelty investigator and he comes and determines that the cat is indeed stuck in the wall. But he doesn't rescue the cat either. Others ask managers, each other, "Will someone rescue the cat?" But no one does. And they keep right on eating their lunches; they keep right on talking and doing those things that people do in break rooms. And meanwhile, the cats' cries are getting more desperate, then weaker and then they finally stop. A short time later, the smell comes: the smell of a decomposing body.

And only then do they complain in earnest. *How can we eat lunch in here, how can we socialize with that smell?* And because it now affects *them*, they do something about it. They cut open a hole in the wall to remove the dead body, while every single one of us wants to scream: *Why didn't any of them tear open the wall when the cat was still alive?* Don't think for a second that this story is unique.

On the following pages of this book are a handful of abuse cases that occurred in our nation's kill shelters over the last few years, as well as some of the efforts undertaken by powerful animal protection organizations to thwart shelter reform. The incidents highlighted here are just a small sampling. There are many more. Moreover, these incidents are not just tragic in and of themselves, but they are set against the backdrop of the killing of roughly four million animals in shelters across the country every year.

Taken as a whole, these facts reveal a distinct pattern, an unpleasant but undeniable truth: willful abuse, careless neglect and even sadistic pleasure in causing animals to suffer and die are the status quo at many of our nation's shelters. The question, of course, is *why?* How is it that agencies filled with people who are supposed to protect animals from harm and rescue them when they are in trouble, people who are paid to care for animals in need, are in fact abusive?

There are a lot of answers to that question: working at a municipal pound is a job, not a mission; animal control lacks accountability; applicants who score the lowest on city aptitude tests get placed in animal control; some agencies are staffed by prison inmates with no oversight; employees who fail in departments deemed more important by uncaring bureaucrats are placed in animal control rather

This kitten was impounded by a shelter and then "lost." She was later found with no food or water on the verge of death and was killed.

than fired; city officials sign draconian union contracts that make it difficult to fire neglectful and abusive staff; lazy managers won't do the progressive discipline necessary to fire them (and workers know this); some people just don't care; and some people are just callous and cruel.

In addition, neuroscientists who study morality believe they have part of the answer. Their studies demonstrate that even normally circumspect people turn off their natural compassion when placed in unnatural environments. People who might be "kind" or "decent" in a normal environment can be cruel when placed in a context in which cruelty is the norm. And what could be more unnatural or cruel than an animal shelter designed to warehouse and then kill animals? Although the large national groups try to assure us that the killing is done humanely, not only do the facts prove otherwise, but the very notion of "humanely euthanizing" a healthy animal is a contradiction.

Studies of slaughterhouse workers have found that in order to cope with the fact that they are paid to kill day in and day out, self-preservation motivates them to devalue animals in order to make what they are doing less morally reprehensible. In other words, the workers make the animals unworthy of any consideration on their behalf. The two most common methods of achieving this are indifference to animal suffering and even intensifying it, becoming sadistic toward the animals. In too many communities, the implications for shelters are frightening: shelters are often little more than slaughterhouses. And therefore by its very nature, shelter killing breeds a lack of compassion and caring for animals.

But while all of the preceding factors contribute to needlessly high rates of killing and a culture of neglect, they alone (or even in combination) do not fully explain how it was that every single person at Dallas Animal Services was complicit in the death of a cat because they failed to take the necessary action to save his life. Nor do they explain fully why this kind of indifference to suffering is endemic and epidemic in shelters across the country. To

This kitten arrived at a shelter healthy. The shelter did not feed her and she became emaciated.

Shelter workers hold a dog down by a catch pole, a hard wire noose wrapped around the dog's neck, and then repeatedly kick him.

understand why they failed to do what every single one of us would have done, we have to look to the very nature of shelters themselves and the kind of people who apply to work in them.

What Would HENRY Do?

One afternoon more than 120 years ago, passersby could hear a cat meowing in distress at a construction site, but they couldn't find her. Concerned for her safety, one of those people knew exactly what to do: tell Henry Bergh.

Widely known for his dedication to animals, the father of the humane movement in North America and a famous fixture of late 19th century New York City (see page 100), Bergh could be seen patrolling the streets every day and night in search of animals in need of his protection. So when he was told a cat was crying out for help, Bergh was quick to act.

When he arrived on the scene, he realized that the cat was stuck inside a wall. Perhaps she had crawled inside to sleep and the construction workers, unaware, had sealed her inside. Bergh asked the owner of the construction company to make a hole in the wall to allow the cat to escape. He refused, saying it would cost too much money to punch a hole and then reseal it. So Bergh took matters into his own hands and demanded that the workers immediately make a hole or he would do it himself. They did. Legend has it that the cat climbed out of the wall, and as if to thank him, rubbed against Bergh's legs before darting away.

Because shelter workers understand that they have the power to kill shelter animals, and will in fact kill many of them, every interaction they have with those animals is influenced by the perception that their lives do not matter, that their lives are cheap and expendable and that they are destined for the garbage heap.

PENNSYLVANIA

Garbage bags full of dead animals destined for the landfill.

TEXAS

EMPLOYEES WANTED TO COMMIT DAILY VIOLENCE TOWARD ANIMALS

Killing is the ultimate form of violence. While cruelty and suffering are abhorrent, while cruelty and suffering are painful, while cruelty and suffering should be condemned and rooted out, there is nothing worse than death, because death is final. An animal subjected to pain and suffering can be rescued. A traumatized animal subjected to savage cruelty can even be rehabilitated, as the dog fighting case against football player Michael Vick demonstrates (see pages 140-141). Dogs who HSUS lobbied to have killed because they claimed they were dangerous as a result of the abuse went on to loving, new homes and some even became therapy dogs, bringing comfort to cancer patients. Where there is life, there Is hope, but death is hope's total antithesis. It is the eclipse of hope because the animals never wake up, ever. It is the worst of the worst—a fact each and every one of us would immediately and unequivocally recognize if we were the ones being threatened with it.

And not only do people in shelters work at a place that commits this ultimate form of violence, they have, in fact, been hired to do exactly that. Can we really be surprised when they don't clean thoroughly, don't feed the animals, handle them too roughly, neglect and abuse them or simply ignore their cries for help while the animals slowly starve to death or die of dehydration? How does shoddy cleaning or rough handling or failing to feed the animals compare with putting an animal to death? Because shelter workers understand that they have the power to kill shelter animals, and will in fact kill many of them, every interaction they have with those animals is influenced by the perception that the animals do not matter, that their lives are cheap and expendable and that they are destined for the garbage heap.

The reality is that truly caring people, people who actually love animals, either do not apply to work at these agencies or if they do, they do not last. They quit when they realize that their efforts to improve conditions and outcomes are not rewarded, that their fellow employees are not held accountable, that neglect isn't punished, and in fact, *they* will be for trying to improve things.

In Philadelphia a number of years ago, a whistleblower not only had his car vandalized, but was threatened with physical violence by a union-protected thug. Who outed him? Philadelphia's then-Health Commissioner, who oversaw the shelter and wanted to silence critics. In King County, Washington, a whistleblower was transferred to another department for her own safety. In Miami, the whistleblower that stood up to cruel methods of killing was simply fired. In Indianapolis, a shelter

director who tried to transform the local animal control facility had his car vandalized and was subject to threats of violence.

Shelters today are places where the normal rules of compassion and decency toward animals to which the vast majority of people subscribe simply do not apply. And most ironic of all is that this system of death camps is defended and celebrated by the nation's largest animal protection organizations: HSUS, the ASPCA and PETA. These organizations tell us that the killing is not the fault of the people in shelters who are actually doing the killing, even while they ignore the systematic neglect and abuse which frequently precedes it.

Cats at this Georgia shelter are placed in outdoor pens with no protection from the elements. On record cold nights, cats have died from exposure. After volunteers complained about conditions, several of the cats were poisoned with antifreeze. This shelter is run by prison inmates.

NO GOOD DEED GOES UNPUNISHED

In 2009, a new shelter director committed to reform was hired to run Indianapolis' animal control shelter. After he began instituting badly needed changes, shelter employees—angry at being held accountable for their poor job performance—fought back, not only threatening him with the warning "You better watch your back," but vandalizing his car as well. Dog food was dumped on his windshield (ABOVE LEFT) and then it was smashed (ABOVE RIGHT).

But it *is* their fault. They are the ones who do it. It is right in their job description. They signed up for it. And because people who care don't, that leaves animals, like the trapped cat in Dallas, at the mercy of an entire department of employees who do not care enough to do anything about it.

The systematic killing of animals in U.S. shelters is not "necessary" or simply "lamentable." And it is certainly not a "gift" as the heads of HSUS, the ASPCA and PETA have indicated to one degree or another. The system is ugly, broken, regressive and violent. And it is so by design. The sooner we recognize that, the sooner we can focus our energies on fixing it. By making our shelters the safe havens they should be, we make them safe for animal lovers to work at, too. But it is taking far too long, and too many animals are being subjected to systematic and unrelenting violence, because the large national animal protection organizations are defending and protecting the status quo.

These organizations fight progressive legislation to save tens of thousands of animals every year from those brutal environments, as the ASPCA did in defeating Oreo's Law (see pages 89-95). They send letters and staff members to fight shelter reform, as either HSUS or the ASPCA have done in San Francisco, California, Austin, Texas, Eugene, Oregon, Page County, Virginia and elsewhere. They defend the killing with circular reasoning, fuzzy math and regressive, antiquated dogmas as AHA recently did. Or, like HSUS does with their annual "National Animal Shelter Appreciation Week," they celebrate these agencies when they should be holding them accountable. And, in doing so, they abdicate their mission to protect animals through oversight of shelters in order to defend harm by providing those who abuse and kill animals political cover.

And not one by one or two by two or a thousand by a thousand or even by the tens of thousands, but millions upon millions of animals are marched to their needless deaths while these national organizations, just like every single employee in the Dallas shelter, continue to ignore their plight.

So we must do it in spite of them. Ending the routine and casual killing of animals will not only save the lives of four million animals every year, but it will bring decency and compassion to our nation's shelters where—as the cases of cruelty and neglect highlighted in this book reveal—these virtues are in tragically short supply.

This bumper sticker is on the car belonging to a Texas shelter employee.

The systematic killing of animals in U.S. shelters is not "necessary" or simply "lamentable." And it is certainly not a "gift" as the heads of HSUS, the ASPCA and PETA have indicated to one degree or another. The system is ugly, broken, regressive and violent. And it is so by design.

SOUTH CAROLINA

HELL ON EARTH: This shelter in Marlboro County, South Carlina has three banks of cat cages—all of which are located in a room without light; the cats at this shelter are kept in darkness. Dogs are forced to drink from algae-filled buckets. The chances of an animal making it out alive are slim because it is only open for adoptions and reclaims of lost animals for two and a half hours a day and at times when most people are either just waking up or in the middle of their work day.

The cat room as seen from the inside.

ANIMAL SHELTER
ADOPTION HOURS
7:30 AM - 9:00 AM
2:00 PM - 3:00 PM

NEW JERSEY

Filthy kennels are the norm at these shelters in New Jersey (ABOVE LEFT AND RIGHT) and California (BELOW LEFT AND RIGHT) where dogs are forced to languish in their accumulated waste, often becoming covered in it.

CALIFORNIA

An animal control officer lets animal lovers know what he thinks of their protest against the high rates of killing at the Los Angeles shelter where he works.

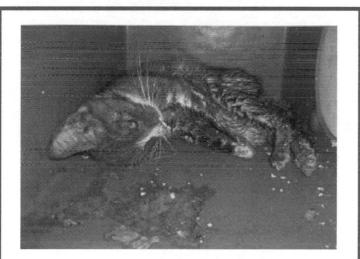

Impounded by a shelter on a day of extreme heat and humidity, this kitten was left in a carrier in direct sunlight with no food or water for three days. This is how they found her. She was dead.

ᴀYEAR IN THE LIFE (and death) 2011

AT AMERICA'S ANIMAL "SHELTERS" AND ANIMAL "PROTECTION" ORGANIZATIONS

JANUARY

A state agency discovers that the Robeson County, North Carolina, pound is sending live animals along with recently killed ones to the dump. The veterinarian contracted to kill animals at the pound failed to properly verify death before the animals were taken to the landfill.

In Amherst County, Virginia, a pound takes a family's two dogs into custody after their house burns down. When the family contacts the shelter to pick up the dogs, they are informed that they have already been killed.

HSUS claims to rescue dogs and after publicizing the "rescue" to the press, activists discover that HSUS shipped some of them to a North Carolina pound where they were gassed.

FEBRUARY

Shelter reform legislation is Introduced In Texas which would ban the gas chamber, require shelters to work with rescue groups, end killing when cages and kennels are available, require shelters to make their rates of killing public and end killing based on arbitrary criteria such as what color the animals are, how old they are or what breed they are. HSUS defeats the bill.

At the same time, HSUS introduces legislation in California that is not designed to save a single life or to improve conditions at shelters. The HSUS-sponsored bill would have changed the language of California's animal shelter laws to replace the word "pound" with "animal shelter," "pound keeper" with "animal shelter director," and "destroy" with "humanely euthanize." The legislation has one purpose: to excuse and exonerate those who harm animals by codifying euphemisms that obscure the truth and make the task of killing easier.

MARCH

In Chesterfield County, South Carolina, shelter staff use dozens of dogs for target practice at a local landfill, taking turns trying to shoot them in the head. A former inmate assigned to work at the shelter tells local media that they also beat cats in the head with pipes.

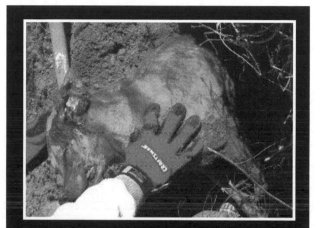

This dog died from a gunshot wound to the head. He was killed by staff of an animal control shelter who used dogs for target practice in Chesterfield County, South Carolina.

A video surfaces on YouTube showing staff at the Hempstead, New York, pound abusing a kitten while a voice chants "Kill the kitty! Kill the kitty!" One of the staff members in the video is subsequently promoted to shelter manager.

In Brown County, Ohio, a dog warden impounds 37 dogs and immediately stuffs them into a homemade gas chamber, killing them.

APRIL

The Charlotte-Mecklenburg, North Carolina, pound tells a TV interviewer the facility is low on cats for adoption, failing to mention why: almost every cat who comes through the door is killed.

CRISIS OF CRUELTY & UNCARING

"Kill the kitty!"

In the video from which this image was taken, an animal control officer hangs a kitten by the neck while another asks, "Debbie, do you want to kill a kitten? You wanna kill another kitty? Pass the needle..." Off camera, another officer chants, "Kill the kitty!"

A rescuer in Hoke County, North Carolina, repeatedly offers to pay for veterinary care for an emaciated dog at the pound, but is refused. The pound ignores the dog's suffering, allowing the animal to slowly die over a period of several weeks.

MAY

A cat lover takes 11 homeless cats to the Harlingen Humane Society in Texas so the shelter can find them homes. After learning that the cats would be held for three days then killed, the cat lover finds an alternative shelter for the cats and attempts to retrieve them. She learns that all 11 cats were killed immediately on intake.

A webcam at Memphis Animal Services in Tennessee captures a mama dog and her litter of four puppies being surrendered. A few days later, the webcam shows the staff putting the puppies—who were never offered for adoption—into a trash can which is then wheeled into the kill room.

JUNE

The Memphis City Attorney threatens to sue a No Kill blogger who is publicly exposing the repeated images of animal cruelty caught on the webcams at Memphis Animal Services. Meanwhile, the webcams capture a worker hanging a cat by the neck prior to killing. The Mayor ultimately decides to protect abusive employees by removing the webcams.

Kapone, a family's beloved "Pit Bull," goes "missing" after being picked up by a Memphis animal control officer when he escaped their yard. Suspicion centers around the dog catcher (hired by the city even though they were aware she had numerous felony convictions) after neighbors saw her pick up the dog, yet cameras at the shelter did not show her impounding him.

JULY

Whistleblowers at the New York City pound come forward to document animal suffering: injured animals receiving no pain relief, animals languishing in filth, animals being denied needed medical care, healthy animals being put to death and kittens going long periods of time without food or water. Meanwhile any volunteer who expresses concern about conditions is terminated.

Kapone with his family

AUGUST

The Okefenokee Humane Society in Georgia admits that 14 dogs died of heatstroke in the preceding three months, including a seven-month-old puppy. Despite oppressive humidity and high temperatures, the shelter doesn't have any air conditioning or fans in the kennels. In fact, it doesn't have any electricity.

SEPTEMBER

In response to a concerned citizen providing photographic evidence of abuse at a pound in Jeffersonville, Indiana, the city enacts a new policy to protect the abusers by banning the public from the kennels.

An investigation of the shelter in DeKalb County, Georgia, concludes it is an "abomination" and a "chamber of horrors." A report details widespread filth, "puppies and kittens left to die" and "workers [killing cats] by holding them down with a foot on the back, sometimes breaking their bones."

OCTOBER

The staff at Bay County Animal Control in Florida attempt to justify the facility's outrageous 76 percent kill rate by blaming the public, even though they kill despite having numerous empty cages.

NOVEMBER

The Wake County Animal Center in North Carolina takes a dog to a local TV studio for a "pet of the day" segment, then returns to the pound and immediately kills her. When people call to adopt her, she is already dead.

An emaciated dog wanders into a hardware store in Detroit, Michigan. The hardware store owner, thinking he is helping the dog, calls Detroit Animal Control. Although the dog is friendly, the pound announces it will kill the dog. Despite appeals from concerned citizens, offers to save the dog by rescue groups and a judge's order barring the shelter from killing him, the city kills the dog anyway.

DECEMBER

The Arizona Humane Society convinces a man who cannot afford veterinary care for his injured kitten to surrender his beloved pet in exchange for the promise of prompt treatment. Although the man's mother offers to give her credit card number over the telephone and even offers to wire cash to her son the following day, they refuse. The kitten is killed despite the promise to treat her.

Two former employees of Calhoun County Animal Control in Alabama claim that animals are beaten to death, dogs are put in garbage bags alive and that, after botched attempts to give them a lethal injection, puppies are thrown in sinks filled with urine, feces and blood to die slowly.

CAUGHT ON CAMERA
MEMPHIS ANIMAL SERVICES

Throughout 2011, webcams at Memphis Animal Services (MAS) in Tennessee captured images of dogs being cruelly dragged with a "catch pole" or "control pole" (a device that wraps a hard-wire noose around the animal's neck), a cat being hung by his neck, sick animals denied basic medical care and healthy puppies being killed without ever being offered for adoption. In response to public criticism, the city turned off the cameras to public view.

An independent investigation of the shelter revealed a broadly held suspicion that MAS employees have ties to dog fighting. And in 2012, an undercover police

MAS employees were routinely captured on webcams handling animals roughly and cruelly. A dog is dragged by a catch pole that is choking him as he urinates on himself (ABOVE). A cat being taken to the kill room is hung by the neck (BELOW).

investigation at the shelter resulted in the conviction of several employees on charges of aggravated animal cruelty. In one instance, according to a newspaper report,

A small, timid Chow dog was scheduled to die at the Memphis Animal Shelter with a sedative injection followed by a lethal solution injected into the heart... "Now you want to act stupid?" former shelter worker Archie Elliott III said to the Chow as he pulled the uncooperative leashed animal into the euthanizing room. "I know how to take care of this. This is my sedation." Elliott then lifted the dog off the ground and held the choking animal over a sink as it urinated and defecated while gasping for air, according to court papers.

A litter of puppies who were never offered for adoption are placed into a garbage can to be wheeled into the room where they are killed (RIGHT).

BEFORE

This puppy entered MAS healthy. He was never fed and died of starvation. At least two other dogs met similar fates.

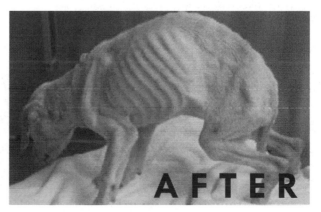

AFTER

WATCHDOGS OR CHEERLEADERS?

HSUS describes itself as the nation's *"strongest advocate"* for shelters and tells the public that they owe a debt of gratitude to the *"dedicated people"* who work at them.

> *In 1996, The HSUS launched National Animal Shelter Appreciation Week... This campaign was designed to acknowledge and promote the invaluable role shelters play in their communities... During National Animal Shelter Appreciation Week, the first full week of every November, The HSUS promotes and celebrates animal shelters across the country through media and public outreach.*
>
> **- HSUS**

A PICTURE IS WORTH A THOUSAND WORDS

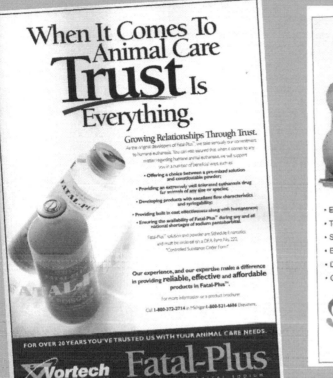

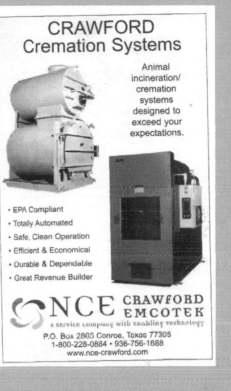

Shelter Pages is a magazine for sheltering professionals published by HSUS. Here are some of the products advertised in the 2012 edition: Fatal-Plus, the drug used to kill animals ("Because When It Comes to Animal Care, Trust Is Everything") and animal incinerators ("designed to exceed your expectations") to dispose of their dead bodies. Running these ads is the equivalent of peddling slaughterhouse equipment, hunting rifles or restraining devices for animals used in scientific research. Yet they are very lucrative for HSUS, with the largest of them costing advertisers several thousand dollars.

WHY ARE THESE CAGES EMPTY?
CONVENIENCE KILLING IN AMERICAN SHELTERS

THERE IS LITTLE REASON WHY MOST PEOPLE, your average animal lover in the United States, would know that shelters kill not out of necessity, but out of convenience. The one fact that would demonstrate that is something they almost never see because they do not go to shelters every day. But animal rescuers see it. What do they see every time they go into animal shelters? They see empty cages. Shelters kill animals every single day, despite empty cages.

Leaving cages empty means less cleaning, less feeding, less work. Some shelter directors do it for this very reason. Others do it because they falsely believe that no one will adopt the animals anyway. Others follow protocols embraced by national organizations which dictate that there should always be cages ready for intake, even if it means killing the animals who are currently in them.

Empty cages mean less cleaning, less feeding, less work. In line with the recommendations of large national animal protection groups, shelters across America kill animals every single day, despite having empty cages.

ANIMAL SHELTERING'S DIRTY SECRET

Given that dozens of No Kill animal control shelters do not keep cages empty, the protocols promoted by national and state sheltering organizations demonstrate that they endorse killing out of sheer convenience. More to the point, it shows how little the groups and the shelters which follow this recommendation actually care about the lives of animals. They may claim that killing is a last resort, but that is a lie. How else can you explain a policy that prioritizes having an empty cage over the life of the animal currently inside it?

A THOUGHT EXPERIMENT

Imagine you are a shelter director. All your cat cages and dog kennels are full, and it is your job to pick which animals die so you can have your empty cages for tomorrow's intake. You enter the cat room and look around. Will you kill that black cat over there? How about that little orange tabby? Or what about that kitten making such a racket, sticking his paw outside the cage, begging for some attention? Yes, that little kitten has to go. You instruct an employee to take him to the kill room. The kitten gets excited thinking he is going to play, but he is killed instead. Once you are done killing that kitten, you clean that cage so it can be ready just in case an animal should need that cage tomorrow.

Then it is on to the dog kennels. Who will die today? Will it be the little Jack Russell jumping

up and down excitedly, hoping you might take him for a walk? What about that quiet and shy chocolate Lab lying on his bed? Yes, how about him? And, again, you instruct a staff member to lead him to the kill room, and then clean the kennel so it is ready for a dog who may or may not arrive. The dog looks up at you, shyly at first, but once the leash is on, he starts to walk with more confidence. He's going for a walk! He's going home!

Instead, he is taken into a room, a room filled with the smell of antiseptic. If he sees the other dead dogs, he'll panic and resist. He may have to be forced down, one person holding him while he struggles and another administering the fatal dose. But either way, he's going to die. You ordered him killed even though another dog might get adopted at any moment, also freeing up that kennel organizations like HSUS tell you is necessary to have ready. Or maybe that dog's family will arrive to reclaim him, ten minutes too late. Perhaps someone would have been moved seeing how sad he was, and chosen to adopt him, but it's too late for him now. He's already dead, his body in the freezer, stacked on top of the large pile of dead dogs that were killed to make room for other dogs over the last few days, including the one that was killed to make room for him.

Then it is on to the rabbits, then the gerbils, and the animals are dead, the cages are clean and there they are, sitting empty and ready for the animals who may or may not come through the doors the next day. This is the status quo at kill shelters throughout the country. And just as it has broken your heart to read it, it breaks the hearts of the employees that care. And that is why they leave.

If animals need to be doubled up in a cage so that no one dies, that is what ethics compel. And no one outside the sheltering profession would ever think, for a moment, that that wasn't the proper thing to do. In fact, the suggestion that a shelter should kill an animal to free up a cage that might or might not be needed would be met with horror by just about everyone who hasn't been in the field long enough into accepting the unethical policies and the tragic results they produce.

Preemptive killing for empty cages demonstrates a lack of creativity on the part of a shelter director. It is a shelter director's job to come up with life-affirming solutions. But if the animal protection groups to which shelters turn for guidance encourage them to do the easy and convenient thing—kill—then that is what they will do.

In addition, it is a shelter director's job to come up with life-affirming solutions. But if the animal protection movement gives them absolution to kill, then that is what they will do, every time. That is why roughly four million animals are killed in shelters. Killing is easy and killing is convenient, so why bother with researching or implementing proven alternatives?

In fact, if you were to ask the average person off the street to come up with 10 creative things that could be done with the cat in the cage or the dog that might come through the door that do not involve killing, they would neither hesitate nor fail given what's at stake. Yet ask the nation's animal protection groups, statewide animal control associations or local shelters to support a law requiring paid staff at these organizations to do the same, you'll get a litany of excuses about why it is a bad idea (see pages 214-217). They will fight your efforts to require it. They will fear monger to the press and public. They will lie to legislators. And they will do everything in their power to make sure that the scenarios you just read about continue unabated—day in, day out.

WHO WOULD YOU KILL?

You are a shelter director following **HSUS** guidelines. All your cages are full and HSUS recommends that you always have an empty cage ready. Who would you kill? Go ahead. Pick one.

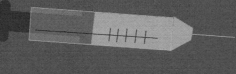

Will you kill the shy gray and white cat?

Or how about that 8 week-old kitten with her whole life ahead of her?

Or will it be the mama cat and her litter of newborn kittens? After all, those kittens are going to grow up and will need cages of their own some day. Maybe better to just kill them now and free up several future cages. That would be the more convenient thing to do, and it's all about convenience.

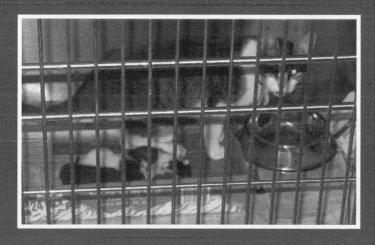

EASIER DEAD THAN FED

Los Angeles shelters kill tens of thousands of animals every year. But in 2005, when a staff veterinarian who ran one of the six shelters in Los Angeles tried to keep more animals alive by ordering her staff not to kill animals if there were empty cages available, she was fired due to numerous staff complaints of "too much work." In Eugene, Oregon, during the busy summer "kitten season" in 2006, all but six cat cages were intentionally kept empty, while shelter staff blamed the killing of 72 percent of all cats on "lack of space."

In 2007, over a period of several weeks, 73 cats were taken off the adoption floor of the Dane County Humane Society in Madison, Wisconsin, to a room outside of public view. One by one, each was given an overdose of barbiturates. One by one, their bodies went limp and slumped to the table. One by one, each was put to death. They were killed because the shelter decided it was going to keep every other cage empty, reducing the number of cages on its adoption floor by half.

In Shreveport, Louisiana, the pound killed 92 percent of all cats, while keeping room after room of cat cages empty. On a January afternoon in 2009, only one cat was available for adoption.

These photos of empty cages were taken at shelters throughout the country. On the day they were taken, these shelters claimed they had no choice but to kill animals for "lack of space."

An Open Door to

DEATH

It is one of the most effective lies they routinely tell: the idea that "open admission" shelters cannot be No Kill. Despite the constant drumbeat by the ASPCA, HSUS, PETA and others that No Kill means limiting intake, there are, in fact, dozens of open admission, No Kill animal control facilities serving hundreds of cities and towns across the United States, with more being achieved all the time.

NO KILL SHELTERS CAN BE PUBLIC OR PRIVATE, large or small, humane societies or municipal agencies. But national organizations like the ASPCA, HSUS and PETA routinely mislead people that so-called "open admission" animal control facilities cannot be No Kill. The ASPCA has written that, "A no-kill shelter really can't have an open admission policy. It must limit its intake if it wants to adopt out animals and not kill them." This is false. A No Kill shelter can be either "limited admission" or "open admission." And there are plenty of No Kill animal control shelters and thus No Kill communities which prove it.

YES! "Open admission" shelters *can* be No Kill.

NO! "Open admission" does not mean "more humane" when the end result is killing.

An "open admission" shelter does not have to—and should not—be an open door to the killing of animals. In addition, using the term "open admission" for kill shelters is misleading. Kill shelters are *closed* to people who love animals. They are *closed* to people who might have lost their job or lost their home but do not want their animals to die. They are *closed* to Good Samaritans who find animals but do not want them killed. They are *closed* to animal lovers who want to help save lives but will not be silent in the face of needless killing. And so they turn these people and their animals away, refusing to provide to them the service they are being paid to perform.

Ironically, kill shelters are so enmeshed in their so-called "open door" philosophy that they are also blind to any proactive steps that might limit the numbers of animals coming in through those doors, like pet retention programs, or that might increase the numbers of animals adopted, like comprehensive marketing campaigns. "Open door" does not mean "more humane" when the end result is mass killing.

DO THE MATH

For too many years, the killing of millions of animals in our nation's pounds has been justified on the basis of a supply-demand imbalance. We've been told that there are just "too many animals and not enough homes." In other words, pet overpopulation. But does pet overpopulation exist?

SUPPLY vs. DEMAND

Number of animals entering American shelters every year:

8,000,000

Number of animals killed annually in our nation's shelters:

4,000,000

Of those, the number killed but for a home:

3,000,000

Number of animals acquired by Americans every year from all sources:

23,500,000

Of those, the number who have not yet decided where they will get an animal and can be influenced to adopt from a shelter:

17,000,000

PET OVERPOPULATION: IT JUST DOESN'T ADD UP

THE NO KILL EQUATION

Lifesaving Alternatives to Killing That Harness Community Compassion

TWO DECADES AGO, the concept of a No Kill community was little more than a dream. Today, it is a reality in many cities and counties nationwide and the numbers continue to grow. And the first step is a decision by a shelter's leadership: a commitment to reject kill-oriented ways of doing business, to replace a regressive, anachronistic 19th century model of failure with 21st century innovations by implementing the No Kill Equation. No Kill starts as an act of will.

Animals enter shelters for a variety of reasons and with a variety of needs, but for over 100 years, the "solution" has been the same: adopt a few and kill the rest. The No Kill Equation provides a humane, life-affirming means of responding to every type of animal entering a shelter, and every type of need those animals might have. Some animals entering shelters are feral cats. At traditional shelters, they are killed, but at a No Kill shelter, they are neutered and released back to their habitats. Some animals entering shelters are motherless puppies and kittens. At traditional shelters, these animals are killed as well. At a No Kill shelter, they are sent into a foster home to provide around-the-clock care until they are eating on their own and old enough to be adopted. Some animals have medical or behavior issues. At a traditional shelter, they are killed. At a No Kill shelter, they are provided with rehabilitative care and then adopted. Whatever the situation, the No Kill Equation provides a lifesaving alternative that replaces killing.

While shelter leadership drives the No Kill initiative, it is the community that extends the safety net of care. Unlike traditional shelters—which view members of the public as adversaries and refuse to partner with them as rescuers or volunteers—a No Kill shelter embraces the people in its community. They are the key to success: they volunteer, foster, socialize animals, staff offsite adoption venues and open their hearts, homes and wallets to the animals in need. The public is at the center of every successful No Kill shelter in the nation. By working with people, implementing lifesaving programs and treating each life as precious, a shelter can transform itself.

NKE PROGRAMS & SERVICES

- ✓ Volunteers
- ✓ Rescue Partnerships
- ✓ Foster Care
- ✓ Trap, Neuter, Release
- ✓ Comprehensive Adoption Programs
- ✓ Medical & Behavior Prevention & Rehabilitation
- ✓ Pet Retention
- ✓ Public Relations/Community Involvement
- ✓ Proactive Redemptions
- ✓ High-Volume, Low-Cost Spay and Neuter
- ✓ Compassionate, Dedicated Leadership

VOLUNTEERS

Volunteers are a dedicated army of compassion and the backbone of a successful No Kill effort: they walk dogs, socialize cats, assist potential adopters and more. Volunteers make the difference between success and failure and, for the animals, life and death.

An adoption or transfer to a rescue group frees up cage and kennel space, reduces expenses for feeding, cleaning and killing and improves a community's rate of lifesaving.

RESCUE PARTNERSHIPS

FOSTER CARE

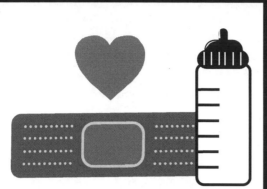

Volunteer foster care is a low-cost, and often no-cost, way of increasing a shelter's capacity and caring for sick and injured or behaviorally challenged animals, thus saving more lives.

Trap-Neuter-Release (TNR) programs provide feral cats who enter shelters a vital alternative to killing (see pages 202-203).

TRAP, NEUTER, RELEASE

COMPREHENSIVE ADOPTIONS

Yes! We're OPEN

By implementing comprehensive adoption programs—including more convenient public access hours, offsite venues and incentives—shelters can replace killing with adoptions.

HOLIDAY SPECIAL!

Adopt Today

MEDICAL & BEHAVIOR REHABILITATION & PREVENTION

Shelters need to keep animals happy and healthy and moving efficiently through the facility. To do this, shelters must put in place thorough vaccination, handling, cleaning, socialization and care policies to prevent illness and rehabilitative efforts for those who come in sick, injured, unweaned or traumatized.

Some of the reasons people surrender animals to shelters can be prevented if shelters work with people to help them solve their problems. Saving animals requires shelters to embrace innovative strategies for keeping people and their companion animals together.

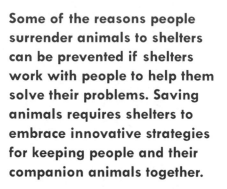

PET RETENTION

PUBLIC RELATIONS & COMMUNITY INVOLVEMENT

Increasing a shelter's public exposure through marketing, public relations and partnering with community groups and businesses increases adoptions, volunteers, donations and other support.

PROACTIVE REDEMPTIONS

One of the most overlooked opportunities for reducing killing in animal control shelters is increasing the number of lost animals returned to their families. This includes matching reports of lost animals with animals in the shelter, rehoming animals in the field and use of technology such as posting lost animals on the internet.

No-cost and low-cost, high-volume spay/neuter programs increase the number of animals sterilized and reduce the number of animals entering the shelter by removing the primary barrier preventing more people from having their animals altered: cost.

HIGH- VOLUME LOW-COST SPAY/NEUTER

COMPASSIONATE, HARD-WORKING SHELTER DIRECTOR

The final element of the No Kill Equation is the most important of all, without which all other elements are thwarted—a hard-working, compassionate shelter director who is not content to continue killing while regurgitating tired clichés about "public irresponsibility" or hiding behind the myth of "too many animals, not enough homes." Such a director implements the programs and services of the No Kill Equation comprehensively and with integrity while holding his or her staff accountable to results and high standards.

Keeping Score:

WHAT DO YOU MEAN YOU'RE THE "EXPERTS" ?

> **ex·pert**
> [n., ek-spurt]
> A person who has a comprehensive and authoritative knowledge of or skill in a particular area.

TO THE MEDIA, to the public and to legislators, our nation's large animal protection organizations are often seen as undisputed sheltering "experts." It is a distinction deeply at odds with their actual accomplishments or, more accurately, lack thereof. For behind their hallowed, pedigreed names is a tragic and sordid history of undermining, rather than leading, the very cause they were founded to promote. Of the numerous communities across the nation which have ended the killing of healthy and treatable animals, *not a single one* achieved success by following the recommendations or guidance of these groups. In fact, in many cases, animal lovers had to fight one or more of these organizations in order to succeed.

The national animal protection organizations frequently cite the slowly declining overall death rate as proof that their work is having a positive impact. In reality, the programs and protocols that have led to this decline—TNR, foster care, proactive adoption programs, volunteer programs, low cost spay/neuter and working collaboratively with rescue groups, among others—were all opposed by the large organizations when grassroots activists pioneered them. The national death rate is declining *in spite* of these organizations and not because of them.

DR. SEMMELWEIS, I PRESUME?

Understanding the Opposition to No Kill

The Semmelweis Reflex
A sociological term used to describe mob behavior in which a discovery of an important scientific fact is punished rather than rewarded.

SHELTER KILLING IS THE LEADING CAUSE OF DEATH for healthy dogs and cats in the United States—millions are losing their lives every year. In scale and scope, this killing can only be described as an epidemic. In light of this, one would predict and hope that leaders running shelters killing thousands of dogs and cats every month, or those in charge of multi-million dollar national organizations formed to protect companion animals, would work to replicate the programs and services that make it possible to stem the tide of animal killing.

It is, at the very least, worth a try, even if they are not convinced of its potential. Mitch Schneider, the former-head of Washoe County Regional Animal Services in Reno, Nevada, describes what the shelter was like when he started:

We [killed] thousands of animals each year. In fact, we had two full-time staff members doing that most of the day. That meant a freezer full of dead pets—fifteen barrels full.

Every day, a renderer came to empty the freezer, and every day we filled it up again.

When urged to shift toward a No Kill orientation, he said:

I didn't believe it could work, at least not in Reno. I did the math and remember thinking that maybe it would work in a more affluent community but we had a more transient population and a high intake rate.

[But] no matter what any of us believes, we ultimately won't know if we don't try. On top of that, if in fact No Kill failed, I didn't want it to be because our agency refused to think outside the box or because I didn't like the term. Even if we didn't achieve the ultimate goal, I knew it could still be better than now. We could save more animals. And that would make thousands of animals pretty happy, and it would make thousands of animal lovers pretty happy.

In less than one year, Washoe County shelters reduced the killing by over 50 percent. When Schneider retired, Washoe County had a 94 percent save rate communitywide, despite a per capita intake rate over two times higher than the national average, four times higher than Los Angeles, five times higher than San Francisco and 10 times higher than New York City.

Being open to new information and new ways of doing things—what Schneider calls "continuous process improvement"—is how people behave when they're dedicated to doing the best job possible. And when it comes to those who are making life and death decisions, it is what ethics demand. But, unlike Schneider, shelter directors in the vast majority of American communities resist, rather than embrace, innovation. Instead, the "old guard" animal shelter directors ignore and/or denigrate the programs that make lifesaving success possible, while animals continue to be needlessly killed by the millions.

Historian John Barry writes that,

> Institutions reflect the cumulative personalities of those within them, especially their leadership. They tend, unfortunately, to mirror less admirable human traits, developing and protecting self-interest and even ambition. They try to [create] order [not by learning from others or the past, but]... by closing off and isolating themselves from that which does not fit. They become bureaucratic.

In short, they focus on self-preservation at the expense of their mission. And in the case of animal shelters and the national allies who support them, this bureaucracy leads to the unnecessary killing of animals. They put the

> **Being open to new information and new ways of doing things is how people behave when they're dedicated to doing the best job possible. And when it comes to those who are making life and death decisions, it is what ethics demand. Yet shelter directors in the vast majority of American communities resist, rather than embrace, innovation.**

interest—*indeed the very lives*—of the animals aside, instead promulgating an anti-No Kill rhetoric with a surprising level of venom and with no valid basis for doing so. Why?

Sociologists have coined the term the "Semmelweis Reflex" to describe "mob behavior in which a discovery of an important scientific fact is punished rather than rewarded." It is named for a 19th century physician, Dr. Ignaz Semmelweis, who experienced this troubling aspect of human nature first hand when he tried to educate other doctors about the importance of hand washing and instrument cleaning before treating patients.

Dr. Semmelweis observed a higher incidence of deaths due to puerperal fever in maternity wards associated with teaching hospitals than in births attended by midwives. In trying to figure out why puerperal fever was a hazard of giving birth in a hospital rather than at home, Semmelweis opined that students and doctors might be carrying diseases from autopsies they performed, while midwives who did not

> **The archaic voices of tradition in sheltering are acting the same way as the doctors who put their own reputations above their patients. They refuse to innovate and modernize because they are threatened by the growth of the No Kill philosophy and what this means for their own stature in the humane movement.**

perform such procedures were not. Semmelweis also found that rigorous instrument cleaning and hand washing could bring the fever rate down to zero. Had doctors known at the time that germs caused disease, this finding would have been unremarkable.

Unfortunately, Semmelweis' discovery predated the germ theory of disease. At the time, no one knew that asepsis was important. According to Semmelweis' critics, hand washing wasn't needed when they could clearly see that their hands had nothing on them. And, tragically, doctors ignored his recommendations and continued with business as usual, with deadly results for their patients. Once germ theory became known and established, however, Semmelweis was vindicated for his foresight. Sterility through instrument cleaning and hand washing has since become the norm.

In the field of animal sheltering, the housing, socialization, adoption, foster care, cleaning and vaccination protocols, medical and behavior rehabilitation and other efforts pioneered in communities across the country offer a better, more humane model of sheltering. They provide an alternative way of operating a shelter that delivers high-quality care and reduced disease rates, while vastly increasing rates of lifesaving.

Rather than attack Semmelweis, doctors should have simply washed their hands, since Semmelweis pointed out that this eliminated deaths, even though, at the time, no one could explain why. Similarly, rather than attack the methods of sheltering which allow the vast majority of animals to be saved, shelter administrators likewise should copy its precepts because it has been shown to work in other communities.

Unfortunately, something more nefarious was at work in Semmelweis' time than a failure of understanding about germs, and it is the same "reflex" which is at work in sheltering today. Semmelweis was fired because doctors felt he was criticizing the superiority of hospital births over home births, something that threatened their position in the social hierarchy. And therein lies the rub. The archaic voices of tradition in sheltering are acting the same way as the doctors who put their own reputations above their patients. They refuse to innovate and modernize because they are threatened by the growth of the No Kill philosophy and what this means for their own stature in the humane movement.

The No Kill movement threatens to expose these individuals as failures. They kill when they don't have to. And that makes them unworthy of their proclaimed expertise and not the leaders they have for so many years claimed to be. No Kill is a threat. And despite the body count that accompanies their resistance, it is threat that they will not accept without a fight.

ANIMAL SHELTERING IN AMERICA
"SPINAL MONDAY"

THE STAFF CALLED IT "SPINAL MONDAY." In March 2005, a volunteer found a rabbit with an exposed spine at the Los Angeles County Department of Animal Care & Control (LACDACC) shelter in Carson, California. A subsequent investigation uncovered that the rabbit had been left alive in her cage for approximately one week with her spine exposed. Also discovered in the cage were a dead rabbit, his decomposing body covered with flies, and another rabbit with an eye popping out of his socket who was being attacked by the others. None of the rabbits had food or water. Shelter employees claimed to be unaware of these conditions, even though they are required to clean the cages every day. Nor did being made aware of the neglect and suffering which the rabbits endured lead them to improve conditions. During an unannounced visit to the same shelter two years later, No Kill Advocacy Center attorneys found filthy rabbit cages and empty water bowls, apparently once again "forgotten" in an out-of-the-way back room.

(ABOVE) A rabbit tries to drink water from an empty container at LACDACC.

How Do They Measure Success?

THEY DON'T

IN A 2011 RADIO INTERVIEW, Dori Villalon, then the Vice President of Animal Protection for the American Humane Association and their resident sheltering "expert," was asked whether she believed shelter directors were doing a good job. Villalon stated that,

I've been a shelter director. I admire so many shelter directors out there. I have met people who are working so hard in states where they are challenged with every turn, from political to financial, yet they are doing whatever they can to save animals. So I tend to feel that anyone who gets into this business, I'm giving you the benefit of the doubt. We are all trying to do the same thing.

On its website, AHA claims to be a resource for animal welfare professionals, offering them "the education and training to provide the best animal care possible." But when asked whether those who have the power of life and death over animals are actually providing "the best animal care possible," she offered a cliché, stating that no one wants to kill while admitting

that shelter directors are given the "benefit of the doubt"—in other words, a free ride—by her organization rather than being held to measureable standards and goals.

Despite overwhelming evidence to the contrary in communities across the United States, Villalon ensured listeners that shelter directors are "doing whatever they can to save animals." As a representative of an organization which claims to be ensuring that our shelters are run humanely and effectively, it was Villalon's obligation not only to admit that our nation's shelters are broken and highly dysfunctional, but to provide listeners with substantive guidelines which they could use to measure how well their local shelter is meeting its obligations.

Indeed, there are many indicators that can be used to judge how humanely and compassionately a shelter is operating—the most significant one being how many animals the shelter kills. Does the shelter have the programs of the No Kill Equation and how fully have they been implemented? Is there a safety net in place for all species entering the shelter, such as rabbits, birds, wildlife and other animals in addition to dogs and cats? Do sick and injured animals receive quality veterinary care? Does the shelter follow the latest vaccination and cleaning protocols to ensure the health of the animals? Are the animals well-socialized and do they receive plenty of exercise to reduce stress and anxiety? And is the shelter well-regarded by the community it serves? Of course, there are many more.

And given that the answer to these questions in most communities is, "No," then the answer to the overall question that Villalon was asked should have been, "No," too. Moreover, why didn't Villalon offer a single one of these benchmarks, rather than generalize that shelter directors have a responsibility to have a strategic plan in order to increase lifesaving and reduce killing? Why don't any of the national organizations hold shelter directors to these standards? Why don't they teach them how to recognize and learn from the hallmarks of success? The answer is simple.

If you are an agency that is supposed to be providing oversight and you intentionally fail to, standards are a threat. Standards invite comparison and comparison can compel criticism. So while questions that attempt to gauge success and highlight areas of deficiency are important if you are seeking improvement and accountability, if you are not—that is, if no matter what the answers, you do not intend to do anything about it—then they are dangerous questions to be asking. Because not only can the answers to such questions be used to criticize your friends who run shelters, but they could be used to criticize you for failing to hold them accountable, too. And that is why they are very careful never to ask them.

Don't Ask Don't Tell

While questions that attempt to gauge success and highlight areas of deficiency are important if you are seeking improvement and accountability, if you are not, then they are dangerous questions to be asking. And that, quite simply, is why they don't.

HOW TO TELL IF A SHELTER IS DOING
A GOOD JOB

FOR WELL OVER A CENTURY, the killing of dogs and cats has been a central strategy of most animal control agencies, as well as private SPCAs and humane societies which contract with cities and towns to run their pounds. They even created a euphemism—"putting them to sleep"—to make the task of killing easier. In the end, that's exactly what the humane movement has become: a movement of "euphemisms"— euphemisms such as "euthanasia" and "humane death." In the age of No Kill, add one more: "unadoptable."

To shelters mired in killing, the term "unadoptable" is interpreted very broadly. Some shelters, for example, consider a kitten with a minor cold or a dog older than five years to be unadoptable. And with national organizations telling communities that they are each permitted to define for themselves which animals are healthy or treatable, that each community must determine for itself its lifesaving commitment (see pages 61-62), shelters now claim that they are No Kill by simply defining the animals away.

Even though 95 to 98 percent of all animals entering shelters are healthy and treatable, the Michigan Humane Society claimed it was saving all "adoptable" animals despite killing roughly seven out of ten (including 68 percent of puppies and kittens). Likewise, the Los Angeles County animal control shelter claimed it was saving over 90% of "adoptable" animals despite killing half of all dogs and eight out of ten cats.

Only when a shelter truly "zeros out" deaths of healthy and treatable animals do we get closer to euthanasia's dictionary definition: "the act or practice of killing or permitting the death of hopelessly sick or injured individuals (as

CALCULATING A SHELTER'S SAVE RATE

Some shelters are adopting the language of No Kill but not the programs and services which save lives. As a result, they may be killing as they have always done, but call themselves "No Kill" after unfairly labeling animals as "unadoptable." They may claim they are saving all the animals who can be saved, but do not count feral cats, animals who have died on their own, animals with highly treatable medical or behavior conditions, animals who they consider "too young" or "too old," or animals they claim have been killed at the request of the people surrendering them. To determine whether a shelter is doing a good job, calculate their save rate for yourself. If they refuse to provide the statistics you need to do so, they are almost certainly not No Kill.

ACQUIRE THE FOLLOWING STATISTICS:

 A: All animals who were in the shelter's custody at the beginning of the reporting year and all live intakes including those considered "owner requested euthanasia" with only the following exception: animals brought to a shelter's medical clinic for procedures such as vaccines or sterilization where it was understood that the person was going to retrieve their animal following the medical procedure.

 B: All deaths: animals who were killed (including "owner requested euthanasia"), animals who died in the shelter's custody or constructive custody (such as foster care) and animals who are missing and unaccounted for.

 C: All animals who are alive: those adopted, reclaimed by their families, transferred to No Kill rescue groups or other shelters (where they are not at risk for being killed) and those still in the shelter's custody.

THEN CALCULATE:

The save rate is calculated as follows: C divided by A. For example, if a shelter takes in 100 animals a year and 80 are adopted, reclaimed, transferred to No Kill rescue groups or still on hand, the shelter save rate is 80 percent. Conversely, its death rate (B divided by A) is 20 percent. The save rate plus the death rate should always equal 100 percent of live intakes.

LOOK FOR A SAVE RATE OF ROUGHLY 95%

persons or domestic animals) in a relatively painless way for reasons of mercy." But getting close to the actual definition is not the same as achieving it. Nor is the definition itself beyond questioning or even static. Today, the No Kill movement seeks to save all healthy and treatable animals. The fact that the remaining five percent are hopelessly ill or are vicious dogs, however, doesn't mean that their killing isn't ethically problematic. Obviously, aggressive dogs beyond the reach of even the most innovative behavior rehabilitation protocols are not suffering. To categorize their killing as "euthanasia" is inaccurate. Such animals are currently killed for *our* convenience, not their needs.

In addition, while animals entering shelters who are diagnosed with fatal conditions are categorized as "untreatable," many are not yet suffering and can continue living for months or even years with palliative care. For example, a cat with kidney disease can enjoy a good quality of life with fluid therapy and a dog's malignant form of cancer might be slowed with chemotherapy and other drugs. In fact, as some in the sanctuary and hospice care movements argue, the killing of any animal who is not "irremediably suffering"* is unethical.

As more and more people are calling the killing into question as well as proving that viable, humane alternatives do exist, they are increasingly forcing our shelters to reject the system of casual convenience killing that is now the norm. Moreover, as we succeed at building a culture in which the lives and needs of each individual animal is paramount, the more obvious the gaps in the safety net will become.

---

* An irremediably suffering animal is any animal with a medical condition who has a poor or grave prognosis for being able to live without severe, unremitting pain.

THE GAS CHAMBER

LEGAL ANIMAL TORTURE

A GAS CHAMBER is one of the cruelest methods of legally killing an animal. Animals are often crammed into the small chambers, piled one on top of the other. When the chamber is then filled with poisonous carbon monoxide gas, the animals inside gasp for breath, feel searing pain in their lungs and often claw at the chamber door or throw themselves against the sides in a desperate attempt to escape. Perhaps worst of all, this process can last up to 30 minutes. Even though HSUS has criticized gas chambers for their notorious cruelty, their professed "opposition" to gassing did not stop them from sending dogs they claimed to have rescued to a shelter that used a gas chamber to kill them (see pages 96-97). Nor did it stop them from giving another shelter an award as a "Shelter We Love" that also uses one, killing nine out of 10 animals they take in that way (see pages 98-99).

At one time, HSUS provided shelters a step-by-step guide to building their own "homemade" gas chamber. Some of those devices are still in use today. While a small number of states have outlawed their use for all animals, the gas chamber remains legal in most. In 2011, HSUS led a coalition of organizations to defeat legislation that would have banned the use of the gas chamber in Texas.

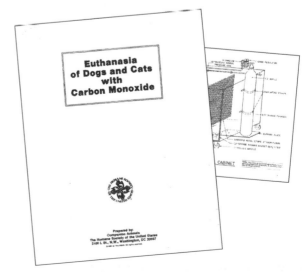

Euthanasia
of Dogs and Cats
with
Carbon Monoxide

MOTIVATED BLINDNESS

Motivated Blindness
A term coined by psychologists to describe behavior in which people ignore situations which they find uncomfortable to address.

IT HAS BEEN OVER A DECADE since the achievement of the first No Kill community in the United States. More than ten years have passed since a shelter actually achieved what the animal protection movement, for nearly 50 years prior, had been claiming was one of its most pressing goals: *ending the killing of animals in our nation's shelters*. And yet despite this achievement and the dozens of communities nationwide which have since followed its model and realized the same level of success, large animal protection organizations like HSUS and PETA have never acknowledged, let alone celebrated, this important milestone. It is as if the key to ending the killing has yet to be discovered; the heads of these groups forge on as before, mired in disproven dogma, intentionally blind to existing success and the valuable lessons it holds for every shelter in America.

Psychologists have coined the term "motivated blindness" to describe behavior in which people ignore situations which they find uncomfortable to address. Were leadership at groups like HSUS or PETA to actually acknowledge No Kill success to the public, it would immediately create an expectation that they would champion it. And because championing No Kill would require sincerity, dedication, hard work and, most threatening of all, acknowledging that their friends and colleagues who are currently running shelters are not meeting these standards or that they themselves failed to do so when they ran shelters and needlessly killed animals, they don't acknowledge it or the effort required to make it happen elsewhere. In fact, they fight it.

KEEPING STANDARDS LOW BY CELEBRATING FAILURE

In 2004, a contingent of 20 killing shelters and their allies, under siege by the growing No Kill movement, met in a Northern California community to pen what they dubbed, "The Asilomar Accords," a document outlining shelter policies which they stated were designed to further "goals focused on significantly reducing the euthanasia of healthy and treatable companion animals in the United States." Yet, in contrast to this stated mission, the policies they actually agreed upon sought to cement the status quo and undermine No Kill efforts.

They reaffirmed some of the most egregious sheltering policies by allowing for the round-up and killing of feral cats, refusing to work with rescue groups and promoting draconian animal control laws which have been proven time and again to exacerbate, rather than lessen, shelter killing (see pages 212-213). The groups also ignored the central lesson of existing No Kill success, that in order to end the killing of animals, shelters were obligated to comprehensively implement the No Kill Equation. Instead, the groups claimed that no one should require shelters to implement any programs they did not want and that each shelter director would be allowed to determine for himself how their shelter would operate. In short, the status quo.

It is as if the key to ending the killing has yet to be discovered; the heads of these groups forge on as before, mired in disproven dogma, intentionally blind to existing success and the valuable lessons it holds for every shelter in America.

As was true before the Asilomar Accords, if an animal enters a shelter with a caring and compassionate director, the animal will live. If she is not so fortunate, the animal will die. In fact, it could also depend on who is in charge of a particular shelter at a particular time.

Macon County, Georgia's dog pound was a slaughterhouse, roughly 85 percent of dogs were killed. But when the shelter director was fired, and an interim director appointed, the killing immediately stopped. Every day for the 49 days he was in charge, the animals went home alive—every single one of them. But the county was ordered to reinstate the old director following a lawsuit and he was once again put in charge of the pound.

As a result, the killings started again: first it was six, then 17, and then on a day where there were banks of empty cages, 14 animals were put to death anyway. To the ASPCA, HSUS and all the other signatories of the Asilomar Accords, this is as it should be.

The Asilomar Accords also directed that shelter reformers must stop using the term "No Kill," labeling it as "hurtful and divisive" and ignoring the fact that by following the model of successful communities, every shelter could be a No Kill shelter and the criticism would come to an end. The policies agreed upon in the Asilomar Accords reflect the paradigm that predominates in animal sheltering today: keep the public ignorant and expectations low by championing mediocrity and failure.

This explains why in 2002, HSUS rallied around the New York City animal control shelter even after the comptroller's audit found "a number of allegations of animal neglect and abuse," "many animals didn't have regular access to water and were often left in dirty cages" and nearly 70 percent of dogs and cats killed. It also explains why in 2012, HSUS gave Davidson County, North Carolina's pound an award for being a "Shelter We Love." The Davidson County shelter kills nine out of 10 animals in one of the cruelest ways possible—by gassing them to death. It also kills animals illegally and sadistically, putting different species into the gas chamber so that employees can watch them fight before they are killed (see pages 98-99).

Not to be outdone, the ASPCA named the Houston SPCA the nation's "Shelter of the Year" in 2006, even though that shelter's regressive policies, breed discrimination, antagonistic relationship with rescue groups, lack of transparency and failure to comprehensively implement alternatives to killing make it the antithesis of a well-run, compassionate and successful animal shelter.

The Houston SPCA kills seven out of 10 animals and fights reform efforts in that city and throughout Texas. When the Texas Companion Animal Protection Act was introduced in 2011—a law which would have stopped breed discrimination, convenience killing and gassing—the Houston SPCA was part of a coalition of kill shelters and animal protection organizations (including HSUS) which banded together to successfully defeat it. The actions have made the Houston SPCA a target of criticism by animal lovers in that community, a symbol of the uncaring, cruelty and corruption of its mission that predominates today. None of that would stop the ASPCA from making it its choice as America's best shelter.

ANIMAL SHELTERING IN AMERICA
MEET HOPE

Hope entered a Texas shelter in need of veterinary care and pain control. For three days, the shelter director wouldn't let a rescue group help her. When the rescue group went public about her plight, the director retaliated by killing another dog they had also offered to save.

MEET HOPE. Hope entered the pound in Harris County, Texas with severe injuries. A rescue group offered to immediately take Hope to a private veterinarian at their own expense and give her not just the medical care she desperately needed, but pain control to relieve her of her immense suffering. The pound's director refused. The group then offered to pay for the care if the shelter provided it. Once again, the pound's director refused. Instead, Hope was allowed to languish with little relief for three days during the state-mandated stray holding period. By the time the holding period ended, so did Hope's life: rescuers rushed Hope to the veterinarian but she could not be saved. Hope was not an aberration.

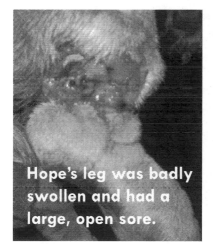

Hope's leg was badly swollen and had a large, open sore.

The Harris County pound kills eight out of every 10 animals. It kills mothers in front of their kittens and puppies, and kittens and puppies in front of their mothers. An investigation by the Harris County Attorney's Office found rampant abuse including cats "pulled out of kennel cages, injected in the chest cavity and then dropped on the floor to die." In one case, a dog who shelter staff ineptly tried to kill was placed in a garbage bag and taken to the freezer with the dead bodies. But the dog was not dead, and clawed and chewed his way out of the garbage bag in a bid to escape. When it was discovered he was still alive, an animal control officer offered to adopt him. Instead, the director ordered the dog killed and he was. In fact, when the rescue group went public about Hope, the pound director retaliated by killing another dog they offered to save, too.

The Texas Companion Animal Protection Act, introduced in 2011, would not only have given rescue groups the legal right to save animals like Hope but would also have required the shelter to give Hope needed veterinary care. Known popularly as "Hope's Law," the legislation was defeated by groups committed to business as usual.

How to Become an AHA Certified KILLER

THE AMERICAN HUMANE ASSOCIATION bills itself as "the nation's 'voice' for the protection of animals." And it claims that,

> One of the important ways American Humane helps protect animals is by educating and training people how to provide the best animal care possible. Throughout the year, we host trainings nationwide for animal welfare professionals and for all people who love animals and want to make a difference in their well-being.

What kind of training does AHA provide for those who might want to "make a difference" in the "well-being" of animals? Every year, AHA hosts "Euthanasia by Injection" workshops where shelter employees from across the nation come together to learn how to kill animals. "Whether you've never performed euthanasia or have years of experience with it," says AHA, everyone is welcome—including those who will use the knowledge AHA gives them to kill healthy and treatable animals. AHA holds the workshops at regressive shelters across the country—so there are plenty of animals on hand to kill.

Imagine it. A hall filled with people who are there to learn one thing: how to kill dogs and cats. And although on the very same website that AHA advertises this workshop you can read their official position against dissection which states that dissection is wrong because it teaches children "that it is all right to disregard another's life for the sake of learning," this

AHA opposes dissection because it teaches children "that it is all right to disregard another's life for the sake of learning." That is, unless they are the ones doing the "teaching." At AHA's *Euthanasia by Injection* workshop, not only will AHA teach you how to kill using real animals, not only will they "catch you up" on the "latest techniques and drugs," they'll teach you how to kill animals in a variety of ways, too.

philosophy apparently doesn't apply to *them*. And even though it is not the job of an "animal protection" group to teach people how to kill, at this workshop, not only will AHA teach you how to kill real animals, not only will they "catch you up" on the "latest techniques and drugs," they'll teach you how to kill animals in a variety of ways, too.

They'll teach you how to inject animals with poison in the vein. They will teach you how to inject animals with poison in the gut. And they will teach you how to inject animals with poison straight into the heart. And in case the animals you are killing realize that you are in fact trying to kill them and fight back, AHA will show you how to restrain them so you can get the job done. And then, when you think it's all over and that the animal you just poisoned is dead, they will teach you how to verify that you did, in fact, kill him, just to make sure more poison isn't required.

And what happens if you have a moment of clarity about what is actually happening—how an organization that claims to help animals is teaching you with precise detail how to kill them—and your conscience protests? AHA will soothe your guilt by teaching you how to smother your compassion. With "an entire section" of the conference devoted to dealing with "the unique stress felt by those who perform euthanasia," they'll lull you back into a state of complacency and assure you that you

are, in fact, a hero for helping create that pile of dead dogs and cats. They'll teach you to regard any empathy you might have felt for your victims not as a plea from your better

eu·tha·na·sia
[n., yoo-thuh-ney-zhuh]
The act or practice of killing or permitting the death of hopelessly sick or injured individuals (as persons or domestic animals) in a relatively painless way for reasons of mercy.

Euthanasia is the act of killing for reasons of mercy. When used accurately, it is a term to describe the hastening of impending death to spare pain and suffering. Using the word to describe the killing of healthy or treatable animals in shelters is misleading and untrue. Nonetheless, it is the shelter industry's favorite misnomer, employed to obscure the reality of shelter killing for the American public.

AHA trains people who kill healthy and treatable animals.

nature to reject killing, but as a pesky case of what they call "compassion stress."

And when the weekend draws to a close and the two days of poisoning animals is nearing its end, when you've successfully watched other people kill animals without trying to stop them and you've even proven that you have what it takes to kill animals yourself, you won't leave empty handed. AHA will make sure that your memories of their conference—of that horrifying weekend when you and other people from across the country came together in a hall to kill innocent animals behind closed doors—will last a lifetime. You will get a certificate that proves you are an AHA-certified killer so that everyone who sees it will know exactly what you are capable of doing.

Death at a No Kill Shelter

It is true; No Kill shelter employees must also learn how to kill, even if it is just for irremediably suffering and non-rehabilitatable animals. When Nathan ran the No Kill animal control shelter in Tompkins County, New York, he refused to send employees to similar workshops because they used healthy and treatable animals. Instead, Tompkins County employees were trained using only hopelessly ill and injured animals who were "euthanized" out of compassion. And they were trained on the job, the way those who learn about human medicine are taught at teaching hospitals. Because it was a No Kill shelter saving 93 percent of all animals, what AHA promises to teach in a weekend took months, in some cases a year. But no one complained or would have had it otherwise. And why would they? They were specifically hired for their love of animals and because of that, it simply would not have occurred to them that it should be any other way. Moreover, unlike AHA, Nathan would never have trained someone who would use that knowledge to kill healthy and treatable animals.

REALITY CHECK

In Their Own Words

"Gosh, um, I don't know that number."

Dori Villalon, AHA Vice-President of Animal Protection, KABC Radio, New York City, January 2011

During a 2011 radio interview in which she explained that killing in shelters is necessary because there are too many animals for too few homes available, Dori Villalon, Vice-President of Animal Protection for the American Humane Association, was asked how many homes become available for companion animals every year in the United States. Her response: "Gosh, um, I don't know that number." How can someone claim that there is a supply-demand imbalance in terms of available homes and number of animals without knowing the demand side of the equation? They can't.

In fact, there are over seven times as many people looking to acquire an animal every year than there are animals being killed in shelters. Pet overpopulation, the main excuse given

by national animal protection organizations to defend the killing, does not exist (see page 42). Shelters can adopt their way out of killing and many have.

Villalon went on to say that to end the killing of animals in shelters, every person in America would have to adopt eight animals and even argued that we could do that this year. She cautioned, however, that we would have to do that *every* year. But if every person in America adopted eight animals, that number would equal about 2.4 billion dogs and cats, 600-times the number actually being killed in shelters, but for a home.

If we can adopt out 2.4 billion as Villalon claimed, we can surely adopt out the true number: three million. In fact, using the most successful shelters as a benchmark and adjusting for population, U.S. shelters combined could be adopting out almost nine million animals a year. That is three times the number being killed for lack of a home. In fact, it is more than total impounds.

If we increased the total population of animals in American homes who come from shelters by just three percent, we would end the killing. It is a very feasible goal. And many communities are now proving it. But if you are uneducated about the most basic facts regarding the numbers and causes of animals being killed in shelters, you will not see the vast, untapped potential and—ignorantly believing the problem to be insurmountable, inflating the numbers 600-fold and providing the excuse regressive shelters need to kill—you will not even attempt to fix it.

When the person who does that is Vice-President of one of the nation's oldest national companion animal welfare organizations, a so-called "expert" people look to for guidance, it is unforgivable.

ANIMAL SHELTERING IN AMERICA
MEET PATRICK

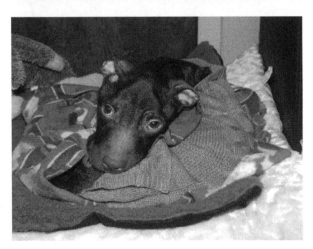

To caring and compassionate people, he is known as Patrick, the horrifically abused dog who was discarded and left for dead in Newark, New Jersey. But to the Associated Humane Societies of New Jersey, he is "trademark registration number 23699" and a "very valuable brand for commercial exploitation and fund-raising."

MEET PATRICK. Patrick is a dog who was starved nearly to death, stuffed into a garbage bag and thrown in the trash at an apartment building in Newark, New Jersey, in 2011. Patrick's ordeal captured the attention and concern of animal lovers nationwide who flooded the veterinary office caring for Patrick with donations. When the Associated Humane Societies of New Jersey (AHS), the organization which contracts for animal control in Newark, realized Patrick's fundraising potential, they

began seeking his custody, even though the veterinarian who had nursed Patrick back to health wanted to adopt him.

In 2003, The New Jersey State Commission of Investigation released the results of a wide-ranging investigation into waste and abuse by AHS. The Commission found that "AHS officials over the years have engaged in questionable financial practices, conflicts of interest, mismanagement and negligent animal care to the extent that the organization effectively lost sight of its core mission." The Commission found that, "the history of AHS' shelter operation has been dominated by deplorable kennel conditions, inhumane treatment of animals by workers, mismanagement and nonexistent or inadequate medical care." The findings included: "Accountability so lax that millions of dollars accumulated in AHS cash and investment accounts while the care and feeding of sick and injured animals went begging."

In 2009, state animal welfare inspectors found even more deplorable conditions for animals including "severe fly and maggot infestation," "overwhelming malodorous smell" and a "large amount of blood... splattered on the floor, walls, and viewing window." They also found animals "exhibiting signs of severe bloody, watery diarrhea and lethargy... not separated or receiving treatment." Of the 4,296 cats taken in, 2,721 were put to death. Another 616 either died or went missing. Of the 3,423 dogs taken in, 806 were killed. Another 60 either died or went missing.

The Mayor of Newark intervened to keep Patrick with the veterinarian, ordering AHS not to have further contact with the dog. In response, AHS sued both the city of Newark and the veterinarian who saved Patrick's life. Instead of seeing to it that Patrick is given the life and love he deserves by staying with the person with whom he has bonded, AHS can only see dollar signs, a conspiracy to "deprive AHS of its property rights" in Patrick. They've asked the superior court of Essex County, New Jersey to award them money damages because the nine million dollars in annual revenues they already take in apparently isn't enough.

According to AHS, saving Patrick's life, trying to keep him in perhaps the only loving environment he has ever known and free from further exploitation is not the right thing to do because, regardless of what might be best for Patrick, it amounts to "interference with [AHS] business activities" and its "economic advantage" resulting in "significant losses." They've not only asked for all the money they could have potentially raised off of Patrick, they've even asked the court to award them the money people donated directly to the veterinarian which went to pay for his medical care, with interest. Their goal is to put Patrick on display in their "zoo" where they can fundraise off him indefinitely, even though doing so would cost Patrick the most important thing in the world: a loving home.

In 2009 New Jersey state investigators found deplorable conditions at AHS' Newark shelter, including rotting animals and floors splattered with blood and fecal material.

A DEADLY SLEIGHT OF HAND

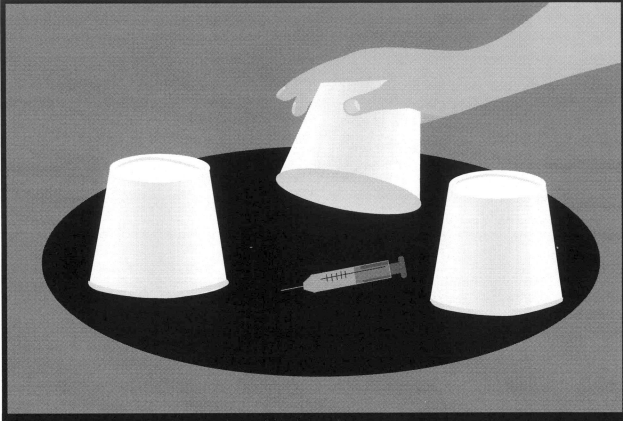

Animal "Rescue" ASPCA/HSUS Style

res·cue
[v. /ˈres.kjuː/]
To free or deliver from confinement,
violence, danger or evil.

ASK PEOPLE WHAT IT MEANS TO "RESCUE" AN ANIMAL and every single one of them will tell you it means to deliver an animal from harm's way and into safety. That, after all, is the common sense definition of the word. It's also the dictionary definition. And it's the one that HSUS and the ASPCA hope you think of when they put out fundraising appeals for the animals they claim to "rescue." In their television commercials, in their publications, on their Facebook page and whenever they reach out to the media to announce their latest campaign—all of which are designed to tug on the heartstrings of Americans—they use the word "rescue" to define their involvement in cases involving animal neglect, abuse, hoarding or exploitation. Yet for many of these animals, a "rescue" ASPCA-style or HSUS-style isn't a rescue at all, but a classic case of out of the frying pan and into the fire.

> **For many of the animals HSUS and the ASPCA claim to "rescue," what they experience isn't a rescue at all, but a classic case of out of the frying pan and into the fire.**

With their combined 300 million dollars in annual revenues and the support of millions of people who love animals, the ASPCA and HSUS have not only the means to provide their own housing and care for animals but also the ability to find them homes. Yet when they assist in a large-scale "rescue," they often dump the animals at local shelters, pocket the donations meant for their care and then walk away. After the photo ops and the fundraising solicitations have been sent out, the animals get shipped off to shelters across the country, where they are either put to death or local animals are put to death so the ASPCA or HSUS animals can be taken in.

In a press release entitled, "The HSUS Names the Top Ten Emergency Placement Partners of 2011," HSUS wrote,

After the HSUS removes animals from abusive situations and provides immediate veterinary care, the organization works with Emergency Placement Partners to care for and place animals. These organizations provide the animals with continued veterinary care, rehabilitation and ultimately, placement in new homes.

Or do they? In fact, in many cases, they do not. Because quite often the shelters to which the ASPCA and HSUS send animals are kill shelters that are as heartless as the circumstances from

which many of the animals have been "rescued." In fact, the shelter at the top of HSUS' List of 2011 Emergency Placement Partners is the Guilford County Animal Shelter in North Carolina, a shelter with a 42 percent rate of killing and where any dog who looks like a Rottweiler, Pit Bull or Chow is killed without ever being offered for adoption— young or old, friendly or scared, healthy or not, they are put to death. And yet despite the killing of nearly half of all animals who pass through the doors of the Guildford County Animal Shelter, HSUS admits to entrusting many animals to their care and publicly lauds them, stating that the shelter goes "above and beyond the call of duty."

Also making the HSUS Top Ten list was the Nashville Humane Association, which took 10 animals from HSUS in December, 2010. When No Kill activists followed up to determine what happened to those animals, reluctant attorneys for the organization ultimately admitted that they had adopted one, killed three and sent the other six to a prison program. The Nashville Humane Association refused to disclose what happened to the six who were sent to the prison program, but their refusal to share this information and to publicly disclose their overall kill rate leaves animal lovers to assume that information must be damning.

Nor was the Nashville Humane Association the only organization to admit to killing animals from HSUS "rescues" in 2011. Some animals "rescued" by HSUS were sent to shelters which ultimately killed them in one of the cruelest ways imaginable: the gas chamber.

Not to be outdone, the ASPCA boasted that it helped rescue 41 animals in South Carolina— but once the fundraising appeals were over, so was any interest the ASPCA had in the animals. They were shipped to three shelters:

- The Capital Area Humane Society in Hilliard, Ohio, which has a kill rate for cats of 85 percent, meaning almost 9 out of ten cats are put to death. The shelter refuses to disclose how many dogs they kill.
- The Bay Area Humane Society in Green Bay, Wisconsin, where 1,619 of the 4,486 animals they took in lost their lives.
- The Animal Humane Society in Minnesota, where local animals are routinely put to death in order to make room for out-of-county animals.

So even if these shelters did not kill any of the ASPCA animals, a dubious proposition in itself, they likely killed local animals to make room. Either way, animals needlessly lost their lives because an agency with annual revenues of nearly 150 million dollars and its own shelter in New York City didn't care what happened to the animals once the money people donated started rolling in.

Even the use of the word "emergency placement" to describe HSUS partners is a misnomer. The ASPCA and HSUS are not only the richest animal protection charities in the U.S., they are among the overall richest charities in the nation. So why is the seizure of some 50 animals an "emergency"? Why doesn't HSUS or the ASPCA find the animals homes themselves among their millions of animal-loving members and what amounts to endless resources? Indeed, not only does HSUS boast over 12 million supporters, but the ASPCA, located in New York City, has immediate access to the single largest adoption market in the country. But HSUS will not place the animals in homes themselves. And despite the millions

Until very recently, "rescues" of this sort were a tidy, efficient arrangement for these organizations. The public's blind faith and trust in the ASPCA and HSUS meant that no one ever thought to ask where the animals ended up or what ultimately happened to them.

hoarded in their bank accounts, the ASPCA has a long, sordid history of a paltry level of adoptions in its own shelter and, worse, of neglecting the needs of the animals suffering in the city pound down the street, even sending animals to be killed there. Kittens and puppies have gone from the ASPCA to one of the most abusive pounds in the nation, only to end up on its nightly "kill list" (see pages 85-88).

Until very recently, "rescues" of this sort were a tidy, efficient arrangement for these organizations. The public's blind faith and trust in the ASPCA and HSUS meant that no one ever thought to ask where the animals ended up or what ultimately happened to them. But that is changing. And as savvy No Kill activists are increasingly uncovering and reporting the heartbreaking truth—that in spite of the feel-good headlines, many of the so-called "rescued" animals actually end up dead or displace others who are then killed—we are left to ask one, inescapable and obvious question: *What the hell kind of rescue is that?*

The answer, of course, is the ASPCA and HSUS kind, and another reason why they are so loath to hold local shelters accountable for their cruelty and their killing. The ASPCA and HSUS

IN THE ARMS OF AN ANGEL

While the ASPCA brings in nearly 150 million dollars a year, owing in no small part to their television ads featuring heartbreaking images of animals set to the soundtrack of Sarah McLachlan's poignant song *"In the Arms of an Angel,"* many of the animals the ASPCA "rescues" are not really rescued at all. The only angel they are delivered to is the angel of death.

rely on these organizations to do their bidding. They need the cooperation of local shelters when they do these sorts of "rescues" because once the media has moved on and the solicitations have been sent out, the animals have lost their usefulness. The local shelters serve as a dumping ground. If the ASPCA or HSUS were to actually hold these shelters accountable for how they operate, they would risk alienating them and losing very valuable allies in these misleading but highly lucrative fundraising schemes.

Welcome to New York City

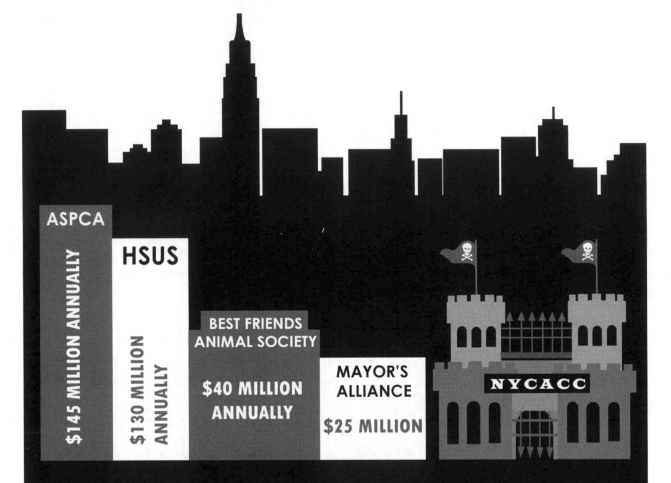

ASPCA — $145 MILLION ANNUALLY

HSUS — $130 MILLION ANNUALLY

BEST FRIENDS ANIMAL SOCIETY — $40 MILLION ANNUALLY

MAYOR'S ALLIANCE — $25 MILLION

NYCACC

New York City is home to four of the nation's largest and wealthiest animal protection organizations, yet its animal control shelter is one of the filthiest and cruelest in the country. So what are these groups doing to change that?

ABSOLUTELY NOTHING

NEW YORK CITY ANIMAL CARE & CONTROL:
A MEDIEVAL HOUSE OF HORRORS

NEW YORK CITY is home to the wealthiest animal protection organizations in the nation: The ASPCA, whose headquarters is there and which takes in nearly 150 million dollars per year; HSUS, which has an office there and takes in over 130 million dollars a year; Best Friends Animal Society, which also has an office in New York City and takes in over 40 million a year; and a group calling itself the Mayor's Alliance for New York City Animals, which has taken in over 25 million dollars. It is home to the single, largest adoption market in the country. It is the center of the nation's wealth. And it is a community with a shelter per capita intake rate that is a fraction of the national average (one-twentieth that of communities which are No Kill). But in a city where the animals should have everything going for them, they have:

this...

(LEFT) The New York City pound is short on compassion and short on staff accountability. This dog was killed after wallowing in a filthy cage filled with feces. Not only does the New York City pound kill healthy animals, it neglects and abuses them in the process.

and this...

(RIGHT) Here, another example of a typical holding pen, a dirty cage filled with feces. This dog died of illness shortly thereafter.

and this...

(LEFT) Volunteers who care for the kittens in the nursery report that were it not for their presence, these most vulnerable and needy of animals would often receive no care at all. Here, a sick kitten with diarrhea is covered in litter and excrement. The kitten ultimately died.

and this...

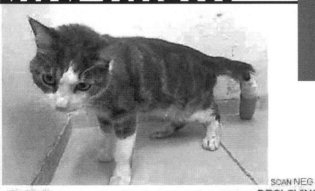

SCAN NEG

NEUTERED QARH PE - MOD STAINING, TARTAR AMB X-4, ROBUST **DEGLOVING WX TO DISTAL TAIL, BANDAGED** VENTRAL ABD AND LEGS STAINED WITH DIED BLOOD **NO PAIN MEDS AVAILABLE** TO GIVE THE CAT

NOSF BECAME AGGITED WHEN TREATING TAIL, NOSF deglving injury to distal tail- painful limited use of tail, but tactile sensation and deep pain appear intact proximal to injury anal tone intact reapplied bandage-recommend amputation surgery of tail temp 102.3, app good, bar *Emily Tahen New Hope Liaison - Manhattan Shelter Animal Care & Control of NYC C: 917-578-6372*

(LEFT) A cat in intense pain as the skin sloughs off of her tail is not provided pain control medication because the shelter claims it does not have the money.

and this.

(LEFT) Lack of oversight, lack of caring, lack of necessary veterinary attention: this is standard operating procedure at the New York City pound. While at the facility, this dog was allowed to chew off parts of his own tail because he did not receive the medical care he needed.

While New York shelter volunteers, rescuers and animal lovers work to reform their broken pound, they must fight not only the inertia of a heartless bureaucracy and the indifference of a hard-hearted Mayor and City Council, but also national animal protection groups which are located in the city. The most cosmopolitan, sophisticated, wealthy and animal-loving city in the nation has a barbaric, regressive pound that can only be described one way: medieval. And every single one of those groups claims the shelter is doing a good job, while turning a blind eye to the animal suffering and killing taking place there.

$
Getting Rich by Peddling False Hope

WHILE THE ANIMALS IN THE NEW YORK CITY pound go without basic care, wallow in waste, receive little socialization and are allowed to suffer with untreated injuries, the ASPCA, the Mayor's Alliance and other groups are collectively raising hundreds of millions of dollars every year by promising a No Kill New York City.

In reality, groups like the ASPCA and the Mayor's Alliance have put up roadblocks to No Kill success. They have fought legislation that would have saved the lives of animals and they have looked the other way while the animals in the city shelter are systematically neglected and abused. They ignore the fact that the city pound kills healthy animals, allows them to languish in pain while they slowly die, does not provide basic care and bans from the premises anyone who tries to reform these practices. In fact, the Mayor's Alliance has misled funders by claiming no healthy animals are being killed, and they continue to falsely proclaim the city shelter is a national No Kill model, giving the pound a legitimacy that it does not deserve and that arguably allows the neglect to continue.

Meanwhile, organizations like Best Friends Animal Society not only hold up the leadership of the Mayor's Alliance as experts, giving them a forum at their national conference, they, too, are also raising money in New York City, while the animals of the city pound endure misery and killing. Why?

Anxious to highlight some semblance of relevance in a movement that is steamrolling ahead without them, Best Friends is willing not only to sell out the animals who are suffering terribly in New York City, but to undermine activists who are working for true reform by

Each of the large animal protection organizations operating in New York City could use their power, their influence and the astronomical amounts of money they raise on the backs of New York animals to foster change at the city pound. But not one of them does.

pretending that the City is poised for success. Their comments provide political cover for the New York City pound director and the government bureaucrats who are supposed to oversee and hold her accountable. Meanwhile, Best Friends continues to raise money feeding into the public's false hope, further enriching their own bloated coffers.

The 99%

In New York City and throughout the country, it is the grassroots that is leading the charge for No Kill. While every national organization ignores the lessons of existing No Kill success and provides political cover for their friends and colleagues running shelters who are neglecting and killing the animals in their care, everyday animal lovers, animal rescuers and shelter volunteers are doing the job they refuse to do: demanding better.

"The American Society for the Prevention of Cruelty to Animals claims it is the voice for defenseless animals: 'We Are Their Voice...' But as long as the ASPCA allows cruelty and neglect to continue in New York City's Animal Care & Control (ACC), the ASPCA has no standing to speak for any animal—most specifically defenseless ACC animals. And it's not as though the ASPCA is unaware of what's going on at the ACC. The ASPCA is located just 18 blocks away from the ACC's Manhattan shelter, and ASPCA employees are frequently in and out of the ACC shelters."

- NYC SHELTER REFORM ACTION COMMITTEE

WHAT THE VESTED INTERESTS SAY ABOUT THE NYC POUND

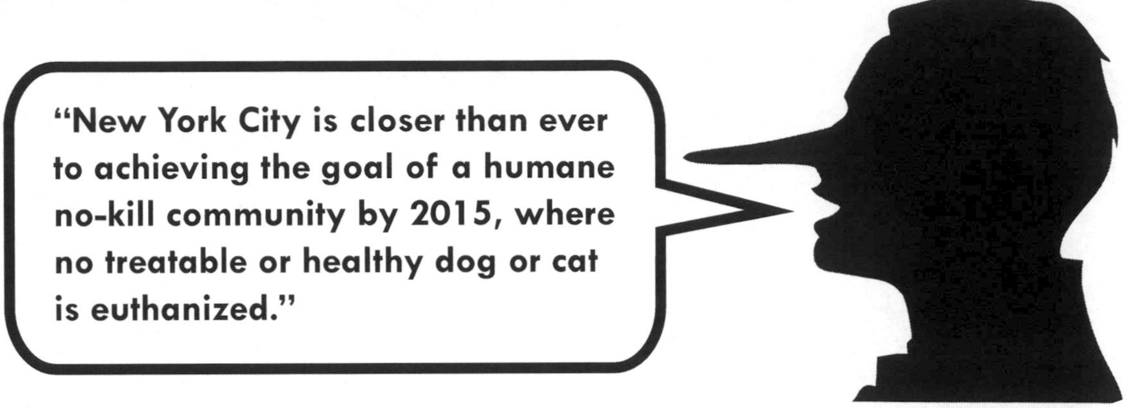

"New York City is closer than ever to achieving the goal of a humane no-kill community by 2015, where no treatable or healthy dog or cat is euthanized."

ED SAYRES
ASPCA
2012

"New York City is well on its way to achieving its no-kill goal under the leadership of Maddie's Fund and the Mayor's Alliance for NYC's Animals."

GREGORY CASTLE
BEST FRIENDS ANIMAL SOCIETY
2012

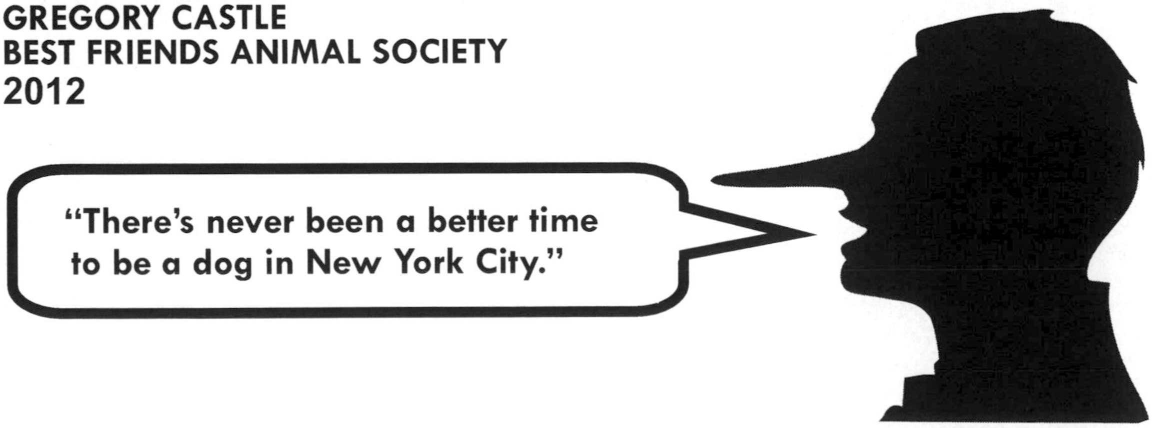

"There's never been a better time to be a dog in New York City."

MICHAEL BLOOMBERG
NYC MAYOR
2010

WHAT VOLUNTEERS & RESCUERS SAY ABOUT THE NYC POUND

"The kitten nursery was the stinkiest, dirtiest place on earth and a textbook definition of misery. The water was dirty, food covered with litter, wet bedding and no clean linen in sight. I found three kittens huddled together in a corner and one separate in a litter box with [his] face in litter. He was cool and limp and covered with feces."

"I don't know which is worse, their lack of care/advocacy for our animals or their duplicity about it. Every time that I go, I feel sick. It is in one word, a disgrace... I think that one would be hard pressed to find anyone who is well-acquainted with them and will say anything positive about them or their animal care."

"The Mayor's Alliance has been unable to significantly influence NYCACC management or procedure and so the internal incompetence and indifference continues unabated. One cannot fix a system that does not want to be fixed."

"New York City's shelters are infamously abusive. No Kill is not a ghost of a thought in the minds of the staff. Why continue to promote this myth of success?"

"The temporary cages are always filthy—covered with feces and no food or water. I know that some dogs or cats can be messy, but I'm usually at the shelter for several hours straight, and I check on these cages when I arrive and when I leave, and they stay the same: filthy with vomit, diarrhea, dirty or no water."

"[A]nimals will more than likely be ridden with disease upon entering the shelter because our shelter system refuses to follow standard procedure and required protocol to keep the shelter sanitary so [as] to conveniently have a reason to deem animals unadoptable..."

"It's horrible. I cry every time I'm there. It's not a national model."

"[T]he night shift is the worst. The staff come in, take a dinner break, play dominoes, or simply disappear for hours. The animals are ignored. But these employees are never penalized because there's no manager around to supervise them and the manager who does come on in the morning never says a word about the cage conditions or animals that died in their kennels during the night... I've caught workers yelling at dogs and taunting them."

HARMING ANIMALS, THREATENING PEOPLE

IN 2010, THE NEW YORK CITY POUND unveiled a new volunteer policy that threatened to expel volunteers for exercising their free speech rights. Specifically, the policy stated that volunteers may not "publicly criticiz[e]" or cast the agency "in a negative light" without permission. It also prohibited them from "[p]osting [criticism] on any internet site such as Facebook, MySpace, Craig's List, etc." It further stated that volunteers are prohibited from sharing their "opinions in regards volunteers, staff, animals, and/or policies to the public." Those who do "will be terminated."

Even though federal law prohibits municipal shelters from taking action designed to prevent people from exercising their First Amendment right to free speech, this tactic is not uncommon. Many shelters across the country which neglect and abuse animals also "abuse"

> **Shelters across the country which neglect and abuse animals in their care frequently "abuse" their volunteers as well through illegal attempts to intimidate and silence them.**

their volunteers through illegal attempts to intimidate and silence them. Los Angeles attorney Sheldon Eisenberg explains:

It can be a cruel "Sophie's Choice" for animal rescuers: observe in silence deplorable conditions and mistreatment of animals in government run shelters or call attention to the plight of the suffering animals and face the possibility of retaliation that can mean being deprived of the ability to save lives. Sadly, this is the reality that rescuers confront when they seek reform from apathetic or incompetent shelter directors and their staffs or, failing that, meaningful oversight from elected or higher level municipal officers to whom the directors report.

Fortunately, there is a legal remedy available to rescuers and volunteers who find that their efforts to improve conditions have led to the suspension or elimination of their rights to visit, monitor and rescue animals from these shelters. A federal statute, 42 U.S.C. Section 1983, best known simply as "Section 1983," can stop governmental officials or employees who retaliate against volunteers. A rescuer not only has the First Amendment right to speak out against abuses and violations of law committed by a governmental entity, he or she also has a constitutionally protected right to demand that the government correct those wrongs.

There would be little progress in improving the conditions at municipal animal shelters if rescuers and volunteers—the people who are most knowledgeable about those conditions—could be intimidated into remaining silent by the threat of retaliation. Thankfully, Section 1983 provides this powerful tool not only to obtain justice for people unfairly treated by government officials, but also to insure that rescuers and volunteers can continue their critically important work of saving lives and educating the public about what goes on behind the closed doors of the local shelter.

THE ASSEMBLY
STATE OF NEW YORK
ALBANY

COMMITTEES
Banks
Cities
Consumer Affairs and Protection
Environmental Conservation
Steering

MICAH Z. KELLNER
65th Assembly District

August 31, 2010

The Honorable Michael R. Bloomberg
Office of the Mayor
City Hall
New York, NY 10007

Dr. Thomas Farley
Commissioner
NYC Department of Health & Mental Hygiene
125 Worth Street
New York, NY 10013

Dear Mayor Bloomberg and Dr. Farley:

It has come to my attention that Animal Care & Control of New York City (ACC) recently unveiled a new volunteer policy that threatens to expel volunteers for exercising their rights to free speech and to petition their government for redress of grievances. Specifically, the policy states that volunteers may not "publicly criticiz[e]" or cast the agency "in a negative light" without permission from ACC. It also prohibits them from "[p]osting [criticism] on any internet site such as Facebook, My Space, Craig's List, etc." It further states that "[v]olunteers are prohibited from distributing their personal information, or opinions in regards [to ACC] volunteers, staff, animals, and/or policies to the public." Those who do "will be terminated." This policy violates the constitutional rights of volunteers.

42 U.S.C. § 1983 states, in relevant part,

Every person who, under color of any statute, ordinance, regulation, custom, or usage . . . subjects, or causes to be subjected, any citizen of the United States or other person within the jurisdiction thereof to the deprivation of any rights, privileges, or immunities secured by the Constitution and laws, shall be liable to the party injured in an action at law, suit in equity, or other proper proceeding for redress.

▪ 834 Legislative Office Building, Albany, NY 12248 • (518) 455-5676, FAX (518) 455-5282
▪ 315 East 65 Street, New York, NY 10065 • (212) 860-4908, FAX (917) 432-2983
E-mail: KellnerM@assembly.state.ny.us

A New York State Assembly Member demands that the Mayor and Health Commissioner of New York City repeal their new policy which was designed to intimidate and silence volunteers. The illegal policy was instituted after animal lovers complained about inhumane conditions.

NYCACC Tells Animal Lovers:

Animal Care & Control of New York City

Volunteer Policy and Procedure Manual

Animal Care & Control of NYC
11 Park Place, Suite 805
New York, NY 10007

SHUT UP OR BE SHUT OUT

---

b. Visual conduct such as derogatory and/or sexually oriented posters, calendars, photography, cartoons, drawings or gestures.

c. Physical conduct such as assault, unwanted touching, blocking normal movement, or interfering with work because of sex, race or any other protected basis.

d. Threats and demands to submit to sexual requests as a condition of continued program participation, or to avoid some other loss, and offers of benefits in return for sexual favors.

e. Retaliation for having reported or threatened to report harassment, or for initiating or assisting in any action or proceeding regarding unlawful harassment or discrimination.

All threats of violence or harassment will be taken seriously. If any volunteer believes that he or she has been unlawfully harassed, that person should submit a complaint to his/her supervisor as soon as possible after the incident. If the volunteer is not comfortable discussing the situation with their immediate supervisor, they may submit their complaint to the Executive Director or the Human Resources Department. The complaint should include details of the incident or incidents, names of the individuals involved, and names of any witnesses. Supervisors will refer all harassment complaints to the Human Resources Department immediately. AC&C will undertake an effective, thorough and objective investigation of the harassment allegations.

Upon completion of the investigation, a determination will be made, and the concerned parties will be notified of the outcome. If AC&C determines that unlawful harassment has occurred, effective remedial action will be taken in accordance with the circumstances involved, including action to prevent any further harassment. This may include counseling for the alleged perpetrator, discipline, and/or discharge of the perpetrator, additional security measures, police involvement, or other appropriate action under the circumstances and as provided by law.

3. AC&C Board of Directors

Members of the Board of Directors of AC&C shall not act as direct service volunteers.

4. Conflicts of Interest

AC&C volunteer applicants who have personal, philosophical, or financial conflicts of interest with the mission of AC&C or any activity or program of AC&C, or develop a conflict of interest during their time of volunteer service, shall not be accepted to serve as a volunteer or will be terminated. Volunteers who find themselves unable to continue to accept the mission of AC&C, and/or AC&C activities or programs will be terminated.

5. Representation of AC&C

Prior to taking any action, or making any statement that might affect or create an obligation for AC&C or publicly criticizing or casting AC&C in a negative light, volunteers must request written clearance from the appropriate supervisory personnel. All media interactions and all fundraising activities must be approved in advance by the Director of Development &

8

Communications. Any adoptions promotions, adoption partner transfers, or temporary foster placements must be approved by the Director of Development and Communications.

Such actions and statements may include, but are not limited to:

a. Posting on any internet site such as Facebook, My Space, Craigslist, etc.

b. Public statements or statements to the press while appearing to represent AC&C.

c. Attempting to create a coalition with other organizations without prior permission from AC&C.

d. Lobby individuals, groups, organizations, or government bodies or representatives (i.e.: rescues, veterinarians, behaviorists, trainers, etc) on behalf of AC&C.

e. Making agreements involving any contractual or financial obligations on behalf of AC&C.

f. Using the AC&C logo, name or animal on any promotional or informational materials.

g. Using the AC&C name to organize meetings, gatherings or social events without prior notification of the appropriate AC&C staff.

h. Fundraising using AC&C's name or animals.

i. Publication or use of any confidential information as described in Section 6 below without written consent from the Director of Development and Communications or the Executive Director.

Volunteers are authorized only to act as representatives of AC&C as specifically indicated within their written volunteer job description, or specifically approved by the appropriate department supervisor on an individual basis. Volunteers are prohibited from distributing their personal information, or opinions in regards to AC&C volunteers, staff, animals, and/or policies to the public. Volunteers are expected to use good judgment when speaking to the public and/or AC&C clients. On occasion you may be asked questions regarding AC&C policies, philosophies, or services that you do not feel comfortable with or are qualified to answer. In these cases, please refer the inquiry to the appropriate staff person.

6. Confidentiality

Volunteers are responsible for maintaining confidentiality of all proprietary or privileged information to which they are exposed while serving as volunteers, whether this information involves a single staff member, volunteer, client, other person or overall AC&C business. Failure to maintain confidentiality may result in termination or other corrective action. All volunteers will be required to sign a Confidentiality Agreement as a condition to volunteer.

Confidential information includes but is not limited to: animal and client information from our computer system, whether gained through the course of volunteer service or from other internal sources, shelter or photographs, all records, files, forms, applications, mail lists, passwords, security codes, correspondence, messages or any other entities belonging to AC&C and/or bearing AC&C's logo and/or name, are the sole property of AC&C and may not be disseminated, used, published or sold without the written consent of the Executive Director.

9

THE TRUTH ABOUT THE ASPCA

MEET 6 NEWBORN KITTENS WHO HAD NO MAMA

This little kitten was one of a litter of five delivered to NYCACC where he and his littermates were killed within hours of arriving, without ever being offered to New York rescue groups ready and willing to save them.

MEET SIX NEWBORN KITTENS in need of a surrogate mama. The first, a healthy three-week old, was delivered to the ASPCA in May 2012, possibly by a Good Samaritan who found him. Perhaps that person had seen an ASPCA commercial on television, had heard the Sarah McLachlan song "In the Arms of an Angel" and believed that by taking him to the organization that bills itself as the animals' "voice," that is the single richest SPCA in America, the kitten would be safe.

Maybe the Good Samaritan even wrote a donation check to thank the ASPCA for taking in the kitten. It is not uncommon for people who bring in orphaned animals to do so. And the ASPCA could then use that money to buy formula, a bottle and a heating pad. Even if the Good Samaritan didn't write a check, no matter, the ASPCA could afford it. It would cost little:

• Powdered kitten milk replacer: $12.99
• Kitten bottle: $5.19
• Heating pad: $13.49
• Towel: donated

Only $31.67 to save this kitten's life, a mere fraction of the ASPCA's revenue. They'd make that back in interest alone before the kitten needed his next feeding. Yes, the kitten was safe. And not only did he have the animals' "voice" protecting him, but this one was easy, a no-brainer, saving lives for dummies. No surgery, no heroic efforts, just your run-of-the-mill, garden variety need for a volunteer, some powdered milk, a two-ounce plastic bottle, a little TLC and 31 dollars and change. There is absolutely nothing that could and would stand in the way of the bright future this kitten had to look forward to.

So how could it be that although this kitten seemingly had everything going for him, that just a few hours later, he was dead? Because once that Good Samaritan walked out the door, naively thinking he had done his good deed for the day, fast on his heels was an ASPCA employee, delivering that very same kitten to the city pound where he was killed just two hours later. Injected with a fatal dose of poison, his little body was then tossed on a pile of other dead animals in a cold, dark freezer. And there his lifeless body sat, waiting to be transported to a crematory.

And although New York rescuers complained that they were never given a chance to save him, the very next day, the city shelter killed five more motherless kittens which they refused to care for, and which, once again, they denied rescue groups the opportunity to save. And who was it at the city shelter that signed off on the death of these five little orphaned kittens? The person who noted that they had "no place to go"? A staff member at the pound who is also a part-time employee of the ASPCA—a person who therefore probably knew, from first-hand experience, that it was futile to expect the ASPCA to save them. And while orphaned newborn kittens continue to be killed at the city shelter in New York, staff who have offered to bottle feed them and take them home until rescue groups can be found have been told by the director that they are not allowed to do so. Instead, they are told to label the kittens as "untreatable" so they can be put to death with impunity, while the ASPCA not only provides them grist for their killing mill, but political cover in the form of public accolades, too.

DEAD ON ARRIVAL

If a truly compassionate person were running the New York City pound, all underage kittens, especially those who were impounded without their mothers, would be listed as "pre-foster." Instead, they are slated to be killed as soon as they come in the door. Status: "Pre-Euth." If it is during the day, rescue groups have an hour or so to respond before the kittens are killed. If it is after 7 p.m., rescue groups are not even called; the kittens are killed right away. If a staff member wants to foster them at no cost to the shelter until a rescue group can be found, the director forbids it. Of course, the pound, the Mayor's Alliance and the ASPCA report those dead kittens as "untreatable." That way they can continue peddling the fiction that New York City is a national model of compassionate care.

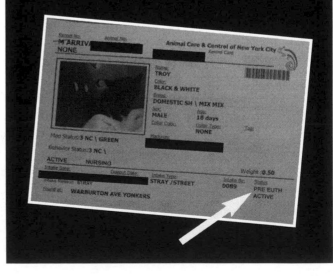

THE TRUTH ABOUT THE ASPCA

MEET 3 KITTENS WHO HAD NO NAMES

MEET THREE NAMELESS KITTENS who arrived at the ASPCA in 2011 with a cold. These kittens had their whole lives ahead of them: years to chase toys, years to take naps stretched out in the warm sun and years to be scratched behind the ears by people who love them. But these kittens almost didn't live long enough to be given names. Because instead of treating them with fluids and some inexpensive antibiotics, the ASPCA shipped them off to be killed at one of the most neglectful and abusive shelters in the nation: the New York City pound.

Although the pound immediately put the kittens on a kill list, rescue groups with a fraction of the ASPCA's revenues stepped up and saved them. This is the same rescue community the ASPCA argues cannot be trusted, the same rescue community that the ASPCA argues are dog fighters and hoarders in disguise (see pages 89-93). And yes, the same rescue community that came to the aid of these sick little kittens, giving them the life that the ASPCA—for all its wealth—and the animal control shelter—despite its public mandate—simply refused to give.

A S P C A :
TREATING KITTENS LIKE LITTER

THE TRUTH ABOUT THE ASPCA
MEET GLORIA

Gloria had been in the "care" of both the ASPCA and the New York City pound for over 2½ weeks with a broken leg before arriving at the rescue facility. Why was she allowed to suffer for weeks with no veterinary attention or pain management?

MEET GLORIA. In 2011, Gloria was abandoned at an ASPCA mobile spay/neuter clinic in Queens, New York. Instead of finding Gloria a home through their own shelter, the ASPCA dumped Gloria at the city pound. Because basic disease prevention protocols are routinely violated, animals who stay at the pound for more than a couple of days frequently become ill. Gloria contracted a cold and was placed on the pound's kill list.

Thankfully, a rescue group saved her. But once in their care, it became immediately apparent that something wasn't right with Gloria. Her appetite was poor and she was lethargic. A veterinarian examined Gloria and found that her leg was broken. Gloria had been in the "care" of both the ASPCA and the New York City pound for over 2½ weeks before arriving at the rescue facility. Why was she allowed to suffer for weeks with no veterinary attention or pain management?

Outraged rescuers publicized Gloria's case and the ASPCA was forced to account. They admitted to knowing that Gloria's leg was badly broken and claimed that they had made the New York City pound aware of it when they left her there. However, Gloria's medical record from her time at the pound does not indicate that they knew her leg was broken. And either way, the ASPCA was implicated in Gloria's neglect. If they did not know about Gloria's condition, they should have. If in fact, they did know, why didn't they treat her to relieve her immense suffering? And why did they send a cat with a broken leg to a place notorious for its neglect and cruelty—a place that refuses to provide pain medication to injured animals, a place where she would be put on a list to be killed, which is exactly what happened?

THE TRUTH ABOUT THE ASPCA
MEET OREO

Meet the abused dog whose killing by the ASPCA was the tinder that lit a fire for legislative reform in New York and caused the ASPCA not only to declare outright war against animal rescuers and animal lovers in that state, but to doom roughly 25,000 animals every year to certain death.

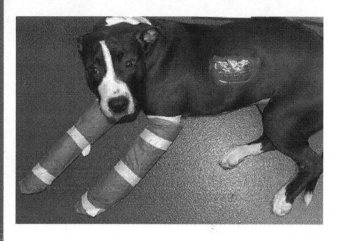

MEET OREO. Oreo was a one-year-old dog who was thrown off the roof of a six-floor Brooklyn apartment building in 2009. Oreo suffered two broken legs and a fractured rib. Several of the neighbors in the building reported having heard the sound of her being beaten. The ASPCA nursed her back to health and arrested the perpetrator. They also dubbed her the "miracle dog" and fundraised off her plight. But the miracle was short lived.

According to ASPCA President Ed Sayres,* when Oreo recovered from her injuries, she started to show signs of aggression. After the money was counted and safely deposited into ASPCA bank accounts, Sayres made the decision to kill her. (Although there were videos taken of Oreo, the ASPCA has refused to release them and the only public documentation of Oreo is photographs of ASPCA employees

hugging her—their own faces inches from hers—which do not demonstrate any aggression). *The New York Times* reported the story the day before Oreo's scheduled execution. The reaction among animal lovers was strong and swift.

If it was true that Oreo was still traumatized and untrusting, who could blame her? She needed time. Although the ASPCA could have cared for Oreo as long as it took to get her to trust again, Sayres refused. But others came forward to offer what the ASPCA would not: time and space to learn that not all humans are

On a cold, Friday November morning in 2009, Oreo was killed; not by her abuser, but by those whose mission it was to protect her.

---

* On July 25, 2012, the ASPCA announced that Sayres would "step down" as ASPCA President.

Oreo's Killer, Ed Sayres

rescue organizations, tired of shelters killing animals they wanted to save, adopted Oreo as their mascot and sought the introduction of a bill that would make it illegal for a shelter to kill an animal a rescue organization was willing to save. The New York State legislator who introduced the legislation dubbed it "Oreo's Law."

Although Oreo's death was the catalyst, the legislation was desperately needed statewide. A survey of New York State rescue groups revealed that 71 percent had been turned away from shelters, which then killed the very animals they had offered to save. In one case, a rescuer described how the shelter manager specifically walked a dog her group wanted to save right past them and into the room where

abusers. A No Kill sanctuary near the ASPCA which specializes in rehabilitating aggressive dogs (and, if that proves impossible, safely caring for them for the rest of their lives), contacted the ASPCA to ask if they could save Oreo. They made numerous telephone calls and sent numerous emails. They were ignored, hung-up on and lied to. Two volunteers of the group even went to the ASPCA but were escorted out after Sayres and others in charge of Oreo's fate refused to meet with them.

On a cold, Friday November morning in 2009, Oreo was killed; not by her abuser, but by those whose mission it was to protect her. The kennel that the sanctuary readied in anticipation of her arrival lay empty and unused that day, filled with a soft bed, a pool of water and several toys for her to play with. Instead, Oreo's body was discarded in a landfill.

As word spread among animal lovers about what had happened, the furor and condemnation of the ASPCA was severe. No Kill

The kennel that the sanctuary readied in anticipation of Oreo's arrival lay empty and unused that day, filled with a soft bed, a pool of water and several toys for her to play with. Instead, Oreo's body was discarded in a landfill.

animals are killed. It was estimated that if Oreo's Law passed, roughly 25,000 animals a year—most of them young, friendly and healthy—would be saved rather than killed by New York shelters.

A PERSONAL VENDETTA

Ed Sayres—spiteful over the backlash against his killing of Oreo—declared that he would use his leverage in the State Capitol to defeat the bill. And although the public support for the bill was overwhelming, with calls to New York legislators shutting down the email servers in the Assembly not once but twice, Oreo's Law was defeated by a coalition of shelters and other organizations including Best Friends Animal Society, spearheaded by the ASPCA.

Oreo's Law was introduced again in 2011 but under a new name—the Companion Animal Access and Rescue Act (CAARA)—with the hope that changing the title of the bill might diminish ASPCA opposition. Again the ASPCA led the effort which defeated the bill. And in 2012, the ASPCA succeeded in defeating CAARA yet

again. But they also found a new tactic to ensure its final demise: introducing competing legislation that would undermine true reform. In other words, Sayres attempted to mollify opposition by passing the ASPCA's own "rescue access" bill.

Although the ASPCA assured the public and the media that their legislation mandated rescue access, in reality, it merely suggested it, and then cleverly codified in law a shelter's right *not* to work with rescue organizations. It stated that shelters "may" give animals to rescue groups rather than kill them, instead of "shall" give the animals to them as required by CAARA—the bill supported by the New York rescue community and tens of thousands of New York animal lovers. And in codifying a shelter's unlimited authority to determine whether a rescue group or particular animal qualifies, the law eviscerated whistleblower protection for rescuers who want to expose cruel and abusive treatment of animals in the shelters they visit but are afraid to do so for fear of losing their ability to rescue.

Oreo, recovered from her physical injuries and shortly before she was killed by the ASPCA

But the worst part of the bill was a provision that went one, egregious step further. The ASPCA legislation attempted to erode one of the few, but most important protections animals in shelters have: mandatory holding periods. Ed Sayres attempted not only to co-opt and destroy efforts at true rescue access legislation but to turn back the clock on animal protection in New York State over 40 years.

The ASPCA-sponsored bill eliminated holding periods for scared and shy animals, granting shelters the authority to kill them the moment they walked in the door. Under the proposed ASPCA law, if shelter staff determined that an animal was in "psychological pain," the animal could be killed immediately.

Not only is it cruel to kill an animal for being scared or shy, and not only is killing an animal who is fearful of being harmed both paradoxical and absurd (a shelter is doing the very thing the animal is afraid will happen), but there was no definition in the bill as to what constitutes "psychological pain" and no standards as to how the provision was to be applied.

Whining puppies in need of socialization, fearful cats or traumatized animals in need of a gentle hand and compassion would instead face instant death. As the bill was written, all it

Other parts of the ASPCA bill which gave the illusion of reform were also worded so as to be merely suggestive. The bill suggested that shelters scan for microchips and post lost animals on the internet only if they found it "practicable" to do so. Again, the real shelter reform bill mandated that these common sense things be done whether a shelter wanted to or not precisely because they are not being done, with shelters already finding them not "practicable" to do.

The ASPCA attempted not only to co-opt and destroy efforts at true rescue access legislation, but to turn back the clock on animal protection 40 years by seeking to eliminate legal protections for animals that have been in place since 1971.

that often characterize lost or stray animals, the ASPCA was trying to grant shelters the authority to kill them immediately upon intake, before their families even had a chance to look for them. In many cases, before their families even had a chance to notice that the animal was missing.

And it was not just New York animals that were threatened by this bill. For the first time anywhere in the U.S., legislation was being sought that would allow shelters to kill animals based on a perceived state of mind— something that is completely subjective and unknowable—eliminating fundamental protections animals entering shelters have had for decades.

Mandatory holding periods are very important. When shelters obey them, they allow people the opportunity to reclaim their missing animals and they afford homeless animals a little time and space to be adopted. Yet the ASPCA was working to expedite shelter killing by eliminating this vital protection.

Were other states to pass similar legislation, the body count would be astronomical. And for what purpose? Not because of a glaring deficiency in New York law regarding holding periods that the ASPCA was honestly and responsibly trying to amend so that the needs of animals in that state could be better served.

Rather, it was introduced as what appeared to be a spiteful vendetta of one heartless person: Ed Sayres of the ASPCA—a man who appears willing to sacrifice tens of thousands of animals to his own blind ambition. And a man who surrounded himself with sycophants and "yes men" willing to do his nefarious bidding in spite of the bloodbath that would come of it.

would take to issue the death sentence would be for any two shelter employees, regardless of their "expertise"—including the janitor, the receptionist or a kennel attendant—to say that they believed that an animal was in "psychological pain."

For those New Yorkers who share their lives with a dog or cat, the threat this bill created was very real: the next time the gardener accidentally left the gate open or the next time the kids forgot to close the front door and their companion animal escaped, it could have been the last time he was ever seen alive. Because being scared or shy are precisely the behaviors

THE ASPCA'S DEADLY "QUICK KILL" BILL

Animal lovers dubbed the ASPCA's proposed legislation the "Quick Kill" bill and New Yorkers fought back and fought hard. They flooded New York State legislators with over 20,000 telephone calls and emails urging that the bill be dropped, while their generosity funded the placement of newspapers ads and the mailing of a postcard against the bill to every household in the hometown of Assemblywoman Amy Paulin, the legislative sponsor. Despite intense public opposition, the ASPCA and Paulin remained defiant for many months, publicly referring to those who opposed the bill as "misinformed" and "uneducated." And while an exodus of 11 of the bill's cosponsors and the bill being stricken in the Senate forced Assemblywoman Paulin to eventually drop the provision eliminating holding periods, she refused to amend those provisions gutting true rescue access. To this day, the ASPCA remains the biggest roadblock to real rescue access legislation in New York State, legislation that would save tens of thousands of animals every year who have an immediate place to go.

Assemblywoman Amy Paulin wants your pet DEAD before you even know he's missing

The next time the gardener accidentally leaves the gate open or the kids forget to close the front door and your pet escapes, it may be the last time you ever see your cat or dog alive. New York Assemblywoman Amy Paulin has recently introduced A05449, the "Quick Kill," legislation that would eliminate holding periods for any animal entering a shelter who shelter staff determines to be scared or shy. Because these are precisely the behaviors that often characterize lost or stray pets, shelters would be granted the authority to kill many animals immediately upon intake, before their owners even have a chance to look for them and, in many cases, before owners even have a chance to notice that their beloved pet is missing.

Assemblywoman Paulin is up for re-election. Let her know that you will not support a candidate who wants to make it easy for people to kill a cherished member of your family.

Please contact Assemblywoman Amy Paulin and ask her to withdraw her cruel and deadly "Quick Kill Bill," A05449.
PaulinA@assembly.state.ny.us
www.facebook.com/assemblywomanpaulin
(914) 723-1115

visit www.protectNYpets.org for more information

(ABOVE) MARCH 2012: Animal lovers nationwide, fearful of the dangerous precedent the ASPCA's "Quick Kill" bill presented by eliminating mandatory holding periods for scared animals entering shelters, chipped in to pay for this half-page ad which appeared in the district newspaper of the bill's sponsor, Assemblywoman Amy Paulin. The bill was ultimately defeated.

(LEFT) JUNE 2012: As Chair of the Agriculture Committee, New York State Assembly Member William Magee voted to pass the "Quick Kill" bill while tabling real shelter reform for two straight years in deference to the ASPCA. When the latter bill came up for a vote for the third time, animal lovers funded this full page ad in his district newspaper, urging Magee to be a hero for 25,000 animals who faced certain death each year.

(RIGHT) JUNE 2012: Despite overwhelming public support for the real shelter reform bill, Assembly Member Magee chose to do the ASPCA's bidding once again and killed it. Once again, animal lovers stood up to make their voices heard, paying for another full page ad in order to educate voters in his district.

THE TRUTH ABOUT HSUS

MEET HARRY, BUDDY, MURRAY AND A DOG THE SHELTER CALLED No. 38805

HARRY

BUDDY

MURRAY

DOG No. 38805

MEET HARRY, BUDDY, MURRAY and a dog whose name we will never know, four dogs gassed at a North Carolina shelter in 2010 after HSUS claimed to have "rescued" them, only to send them to be killed in one of the most brutal ways possible.

When word spread that 44 dogs which HSUS claimed to have "rescued" were sent to various kill shelters, animal lovers demanded an explanation. HSUS issued a statement defending the decision by claiming that they sent the dogs only to shelters with which they are familiar.

Far from getting HSUS off the hook, HSUS' statement was an admission that they knew that they were sending dogs to kill shelters and that the dogs would likely face that outcome if sent there. It also meant that HSUS was aware that dogs already at those shelters would face likely execution in order make room for any dogs HSUS sent. But HSUS didn't care, and shipped dogs to the shelters anyway—four of whom were placed in a small, closed chamber that was then filled with poisonous carbon

monoxide gas, killing them slowly and torturously. Some of the others were killed by lethal injection at the other shelters.

Removing animals from one "compromised" position just to place them into an even graver one that culminates in death is *not* a rescue. In fact, it is the opposite of one. And when you are an organization bringing in over 130 million dollars a year, capable of providing to the animals off whom you fundraise the best quality care money can buy, and when you have a network of millions of animal-loving members to whom you could appeal to for adoption, it is nothing short of obscene.

But what made matters worse were the photographs of the dogs in the home HSUS claimed was a "hoarder." While the individual from whom the dogs were taken had a lot of dogs, the conditions depicted in the photographs were far from filthy. In fact, the surrounding area looked clean, the dogs well fed. And only two of the 44 dogs were sick, illnesses which they could have contracted at the shelter which killed them.

The dogs before they were taken by HSUS and shipped to kill shelters.

THE TRUTH ABOUT HSUS

MEET A PUPPY HSUS SAID WAS VICIOUS AND SHOULD BE KILLED

MEET A PUPPY who was killed before he ever had a chance to live. In February of 2009, over 100 dogs and puppies labeled as "Pit Bulls" were seized from an alleged dog fighter in Wilkes County, North Carolina. Each and every one was systematically put to death over the opposition of rescue groups, dog advocates and animal lovers. This included puppies who were born in the shelter after the seizure. It included two-week old puppies a foster parent had nursed—one of whom is pictured above—after she was ordered to return them to be killed.

As they did in the Michael Vick case and with many other dog fighting busts (see pages 137-138), HSUS led the charge to have the dogs killed. To do so, they perjured themselves before the court hearing the case, testifying that all the dogs, including the puppies who were born in the shelter and had never been exposed to aggression, were irremediably vicious and should be put to death. The court sided with HSUS President Wayne Pacelle's handpicked "experts." Each and every one, including this puppy, was killed. Over 100 victims lay dead, not by a dog fighter, not by an abuser, but at the insistence of HSUS.

Animal lovers call the Davidson County animal shelter "SAVAGE," a "DISGRACE," "DISGUSTING" and "HORRIFIC."

WHAT DOES HSUS CALL IT?

"A Shelter We LOVE"

IN 2010, 3,984 of the 4,133 cats taken in by the Davidson County, North Carolina shelter—96 percent—were put to death. While dogs fared a little better, eight out of 10 were still killed: 2,846 of the 3,625 they took in, including every dog they deemed a "Pit Bull" or "Pit Bull"-mix as a matter of policy. With an adoption rate of only six percent, they don't even try to save lives, choosing to kill them instead. Not only does the shelter do little more than kill animals, they kill them in one of the cruelest ways possible: the gas chamber.

Although the gas chamber is legal in North Carolina, it is illegal for animals that appear to be 16 weeks or younger, pregnant or near death because it takes sick, younger or older animals longer to absorb the gas, resulting in a slower and more agonizing death. The state also prohibits animals of different species from being put in the gas chamber together. But the employees of the Davidson County shelter do not care. And neither does the Sheriff who was supposed to oversee them, but chose to turn a blind eye to the illegal and sadistic killing of animals occurring under his watch.

Davidson County has a history of killing kittens and puppies using the gas chamber in violation of North Carolina law. It has a history of killing elderly and sick animals in that manner, which is also illegal. And, according to an eyewitness, shelter employees also put a raccoon in the gas chamber with a mother cat and her kitten in order to sadistically watch them fight before they died:

The gas chamber has two windows, one on either side. The raccoon and the adult cat started fighting. Then they turned the gas on. The adult cat got on one corner and the raccoon got on the other, and as soon as they turned on the gas, the kitten started shaking and going into convulsions.

A contractor who was working at the shelter told the County Board that he heard the employees laugh when they did it. He said he was sickened by the incident, as were animal lovers nationwide who condemned the shelter, calling it "savage" and "horrific." But it did not sicken the Sheriff. Rather than condemn the staff, the Sheriff defended them, saying the staff are doing a good job ("shelter employees don't want to euthanize animals") and claiming they gas animals because that is "the most humane way to deal" with them. And it did not sicken the Humane Society of the United States. Instead, HSUS gave them an award at a public ceremony, calling the Davidson County facility "A Shelter We Love."

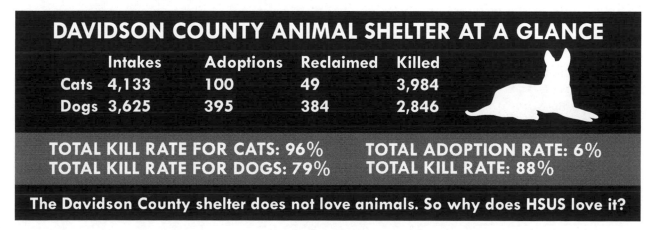

DAVIDSON COUNTY ANIMAL SHELTER AT A GLANCE

	Intakes	Adoptions	Reclaimed	Killed
Cats	4,133	100	49	3,984
Dogs	3,625	395	384	2,846

TOTAL KILL RATE FOR CATS: 96% **TOTAL ADOPTION RATE: 6%**
TOTAL KILL RATE FOR DOGS: 79% **TOTAL KILL RATE: 88%**

The Davidson County shelter does not love animals. So why does HSUS love it?

NOBLE BEGINNINGS, TRAGIC BETRAYALS

THE ANIMAL PROTECTION MOVEMENT in the United States began in earnest in the mid-19th century, when the great Henry Bergh founded the American Society for the Prevention of Cruelty to Animals in New York City. Bergh spent his days and nights patrolling the streets of New York looking for animals in need of his protection. He passed the first anti-cruelty law in the United States, a law the ASPCA enforced with zeal, filing over 12,000 cruelty cases during Bergh's lifetime, including 12 cases of cruelty against city dogcatchers in one year alone.

Bergh's targets were wide and varied: whenever and wherever animals were in need of help, Bergh was there—protecting tired, injured and overworked animals such as the horses who were forced to power the New York horse railway system, advocating for wild animals by opposing hunting and protecting animals used in scientific research by calling for an end to vivisection. But a great deal of Bergh's time and energy was spent advocating for the homeless and stray dogs of New York City. Bergh was a thorn in the side of the cruel and abusive dogcatchers who had Bergh to answer to for beating and starving dogs.

A GREAT AMERICAN HERO

HENRY BERGH
1813 - 1888

> **HSUS does not operate a single shelter, nor is it officially affiliated with any of them. The ASPCA runs one shelter in New York City which saves fewer animals a year than many rescue groups operating on a fraction of the ASPCA's budget.**

Bergh's tenacity, his unwavering commitment and his outspoken defense of animals even against powerful interests earned him a reputation, and the nickname "The Great Meddler." Those with a vested interest in animal exploitation hated him, but everyday people and animal lovers nationwide admired and respected him. His example inspired others across the country to emulate his work and found similar "societies" for the protection of animals in their own communities. By the end of the first decade of the 20th century, virtually every major city in the United States had an SPCA or humane society.

Each SPCA and humane society was a unique entity with its own funding, leadership, staff, policies and governing structure. In other words, no SPCA was (nor to this day is) affiliated with or receives funding from any other SPCA or humane society. But many people believe otherwise—a confusion that the ASPCA and HSUS both welcome and encourage.

Fraudulent Fundraising

Today, many Americans believe that the ASPCA owns and operates shelters across the country. In reality, the ASPCA runs one shelter in New York City which has historically sent the neediest of animals down the street to the pound where they are killed and which, despite being located in a city of eight million people adopts out fewer animals than the Nevada Humane Society in Reno, Nevada, with its 425,000 residents. It adopts out fewer animals than some shelters in communities with 100,000 residents. In fact, it adopts out fewer animals than many rescue groups subsisting on shoestring budgets. And yet it takes in over 140 million dollars a year in revenues partly because many people mistakenly think they are donating to their local shelter when they donate to the ASPCA. And they think that way, in part, because the ASPCA wants them to think this.

Not long ago, the ASPCA went door to door in Seattle, Washington, asking for donations. ASPCA solicitors were told to bring a dog and they were given an "Adopt Me" vest for the animal to wear. The purpose was clear: confuse people into thinking the agency was local and its mission was to save lives locally. The volunteers were given a very specific script from which they were told not to deviate. When one of those hired to fundraise suggested it was misleading, she was asked to leave. This type of duplicity isn't limited to Seattle. Nor is it limited to the ASPCA.

Local and state organizations have complained about such misleading fundraising tactics, even asking the Attorneys General of their states to open an investigation, as was done in Louisiana in the aftermath of Hurricane Katrina. Then, it was HSUS that was the worst offender, raising over 30 million dollars but spending only seven million before their President Wayne Pacelle announced "Mission: Accomplished" and headed out of town, leaving behind thousands of animals in need who were then shipped off to kill shelters nationwide (they had a policy of not working with No Kill shelters), sticking the

A STORM OF CONTROVERSY

In the aftermath of Hurricane Katrina, HSUS raised over 30 million dollars but spent only seven million before their President Wayne Pacelle announced "Mission: Accomplished" and headed out of town, leaving behind thousands of animals in need who were then shipped off to kill shelters nationwide (they had a policy of not working with No Kill shelters), sticking the money Americans donated specificly for Hurricane Katrina animals into HSUS bank accounts.

money Americans donated specifically for Hurricane Katrina animals into HSUS bank accounts.*

Moreover, for a significant fee, HSUS sells its donor marketing list for one time use by shelters, but the list comes with caveats. In addition to others (such as not mailing it out before HSUS sends their own fundraising appeal to those same donors), the one primary stipulation is that: "In order to rent the list, you need to submit the complete mail piece to the list owner for approval."

Over the years, the Nevada Humane Society (NHS) has learned that people are often confused by fundraising appeals from HSUS. Local residents think they are donating to them when they are actually giving money to HSUS. In fact, local residents have told NHS that they have already donated to them, when in fact they gave to HSUS. HSUS and the ASPCA ride the coattails of local shelters and reap the rewards, but when HSUS and the ASPCA behave badly, it is the small, local shelters that

pay the price. When HSUS embraced Michael Vick, the most notorious dog abuser of our generation, earning them a sizeable sum of money from Vick's football team but raising the ire of dog lovers in the U.S. (see pages 132-136), local humane societies took the heat. NHS, for example, was publicly criticized for "embracing Michael Vick"—which they did not. In order to clarify the confusion and to help raise funds for local programs, NHS tried to buy a list from HSUS. And they submitted their proposed mailing for HSUS approval which included the statement:

Nevada Humane Society is a nonprofit organization. We rely upon donations to make our lifesaving work possible. We do not receive funding from national groups or the government.

HSUS denied the request, stating that unless they removed the statement that NHS does not receive funding from national groups, they could not use the list. In other words, HSUS did not want NHS informing their local donors that

---

* In response to the investigation of its Hurricane Katrina fundraising campaign and public censure, HSUS claims it has since spent all 30 million dollars in the Gulf states. In at least one community, HSUS paid to build a room for a shelter to kill animals, not what the donors intended.

> **The fact is that the truth about the ASPCA and HSUS wouldn't sell: the misplaced priorities and defense of killing, the money hoarding, sending animals to kill shelters after they raise money on their "rescue." And so they misrepresent their work, take credit for the success of others and work to keep the American public ignorant of who and what they really are.**

when those local donors give to groups like HSUS, they are not giving money to local lifesaving efforts. Put simply, HSUS was committed to keeping Nevada donors in the dark as to where their money was going.

Why? The fact is that the truth about the ASPCA and HSUS wouldn't sell: the misplaced priorities and defense of killing, the money hoarding, sending animals to kill shelters after they raise money on their "rescue." And so they misrepresent their work, take credit for the success of others and work to keep the American public ignorant of who and what they really are.

A NOBLE LEGACY BETRAYED
Near the end of his life, Bergh often worried about the future of the ASPCA, stating, "I hate to think what will befall this Society when I am gone." It didn't take long for Bergh's worst fears to come true. Shortly after his death, and against his express instructions, the ASPCA traded in its mission of protecting animals from harm for the role of killing them by agreeing to

run the dog pound—something that Bergh rejected during his lifetime: "This Society," he once wrote, "could not stultify its principles so far as to encourage the tortures which the proposed give rise to." He would not allow his ASPCA to do the city's bidding in killing dogs they deemed "unwanted." In fact, Bergh's answer was the opposite: "Let us abolish the pound!" he proclaimed. But after his death, the ASPCA capitulated and took over the pound, becoming New York City's leading killer of dogs (and later cats). It was a terrible mistake, one emulated by humane societies and SPCAs nationwide, with devastating results.

Unwilling to harm the animals they were supposed to be protecting, animal lovers fled from these organizations, and bureaucrats and opportunists with no passion for animals or for saving their lives took them over, paving the way for the crisis of uncaring and killing we have inherited today. What began as a nationwide network of animal protection organizations devolved into dog and cat shelters whose primary purpose became, and in too many communities remains, killing animals, even when those animals are not suffering. And the mighty ASPCA, once a stalwart defender of animals, became a stalwart defender of killing them, beholden not to animals or furthering their best interest, but to a ruthless fundraising machine enriching itself and its leadership at the expense of its founding mission.

BLOATED COFFER$

Today's large animal welfare organizations have built a dependency model where the American public writes them checks and they "promise" to help animals. That has made them very rich and, too often, the animals no better off. They either hoard the money, use it to thwart lifesaving reform, use it to kill animals or waste it on meaningless programs that do not deliver substantive change.

In fact, here's their dirty little secret: These organizations already have enough money to do all the programs they want—if they would choose to do them. Moreover, they are not using the money people scrape together and send them to do more. When people send ten dollars to one of the large, national organizations, they might think it will feed a dog for a week or allow a stray cat a second chance, but the reality is the organizations can already afford to feed all the dogs and give all the stray cats as many chances as they want. But they don't. The additional money goes straight into their bank accounts, where it sits, year after year, making them richer. No additional dogs are fed. No additional cats are given a second chance. Or, worse yet, the donation is used to fight shelter reform efforts, condemning animals to certain death.

COMPARE & CONTRAST

The ASPCA's annual income translates into a stunning $41,000 raised per animal adopted at their New York shelter. Consider how many animals other New York groups would save with the same resources:

In 2010, ASPCA revenues exceeded 140 million dollars. They only adopted out 3,389 animals. That is roughly $41,000 per animal.

By contrast, during the same time frame, a New York No Kill shelter and sanctuary took in $635,000 and saved 2,932 animals. That is $216 per animal—or the equivalent of the ASPCA saving 645,040 animals.

A No Kill animal control shelter in New York took in $439,000 and saved 2,315 animals. That is $190 per animal—or the equivalent of the ASPCA saving 736,842 animals. This amounts to one-fourth of all animals being killed in shelters nationwide, but for a home.

What Would HENRY Do?

On February 8, 1866, to a well-filled room of attendees including the New York City Mayor, Henry Bergh, the father of the humane movement in North America, delivered the first lecture on animal protection in the United States. He called upon the gathering to undertake a moral fight to better the plight of animals: "This is a matter purely of conscience. It has no perplexing side issues... No, it is a moral question in all its aspects." But he later cautioned that,

> The chief obstacle to success of movements like this [is] that they almost invariably gravitate into questions of money or politics. Such questions are repudiated here completely... If I were paid a large salary... I should lose that enthusiasm which has been my strength and my safeguard.

In 2010, the ASPCA paid its president over half a million dollars—$555,824—in salary and other compensation. By contrast, when Henry Bergh founded the ASPCA, he fitted it with what he called "the very plainest kind" of furniture. When the Governor of New York visited the ASPCA, he stumbled over a hole in the old carpet and said: "Mr. Bergh, buy yourself a better carpet and send the bill to me." To which Bergh replied, "No, thank you, Governor. But send me the money, and I will put it to better use for the animals."

HSUS: A PATTERN OF DECEPTION

HSUS deception is not an isolated incident, but part of a recurring pattern designed to misrepresent the truth and raise money off of the work of others.

HSUS ASKED FOR DONATIONS IN THE AFTERMATH OF HURRICANE GUSTAV, CLAIMING CREDIT FOR THE WORK OF ANOTHER ORGANIZATION. ACCORDING TO A MUTTSHACK RESCUE REPRESENTATIVE:

"[We] just completed the largest animal evacuation in the history of the State of Louisiana. After its completion, HSUS took loaded dogs and cats off the MuttShack trucks, shot some footage and has posted it [on their website] as their own rescue."

A MISSISSIPPI RESCUE GROUP WRITES:

"We are a very small group that has been working in Mississippi since just after [Hurricane] Katrina. A couple of puppies that our team had rescued were adopted by some White House staffers and got a ride to their new homes on Air Force One. When US News picked up the story and printed it... suddenly on the HSUS website was a picture of one of the puppies in a HSUS bag with their claim of having 'placed a Katrina puppy in the White House. Please donate to us so we can save more...'

"Needless to say, my e-mails and phone calls to them were never answered. The staffer who allowed the photo had no idea what their real intent was of course and even she could not get them to rescind their web posting."

THE FORMER DIRECTOR OF BAY COUNTY ANIMAL CONTROL IN FLORIDA WRITES:

"[W]e did a horse rescue here In neighboring Jackson County, FL. An HSUS rep came to the scene, stood around for a couple hours watching others work, left... and then [their] news release said "HSUS Rescues 28 Horses" and asked for donations. They never even provided any sweat assistance— much less trailers, vehicles, gas, feed, or anything else. [The] HSUS person on site spent most of her time answering e-mail on her Blackberry."

THE TRUTH ABOUT HSUS
MEET FAY

MEET FAY. In 2009, HSUS set out to raise one million dollars in one month on the back of an abused dog rescued in the largest bust of a dog fighting ring in U.S. history. According to the HSUS fundraiser,

> This is Faye. She survived because of you. I'll never forget Faye's story. I bet you won't, either. Our team met her in Missouri, when The Humane Society of the United States helped rescue hundreds of animals from the horrors of dog fighting. She'd been wounded badly in a fight, and a dogfighter had mercilessly cut off her lips. She was in tough shape, but we found her in the nick of time… Watch our moving video to see Faye's happy ending—then become a Humane Hero with your monthly donation to our 2010 Animal Survivors Fund. Faye's a lucky survivor: She now sleeps in a warm bed in a safe place. To help save thousands of animals just like her in the new year, we're doing something we've never done before, and it's BIG: We're hoping to raise a million dollars online by December 31 for our 2010 Animal Survivors Fund.

They raised 1.4 million dollars. There was only one problem. HSUS did not rescue Fay. They even spelled her name wrong on the solicitation. In fact, HSUS was saying that Fay and the other dogs from that dog fighting bust should face a "pretty certain" death. And while Fay was being cared for and needed surgery, the costs and care were being provided by a small rescue group with limited means. Her foster mom writes:

> I am rather sad that HSUS has chosen to use Fay (not Faye) in their fund drive. Fay has never received a dime from HSUS. How do I know? Because I am the one that is fostering Fay. Fay is currently going through expensive surgeries to recreate medically need lips so her teeth do not fall out, her jaw bone stops deteriorating, and she can live a normal life. HSUS never contacted us regarding Fay.

In response to the criticism and condemnation of this fraudulent fundraising appeal—on blogs, on twitter and including calls for a criminal investigation of HSUS—and with the memory of an investigation for fraud by the Louisiana and Mississippi Attorneys General for Hurricane Katrina fundraising still fresh, HSUS announced that they would give $5,000 dollars for Fay's surgery, less than ½ of one percent of what they raised from the appeal about her.

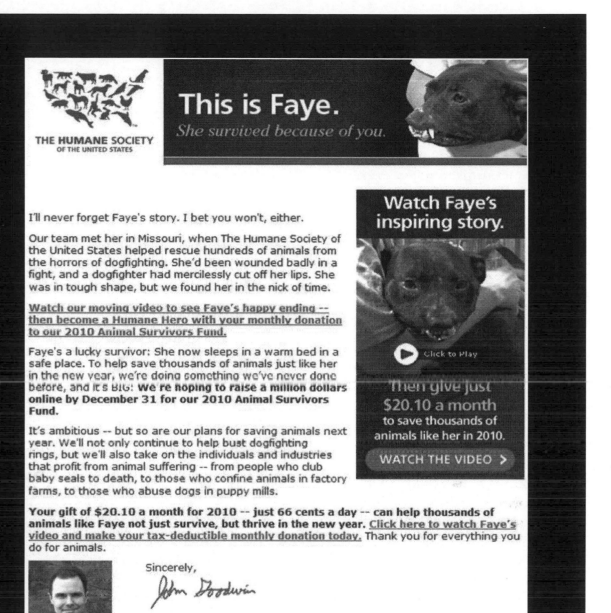

THE HUMANE SOCIETY
OF THE UNITED STATES

This is Faye.

She survived because of you.

I'll never forget Faye's story. I bet you won't, either.

Our team met her in Missouri, when The Humane Society of the United States helped rescue hundreds of animals from the horrors of dogfighting. She'd been wounded badly in a fight, and a dogfighter had mercilessly cut off her lips. She was in tough shape, but we found her in the nick of time.

<u>Watch our moving video to see Faye's happy ending -- then become a Humane Hero with your monthly donation to our 2010 Animal Survivors Fund.</u>

Faye's a lucky survivor: She now sleeps in a warm bed in a safe place. To help save thousands of animals just like her in the new year, we're doing something we've never done before, and it's BIG: **we're hoping to raise a million dollars online by December 31 for our 2010 Animal Survivors Fund.**

It's ambitious -- but so are our plans for saving animals next year. We'll not only continue to help bust dogfighting rings, but we'll also take on the individuals and industries that profit from animal suffering -- from people who club baby seals to death, to those who confine animals in factory farms, to those who abuse dogs in puppy mills.

Your gift of $20.10 a month for 2010 -- just 66 cents a day -- can help thousands of animals like Faye not just survive, but thrive in the new year. <u>Click here to watch Faye's video and make your tax-deductible monthly donation today.</u> Thank you for everything you do for animals.

Watch Faye's inspiring story.

▶ Click to Play

Then give just **$20.10 a month** to save thousands of animals like her in 2010.

WATCH THE VIDEO >

Sincerely,

John Goodwin

John Goodwin
Manager, Animal Fighting Campaign
The Humane Society of the United States

This appeal sent out by HSUS encouraged animal lovers to donate to HSUS to help Fay, a dog who needed surgery to repair a terribly disfigured face as a result of dog fighting. In reality, HSUS did not have custody or care of Fay and suggested that Fay and others like her would face a "pretty certain" death.

ANIMAL SHELTERING IN AMERICA
MEET ZEPHYR

MEET ZEPHYR. Zephyr was a 10-month-old puppy who arrived at the Los Angeles County Department of Animal Care & Control (LACDACC) in Carson, California. She was young, she was healthy and she was friendly and well-behaved. But LACDACC was a shelter notorious for being filthy and inhumane, while routinely failing to provide sick animals with prompt and necessary veterinary care in violation of state law.

Shortly after Zephyr arrived, a rescue group notified the shelter that if she was not adopted, they would take her and find her a home. Unfortunately, Zephyr was never vaccinated at the shelter as required by policy and got sick. As she slowly began to deteriorate, she was left in a cold, barren, dirty kennel. Although the shelter veterinarian prescribed antibiotics for Zephyr, shelter records indicate that she was never given the medication.

Over the course of several weeks, Zephyr's condition worsened. Left untreated, she developed pneumonia and stopped eating. And yet no one took action to ensure that she ate. The rescue group which had offered to take Zephyr was not notified until it was too late. When the rescue group was finally called, one of its members rushed to the shelter to adopt her, only to find Zephyr dead on the

Shortly after Zephyr arrived at the Los Angeles shelter, a rescue group notified the employees that if Zephyr was not adopted, they would take her and find her a home. Yet when Zephyr became ill and stopped eating, no one bothered to treat her or to call the rescue group— until it was too late.

concrete floor of a kennel. None of the staff had even noticed that she had died. The rescuer recounts:

I received a distressed phone call regarding the dog. I drove up to Carson... with the hope that I could get her out and bring her to our vet for emergency care. I found her dead on the outside part of the kennel. No blanket, no heat. I have attached the photo so you can see what being in the L.A. County shelter does to a healthy, young animal. She was just 10 months old.

(ABOVE) Zephyr as a healthy 10 month-old puppy, shortly after she arrived at the Los Angeles County Department of Animal Care & Control in Carson, California.

(BELOW) Zephyr, several weeks after her arrival at the shelter—a shelter notorious for being cold, cruel and filthy. Zephyr contracted pneumonia and stopped eating. She was prescribed medication which shelter staff never administered. No one cared that she was starving to death.

The first time most companion animals experience neglect is when they enter the place that is supposed to deliver them from it.

WHAT THE L.A. COUNTY SHELTER DOES TO A HEALTHY ANIMAL

Rescuers who had offered to take Zephyr shortly after she arrived at the shelter were not notified of her condition until it was too late. When they were told how sick she was, one of them rushed to the shelter to find her already dead. No one on staff had noticed. The cause of death was determined to be pneumonia and starvation ("marked emaciation").

Your tax dollars at work

The Tactics of an Extremist Agenda? Yes, They Are.

IN LATE 2011, the ASPCA released a series of documents on their "ASPCA Pro" website, a website aimed specifically at America's killing shelters and the staff who work in them. Unlike their popular ASPCA website, which is designed for the average American animal lover, the ASPCA Pro page purports to be a "go-to" portal for policies and procedures and guidance on running an "ASPCA-approved" shelter. The documents caused an immediate firestorm.

Why did these documents cause such a stir? Was it because the ASPCA was celebrating the fact that No Kill communities now exist? Were they sharing that good news with other shelter directors so that they could emulate that achievement, too? Was it because the documents revealed that the ASPCA had finally recognized the crisis of uncaring in our nation's shelters and the public discontent it fosters, and was taking decisive action to fix our broken animal sheltering system? Wishful thinking. On the contrary, these documents were a handbook for shelters on how to fight reform efforts and stave off calls for an end to the killing.

The Tactics of the Extremist Agenda

STEP 1: ESTABLISHING A PROXY
A member of a community will begin to adopt the talking points of the Extremist Agenda, using aggressive and divisive language to describe the state of that community's animal welfare organizations.

STEP 2. CREATING A LOCAL ORGANIZATION
The proxy forms an organization (i.e. "No Kill Austin/Louisville/Houston/Philly) that will act as the local brand for the Extremist Agenda and begin to use social networking to expand.

STEP 3: ENGAGING IN LOCAL POLITICS
The no-kill organization lobbies local public officials and candidates regarding the existing euthanasia rates at the municipal shelter. In most cases, there does exist public attention to the need to reform the sheltering system to increase lifesaving.
• The proxy organization will get involved in local elections, circulating questionnaires and financial support to candidates perceived as sympathetic to the Extremist Agenda.

STEP 4: SLANDERING EXISTING ANIMAL WELFARE
The Extremist Agenda slanders the existing shelter director and any local humane organization that is deemed to be sympathetic to the status quo. The aim of the slander is to put enough pressure on the director to step down (which is often achieved).

STEP 5: INSTALLING A PUPPET REGIME
A new "compassionate" director sympathetic to the Extremist Agenda is put in place through effective lobbying. The Extremist Agenda organization will often advocate a candidate with little or no experience who will essentially do as they are told.

STEP 6: SAVING FACE WHEN THE AGENDA FAILS
The Extremist Agenda displaces blame when the program becomes unsustainable by blaming either their own director or local public officials for not backing them sufficiently.

STEP 7: SLANDERING MEDIA
Attacking unfavorable media is commonplace for the Extremist Agenda when a story runs that questions any component of implementing overnight solutions while demonizing hardworking animal welfare organizations.

Engaging Public Officials

Every community is different, and there is no "one size fits all" template for handling local public officials. However there are a few general guidelines that may help you advance a **No Harm No-Kill** (NHNK) message while pointing out the dangers of the Extremist Agenda.

It is important to remember that if the Extremist Agenda establishes itself in your community, there will eventually be a call for policy changes that will implicate your local public officials. The distinction between the Extremist Agenda and NHNK is not only about caring for animals but also about public policy that impacts how a community addresses animal welfare needs.

Emphasize Success
Public officials like it when programs work well. Be sure to highlight the progress your organization and/or community have made in decreasing intake, improving shelter care and increasing live outcomes.

Talk Money and Resources
Public officials are held responsible for budgeting to ensure programs operate effectively. Be sure to stress that achieving a responsible and sustainable NHNK community requires a commitment of money and resources so that it is done right.

In contrast, the Extremist Agenda downplays the importance of financial commitments and dedicating resources, including staffing and adequate capacity.

Provide Face Time and Materials
Meeting face to face with your public officials can leave a valuable impression. When meeting, come equipped with materials that are easy to digest but grounded in data and facts. Such materials may include highlights of your successes in lifesaving and NHNK talking points.

In some cases it may be appropriate to hire a government affairs expert who has greater contact with public officials. Be sure to

provide him or her with presentable materials that advance the NHNK message.

Be Cautious with Officials Sympathetic to the Extremist Agenda
The Extremist Agenda is able to push through resolutions and legislation by finding at least a handful of sympathetic public officials. Public officials who are leaning in the Extremist direction need to be handled cautiously.

It is important to not back them into a corner and provide as much factual information as you can. Use your judgment and decide if it is helpful to provide them with case studies where the Extremist Agenda failed and case studies where NHNK succeeded.

Collaboration, Not Divisiveness
Most public officials are weary to be associated with divisive figures. It may be helpful to point out the slanderous tactics of the Extremist Agenda while maintaining a reasoned, calm and cooperative tone.

Public officials have to win re-elections and try to avoid extremists, even in progressive communities.

In them, the ASPCA admitted "there does exist public attention to the need to reform the sheltering system to increase lifesaving." Nonetheless, the documents attempt to teach shelter directors how to defeat these calls for reform. And they do so by describing No Kill reformers and the democratic efforts in which they engage with the most reactionary of language.

The documents describe local No Kill activists working to end the cruelty and killing occurring at their local shelters as "proxies" of No Kill leaders. It describes their efforts to replace poorly performing shelter directors with compassionate people committed to ending the killing as seeking to "install puppet regimes." And it decries the legal, democratic means No Kill activists use to achieve their ends—educating the public through protest and the media, and working with public officials and legislators to seek legislative reform—as "Tactics of the Extremist Agenda." Shelter directors are especially warned to "be cautious of officials" who are "sympathetic" to this "extremist agenda."

Shocked animal lovers who learned of these documents overwhelmingly condemned the ASPCA. Even a long time ASPCA supporter wrote:

  Instead of cooking up fevered fantasies about an Al-Qaeda-like no-

kill operation that is on the loose and may be coming to a community near you, one would hope that the ASPCA would be rattling the cages of local SPCAs and shelters and using their considerable influence in those circles to get such organizations to address the actual cause of public unrest, which is not an extremist agenda, but the killing of healthy, treatable pets.

Because the criticism even came from the ASPCA's allies, the documents were removed from the website very quickly. Their disappearance was followed by an apology from the ASPCA, explaining that the documents were posted on their website "by mistake." In truth, the only mistake the ASPCA made was in assuming that everyone viewed No Kill reformers with the same scorn and suspicion that they do. As a result, the ASPCA was left with no choice but to pretend that the documents they had written and posted on their own website had nothing whatsoever to do with them. But it was too late.

Animal lovers had a glimpse behind the curtain, and what they saw was not only very, very ugly, but confirmed what No Kill advocates already knew: the ASPCA considers people who love animals and do not want them to be killed or abused in our nation's shelters not as allies in the cause of animal protection, but as enemies to battle and defeat.

One City's Road to a 90% Save Rate and How the ASPCA Tried to Block It

WELCOME TO AUSTIN, TEXAS

Today, in Austin, Texas, over 90 percent of all dogs and cats entering the animal control shelter in that community make it out alive, the largest municipal shelter in the country to cross that threshold. But it wasn't always that way.

In the not-so-distant past, the animal control shelter in Austin was overseen by an individual who killed over 13,000 animals every year despite pleas from animal lovers that she implement the simple, common sense alternatives that today make a life and death difference for Austin's homeless animals.

For years this director ignored their requests, ordering her staff to kill animals instead of adopting them out, ordering her staff to kill animals instead of sending them into foster care, ordering her staff to kill sick and injured animals rather than providing them with veterinary care and ordering her staff to kill animals in spite of empty cages. And for years, she got away with it because the powerful and influential ASPCA defended her, telling the media, Austin's legislators and the Austin public that not only was a 90 percent save rate impossible and not only were No Kill advocates calling for reform dangerous, but that the animals themselves were not worth saving.

The story of how No Kill reformers in Austin succeeded in transforming that community provides many valuable lessons for animal lovers seeking to reform the shelter in their own hometowns, but none more important than this:

IT TAKES A FIGHT.

IN TOWNS AND CITIES across the United States, wherever animal lovers are waging campaigns to reform their local shelters, not only do they have to overcome a hostile, entrenched shelter director who refuses to innovate and remains intent on killing, but they often have to fight one or more of the national animal protection groups which come to that shelter director's

> To launch the campaign, the ASPCA hosted a meeting of animal welfare stakeholders during which they announced that rather than follow the only model that had ever achieved success—the No Kill Equation—Austin would follow a "collaborative" model, one that had never created No Kill but which shielded those in power from valid criticism.

defense. They have to fight PETA, which tracks No Kill reform campaigns nationwide and writes letters to the editor of local newspapers in defense of killing, equates No Kill with hoarding and animal abuse and tells policymakers that they should not give in to reformers even in the face of outright cruelty in the shelter. They have to fight HSUS, which consistently undermines the work of No Kill reformers by urging policy makers to reject progress and maintain the status quo, insisting on the right of shelters to kill animals. And they have to fight the ASPCA, which has labeled reformers as "extremists," has employed people who have labeled them "terrorists" and

which co-opts local No Kill initiatives by stifling dissent and attempting to marginalize any individuals who criticize those in power.

While the resistance of regressive local directors and the influence of their allies at powerful national animal organizations can make the work of No Kill reformers difficult and challenging, they by no means make success impossible. Where activists have succeeded, it is because of their refusal to back down in the face of opposition. They fought back, and over time their efforts and determination systematically exposed what these organizations really are, thereby hindering their destructive influence. And there is no better example of this than the fight waged by the animal lovers of Austin, Texas, who stood up to the mighty ASPCA and won.

MISSION: ORANGE

In February of 2007, the ASPCA announced a campaign in Austin, Texas, as part of what it called its "Mission: Orange"* program. The goal was a combined 75 percent save rate among Austin-coalition partners, including the city shelter, far less than the minimum 90 percent save rate goal at the city shelter championed by No Kill advocates. To launch the campaign, they hosted a meeting of animal welfare stakeholders. The project was doomed from the start. Rather than follow the successful model of the No Kill Equation, the ASPCA told the assembled crowd that "Mission: Orange"

---

* The ASPCA claims that the "color orange is identified with vibrancy and energy." Indeed, the color orange appears to be a favorite among the "aura-reading" crowd. As a result, outgoing ASPCA President Ed Sayres hopes that the public will identify the color "with the welfare of animals." Hence, the name "Mission: Orange." This type of New Age focus also characterized the San Francisco SPCA during Sayres' tenure as its president. Under Sayres' leadership, the San Francisco SPCA spent a significant amount of money on esoteric conferences in posh locations about communicating with dead pets, insects as messengers of the "soul" and other similar topics, instead of focusing all its energy and resources on saving the animals facing death in shelters. Roughly during the same time period, the San Francisco SPCA was cutting critical programs that saved homeless animals due to budget problems created by Sayres' mismanagement.

THEN & NOW
BLUE AS A SUMMER SKY

There was a time when just being a kitten got you killed in Austin, Texas. A local newspaper did a story a few years ago about life and death at the city pound:

A 7-week-old kitten weighs about a pound; his veins are the size of vermicelli. So if you're administering a lethal dose of sodium pentobarbital, an anesthetic agent blue as a summer sky, you'll probably inject directly into his round, spotted belly. If you have five cages of kittens to kill this morning, you don't have time to go looking for slippery little veins.

A kitten with a hand gripping the scruff of his neck and a needle in his belly will squeal in terror, but once you've pulled out the needle and placed him back into a cage with his siblings, he will shake his head and start to get on with his kittenish business. Then he starts to look woozy, and begins to stumble around. He licks his lips, tasting the chemical absorbed into his system. Soon, he becomes too sedated to stand. The animal collapses, and when his lungs become too sedated to inflate, he stops breathing.

The killings begin shortly after 10am on a Wednesday in early October; by 10:32 the shelter is down about a dozen cc's of pentobarbital, and 20 cats are dead.

That was the world of the then-pound director who oversaw the killing with ruthless efficiency. During her tenure, she killed over 100,000 animals, tens of thousands a year, hundreds per month, dozens per day, one animal roughly every 12 minutes the shelter was open to the public. That was also the world of the ASPCA which—through a local spokesperson—not only backed, defended and promoted the shelter director, but worked to ensure that progress would not be made. While the shelter's director and her staff were busy killing animals in the back, the ASPCA was telling legislators, the media, and the community up front that efforts to save more animals were not worthwhile, that the animals themselves were not "desirable" or "placeable" and that the director should not be questioned.

But reformers fought back and they won. It took several years, but they succeeded. They stayed in it for the long haul, and today, the clouds have parted and the only thing as "blue as a summer sky" is the sky itself.

would follow a different approach: New York City's model of "collaboration."

They would follow the model of a city that was still killing half of all impounded animals and that, to this day, is rife with neglect, abuse, rampant killing and fabricated data. In fact, it is not even a true collaborative model: New York City's leadership interprets that to mean that they have all the power and rescuers are only allowed to participate if they say so and keep quiet. This was the same model that the ASPCA representative in Austin used when she was director of the Austin Humane Society and promised the city a No Kill community by the year 2002. The ill-fated "No Kill Millennium" plan fell apart for failure to reach its goals.

At the meeting, the ASPCA ignored the elephant in the room: that the city's shelter director refused to implement programs and services to save lives, choosing to kill the animals instead. Attendees were forbidden from speaking about what programs weren't being implemented or what animals were being killed who needed to be saved. Instead, they were instructed to "brainstorm" about what they would do over the next three years to help animals, including writing an imagined speech from a future U.S. President thanking them for their work. It was, according to attendees, "surreal."

DO AS I SAY NOT AS I DO
The ASPCA also informed the group that no one would be allowed to participate in the initiative if they criticized coalition members including the city shelter. However, it would turn out that the rules only ran in one direction: the ASPCA would spend the better part of the next several years criticizing those who wanted the shelter to implement programs like foster care and offsite adoptions which the shelter's director refused to do. The ASPCA condemned reformers, misrepresented who they were, attempted to assassinate their characters and tried to undermine their public support.

The ASPCA consistently defended the shelter director even in her bid to move the shelter to a remote part of the city, a move which activists feared would reduce adoptions. According to the ASPCA, the problem was not getting more adopters to the shelter; the problem was that the animals in the shelter were not "desirable" or "placeable." In fact, Austin's shelter director argued that only about 35 percent of the animals in Austin's shelter were "adoptable" and that they were saving more than that already. Austin, according to the leadership of the city shelter, was already No Kill. And trying to save more would just mean keeping "unadoptable" animals that no one would want alive, leading to "warehousing." The ASPCA promoted this view both publicly to the media and privately to city officials in their attempt to sabotage the 90 percent save rate goal of No Kill advocates.

Indeed, while acknowledging that their "collaboration" model had not succeeded in New York and had failed several years earlier in Austin, the ASPCA claimed it would succeed this time because of one crucial difference: the ASPCA would bring dollars to the table. That this view was flawed was not hard to see. All the money in the world would not have made a difference at a shelter run by a director who refused to stop killing. In addition, a lack of dollars was not the issue in either New York or Austin during the "No Kill Millennium" fiasco. In both cases, a private foundation granted a significant amount of money to the effort (over 20 million dollars in New York City alone), more than the ASPCA was offering Austin. Moreover, Austin's city shelter had a larger per capita budget than many communities around the country which had already achieved success. And ultimately, the ASPCA did not even spend all the promised money on programmatic improvements at the city shelter as it had implied, but rather on advertising in Austin to promote itself. The results were devastating.

Rather than see a decline in killing in Austin's shelter, killing actually increased 11 percent during the first year of the ASPCA's sham "No Kill" campaign. Animals had *less* of a chance of coming out of the shelter alive in Austin under the ASPCA "Mission: Orange" program than they did just one year before. By contrast, Reno's No Kill initiative, which was based on the No Kill Equation, saw deaths decline by 53 percent during the same period and it cut spending in the process. The contrast in both approaches and results proved a stunning indictment of the "Mission: Orange" program. But no one would have known that by reading the public relations coming out of the ASPCA at the time. By simply not talking about the numbers of animals saved or killed, the ASPCA billed the Austin campaign as an unqualified success. And the ASPCA continued to claim that Austin held promise for the rest of the nation, even as over 13,000 animals were being put to death in Austin yearly.

Rather than see a decline in killing in Austin's shelter, killing actually increased 11 percent during the first year of the ASPCA's sham "No Kill" campaign. Animals had *less* of a chance of coming out of the shelter alive in Austin under the ASPCA "Mission: Orange" program than they did just one year before.

THE MORATORIUM ON KILLING

But Austinites had had enough, and the Austin City Council understood that to continue following the advice of the ASPCA was as foolish as the ASPCA's plan itself. Over the ASPCA's objections, the City Council passed a No Kill plan, modeled after the No Kill Equation. In addition to mandating programs like foster care and officially establishing a minimum 90 percent lifesaving goal for the city of Austin, one of the key elements of the plan was a moratorium on killing savable animals when there were empty cages. A state inspection report had found that the shelter routinely had hundreds of empty cages on any given day, and yet the shelter continued to put healthy and treatable animals to death.

The ASPCA immediately went to work lobbying against the moratorium, arguing it would lead to warehousing of "unadoptable" animals, even though the terms of the moratorium allowed the continued killing of animals who were hopelessly ill, injured or in the case of dogs,

> **When the No Kill mandates went into effect, the shelter director stopped treating sick and injured cats, causing great suffering. Her actions were illegal, tantamount to animal cruelty. Reformers were quick to condemn her. The ASPCA continued to defend her, calling her the best advocate Austin animals ever had in their corner.**

vicious. The director also lobbied against it, arguing that there was no reason to do offsite adoptions or foster care because the city shelter was already saving all the animals who could possibly be saved. Despite the lobbying efforts of both the leadership of the shelter and the ASPCA, the City Council approved it unanimously.

After the plan became law, the shelter director must have realized that she had lost the support of the City Council. What she did next revealed such a callous disregard for the well-being of animals that it would ultimately cost her her job: she stopped treating some sick and injured cats, causing great suffering. Some No Kill advocates believed she wanted to "prove" the No Kill plan was responsible for "warehousing" and "animal suffering," but regardless of her motivations, her actions not only violated the letter and spirit of the moratorium, they were also illegal, tantamount to animal cruelty. Reformers were quick to condemn her. The ASPCA, of course, continued

to defend her, calling her the best advocate Austin animals ever had in their corner. It would prove a fatal mistake. In a very short period of time, the director was "reassigned" and the ASPCA's influence in Austin would be eviscerated.

When the news broke that the shelter director was being removed, No Kill advocates were elated. By contrast, it was news that the ASPCA condemned, calling her departure "horrible" and warning that the animals would pay the price. Immediately, however, the save rate increased. Within a few short months, it had reached 92 percent under an interim director. In other words, Austin achieved its 90 percent save rate goal without even having hired a permanent replacement. They have been saving 90 percent or better ever since. The ASPCA's systematic attempt to derail the No Kill initiative was finally defeated. So what is the ASPCA saying about Austin now?

INFORMATION PURIFICATION PROGRAM
According to the Chair of the Austin Animal Welfare Advisory Commission, "The ASPCA was against the No Kill plan the entire way. They rallied the troops around the director who was committed to killing. If we did not have the opposition of the ASPCA, we would have achieved success earlier." But when Austin finished the year saving 91 percent of all the animals, with save rates hitting as high as 96 percent during some months, the writing was on the wall.

With both the Austin City Council and the general public thrilled to learn that the effort was in fact succeeding, the ASPCA knew it could no longer fight the tide of history. And so they began to rewrite it. Casting themselves as the saviors of Austin's animals and the group responsible for success, today the ASPCA argues that they have both the experience and credibility to lead No Kill efforts in other cities, "just like we did in Austin, Texas." Austin's success, they claim, is their success, despite having fought the effort every step of the way.

THE ASPCA INFORMATION PURIFICATION PROGRAM

"Day by day and almost minute by minute the past was brought up to date... nor was any item of news, or any expression of opinion, which conflicted with the needs of the moment, ever allowed to remain on record. All history was a palimpsest, scraped clean and reinscribed exactly as often as was necessary."

— George Orwell, *1984*

TEN STEPS FORWARD
ONE TRAGIC STEP BACK

The ASPCA's Lingering Legacy In Austin

AUSTIN'S LIFESAVING SUCCESS has inspired communities across the country. At one time, during the height of the ASPCA's influence, the city was saving only four in 10 animals. In 2011, it saved 91 percent despite intakes of roughly 23,000 animals per year, and it is on pace for a similar save rate in 2012. It is not only one of hundreds of cities and towns across the U.S. with save rates in excess of 90 percent, it is the largest one. And there are many who consider Austin one of the most prized jewels in the ever-growing No Kill crown.

But after maintaining a 91 percent save rate the previous year and 93 percent just one month earlier, the city of Austin killed dogs for space one afternoon in May of 2012. According to a local newspaper report, "the Austin Animal Center euthanized 17 dogs Friday and might kill another 20 today to make space in the shelter." Ironically, after the animal-loving Austin public learned about the plight of the dogs and read that the shelter was staying open until 9 p.m. for adoptions, they adopted in droves. Combined with rescue groups which also stepped up to help, the remaining dogs were safe. Nonetheless, the news that 17 dogs were killed "for space" shocked animal advocates across the country.

Why did it happen?

In 2007, Austin had what other communities coveted: a centrally located facility in an area that is a daily destination for thousands of Austinites. By contrast, one of the primary inhibitors to maximizing adoptions in many cities is the remote location of the shelter. Shelters tend to be placed in outlying parts of a city such as in industrial areas, away from the centers of commerce, retail and prime residential neighborhoods. In other words, away from where the vast majority of adopters, volunteers and other members of the community work, live and play. The shelter is out of sight and out of mind which results in failing to meet the community's adoption potential—resulting in missed opportunities and lives needlessly lost.

While most communities were trying to relocate the shelter from remote areas to more populated centers, Austin was considering taking a step backward by doing the exact opposite, taking the shelter from a prime location in the heart of the city and placing it in a more remote location—an action which is contrary to the prescription for a No Kill Austin.

There was no doubt that the existing facility was run down and needed significant capitalization. But instead of arguing for improvements to the existing facility or building a new one at the same location, the then-shelter director enlisted the support of others to move the shelter, pushing for the remote location because although the design included fewer cages and kennels for the animals, it would allow for bigger offices for administrative staff like herself.

It was a call that would be answered by the ASPCA spokesperson in Austin. She urged the city of Austin to move the shelter. HSUS also chimed in, telling Austin officials that locating a shelter in areas where the shelter is likely to see the most adoptions should not be the primary factor in considering a shelter's location. In other words, HSUS supported the move, not because logic compelled it, but because they were asked by a kill shelter to do so. Despite

> **While most communities were trying to relocate the shelter from remote areas to more populated centers, Austin took a step backward by doing the exact opposite, taking the shelter from a prime location in the heart of the city and placing it in a more remote location—an action which is contrary to the prescription for a No Kill Austin.**

the efforts of No Kill advocates to convince them otherwise, the city approved the relocation.

When the reality of lowered adoptions as a result of the move became evident, the city failed to take steps to overcome the challenge. After killing the 17 dogs, a city spokesperson said they would "accelerate" plans to do a better job marketing animals, to open up satellite adoption centers and to boost adoptions. They should have done this from the beginning. Had they done it, the dogs they killed would be alive today.

In fact, they were required by law to do so but did not. Despite a mandate by the City Council that offsite adoption programs—a key program of the No Kill Equation—be implemented to supplement shelter adoptions, the shelter never obeyed this portion of the law, and the city never enforced it until it was too late.

In response to a public backlash, city officials claimed that no healthy or treatable dogs were among those killed. Though the claim is hard to believe because the city specifically pointed to overcrowding, not medical hopelessness for killing and records of the animals killed include dogs described as "easy, cute and playful," any claims of Austin going back to the status quo are misinformed. There is no doubt that Austin killed savable dogs. But this was not a failure of No Kill, but a failure to fully implement the No Kill Equation. In fact, since roughly 95 to 98 percent of shelter dogs are treatable, a 90 percent save rate goal presupposes that some treatable animals will still be killed.

And while in no way should the tragic killing of even one dog killed "for space" be minimized, with a 91 percent save rate in 2011 and being on track for similar save rates in 2012, the claims that the lifesaving initiative has failed in Austin being sounded by No Kill naysayers in order to derail No Kill efforts elsewhere are cynical, self-serving and greatly exaggerated. No Kill advocates once forced Austin to go from a 40 percent rate of lifesaving to a 91 percent rate. Now, they need to force the city to push that even higher so that no savable animal has his or her life taken in Austin, Texas, ever again.*

The City Council has since given Austin Pets Alive, a local rescue group, the use of the old shelter, resulting in more adoptions and higher save rates than ever before.

IN MEMORIAM

Sammie

Gracey

Although Sammie was surrendered to the shelter for fighting with other dogs in her home, according to the shelter, "she did obey 'rules' in both fetch and tug. Knows 'sit,' 'down,' 'roll over,' 'sit up' and 'shake.'" Sammie was one of the dogs killed by the Austin shelter on May 14, 2012. Other dogs were killed that day for being shy, fixated on tennis balls or fearful. Gracey was described as "easy," "cute" and "playful." She would also not be spared.

✓ REALITY CHECK
In Their Own Words

"Ownerless animals must be destroyed. It is as simple as that."

Dr. John B. DeHoff, Baltimore Health Commissioner, *Proceedings of the National Conference on Dog and Cat Control*, May 21, 1974

From May 21-23, 1974, self-proclaimed "leaders" of the animal welfare movement, including HSUS, the ASPCA and AHA, met in Chicago to look for "causes" and to find "solutions" to what they termed "the surplus dog and cat problem." It had little hope of success.

With stated goals of finding "consensus" and adopting a "unified" approach, they involved private practice veterinarians, the American Veterinary Medical Association and the American Kennel Club, ensuring the rejection of any program perceived to interfere with the business interests of these entities. Not surprisingly, the animal welfare groups unanimously rejected high-volume, low-cost spay/neuter for the animals of low-income households in order to

appease the commercial groups. As a result, the meeting turned into the search for a scapegoat to blame for shelter killing, rather than an attempt to see how shelters could operate differently, more efficiently and more effectively at saving lives.

In fact, they unanimously rejected any blame for animal shelters despite a candid admission that "they are destroying 90 percent of the animals received and only placing 10 percent." Instead, the heads of the largest animal welfare agencies in the country blamed the animals themselves and the pubic for the killing. To the ASPCA and others, most of the 90 percent of animals killed in shelters were not worthy of efforts to save them. Their conclusion: "Ownerless animals must be destroyed. It is as simple as that."

Over 7,000 copies of their conclusions and recommendations were sent to shelters nationwide, promoting the notion that an "adopt some and kill the rest" strategy for shelters is not only inevitable, but the only responsible way for shelters to operate.

> *Free-roaming dogs and cats are like "inhabitants of an interstellar craft... brought here with the purpose of disrupting our ecosystem."*

Roger Caras, HSUS Vice-President (and later ASPCA President), *Proceedings of the National Conference on Dog and Cat Control*, May 21, 1974

When the ASPCA, HSUS and AHA met in Chicago, it was Roger Caras who would set the tone for the rest of the conference. In an astonishing keynote address, Roger Caras of HSUS, who would later go on to lead the ASPCA, likened free roaming dogs and cats to "inhabitants of an interstellar craft... brought here with the purpose of disrupting our ecosystem." He described them as a threat of the highest magnitude, damaging property and decimating wildlife and the notion of creating successful programs to save them as so impossible that it was "not worthy of a passing daydream." This view would define the rest of the proceedings, as well as his career in animal welfare. As president of the ASPCA, Caras would go on to lead the fight against the No Kill movement, calling the effort to save more lives a "hoax."

> *"Running on and on about no-kill as the answer is maybe okay in San Francisco, with a population of 70,000, one-third who are gay (the gay community is traditionally the most animal-friendly)..."*

Roger Caras, ASPCA President August 21, 1997

In the mid-1990s, San Francisco had the highest save rate of any metropolitan area in the U.S. and was the only city to end the killing of all healthy dogs and cats. As news of San Francisco's success spread, animal lovers and activists in other communities tried to force local shelter directors to emulate it, asking the question, "If they can do it in San Francisco, why can't we do it here?" In response, regressive shelter directors like Roger Caras and others came up with creative and increasingly desperate answers.

The Deputy Director of the Los Angeles County Department of Animal Care & Control argued that San Francisco's success was the result of its geographic isolation—dogs and cats could not enter the city from outside because it was, he argued, "surrounded by water." In fact, San Francisco is not an island, but firmly connected to the rest of the North American continent. Not to be outdone,

Roger Caras, in a letter to No Kill advocates, not only understated the population of San Francisco by roughly eleven-fold (at the time, its population was 750,000 not 70,000) but also made the absurd and unfounded claim that the only reason San Francisco was successful was because of its population of homosexuals. Together, regressive shelter directors such as

Caras and others vowed to stop what happened in San Francisco from happening in their own communities. Ironically, not only is Manhattan (where the ASPCA is located) actually an island, but the birth of the modern gay rights movement was in New York City. By their own logic, Caras had no excuse for the ASPCA's continued killing.

> **"There is no room for No Kill as morally superior."**

Ed Sayres, ASPCA President, *USA Today*, August 13, 2007

In 2007, the most popular newspaper in America, *USA Today*, published a hit piece on the No Kill movement in which the leaders of some of the largest animal welfare organizations in the nation equated No Kill advocates with mentally ill individuals who hoard and abuse animals. It was not a new tactic. Kill-oriented traditionalists, desperate to maintain the status quo on which their reputations and those of their peers were built, had been portraying No Kill in a disparaging light for over a decade and without much recrimination for doing so. At one time, the story would not have made much of a ripple within the animal protection movement. But much had changed. As a result, the story made headlines on CNN, was circulated by shelters hostile to reform and was even printed overseas. Why?

With the number of communities achieving No Kill increasing and the calls for reform multiplying, directors running killing shelters and those running the national organizations which defended them felt under siege. And they began pushing back like never before.

No quote from the unfortunate article reveals the disparity between No Kill proponents and the defenders of killing more clearly than that by Ed Sayres. By stating "There is no room for No Kill as morally superior," the head of the largest SPCA in North America inferred that killing homeless animals is the ethical equivalent of saving their lives. The viewpoint is astounding enough coming from a person whose job gives him the tremendous responsibility for defining and upholding our nation's moral treatment of animals; it is even more so given Sayres' firsthand experience with No Kill success.

In 1998, Ed Sayres took over as President of what was then the most successful SPCA in the nation. At the time, the hard work of his predecessors at the San Francisco SPCA resulted in the only city and county in the U.S. saving each and every healthy homeless dog

and cat—a guarantee that extended to the city pound. Although he personally was not responsible for that success, he had knowledge of what could be achieved when people passionate about saving lives put aside excuses and focus on building the infrastructure for greater lifesaving.

When he left the San Francisco SPCA to take over as president of the ASPCA in New York City, Sayres also knew that the programs and services which once made San Francisco successful are the same programs and services that have allowed communities across the nation to go further, extending the lifesaving guarantee to treatable sick, injured, unweaned and traumatized animals. Yet while these shelters send thousands of animals every year into foster care, Sayres' asserts that they are no better than the vast majority of shelters which refuse to do so and choose to put animals to death instead.

While No Kill shelters open their doors to rescue groups, the inference of Sayres' comment is that morally, there is no difference between their actions and those of shelters which won't let these groups in the front door, while the animals they refuse to give them go out the back door in body bags. While No Kill shelters have replaced the killing of feral cats with programs to neuter and release them, Sayres' comment suggests that their doing so is no more ethical than the vast majority which not only oppose such efforts, but even send officers to write citations to the caretakers who do, threatening them

with impound—and killing—of the cats those caretakers are trying to protect.

Sayres' claim that "There is no room for No Kill as morally superior" is not only a slap in the face to the dedicated activists and rescuers across this nation working to make a lifesaving difference in their communities, but also to the American public which donates hundreds of millions of dollars a year to agencies like the ASPCA with the expectation that they will work to promote—and not hinder and undermine—the welfare of animals.

But most significantly, Sayres' statement reveals a lack of caring and concern for animals—qualities that should be defining characteristics of anyone who has been given the important trust of leading one of our nation's largest animal protection organizations. Supporting reactionary shelter leaders, rather than the animals, should not be the mission of the ASPCA.

Were the leader of another social conscience movement to reveal an opinion on par with Sayres' in *USA Today*, the calls for that leader's resignation would be widespread. Imagine what child welfare activists would say if the head of the nation's largest child protection agency stated, "People who treat their children kindly are not morally superior to those who abuse them." Americans should not tolerate it when the head of the ASPCA boldly asserts in the most widely read newspaper in the country that No Kill is not morally superior to killing.

> **"All right, I'm going to talk about the elephant in the room."**

Ed Sayres, March 11, 2010

In 2010, the city of Austin passed a shelter reform law mandating a 90 percent save rate at the city pound. Instead of faithfully implementing the plan, the shelter director allowed cats to get sick and suffer as a result. One rescuer who cared for a seriously ailing cat saved from the shelter describes how she woke up several times every night to care for and force feed the cat whom she was nursing. She recalls the anxiety she felt every time she peeked under the bed where the cat was hiding, fearful that she would discover he had died. Thanks to her efforts, the cat pulled through. But other animals who became sick were not so lucky. In fact, if the cats were feral, the director refused to provide medical care. In other words, the city shelter was now neglecting and arguably abusing animals in its care.

Yet rather than condemn the woman who intentionally caused animals to suffer and die, Sayres publicly lamented that she had lost her job as a result. At a public speaking engagement in Austin not long after the director was "reassigned," Sayres made it clear where he stood on the issue, and it was not on the side of the animals. "All right," he said in the middle of his speech, "I'm going to talk about the elephant in the room." He then went on to describe how "horrible" it was that "divisive incivility" in Austin led to the shelter director's reassignment. He stated that people who criticized her "wasted the time of everyone actually helping animals" and then went on to blame No Kill advocates—the very people who had worked to stop the director from killing and the very people who had nursed and cared for the animals who became ill as a result of her policies—for the killing of animals at the pound.

Sayres' statements reveal a lack of caring and concern for animals—qualities that should be defining characteristics of anyone who has been given the important trust of leading one of our nation's largest animal protection organizations.

MEET SCRUFFY

MEET SCRUFFY. Scruffy was an orphaned kitten rescued by a man named Daniel in Phoenix, Arizona. Daniel bottle-fed Scruffy several times a day, every day, until she was old enough to eat on her own. Every night, Scruffy slept on Daniel's pillow. Daniel credited Scruffy with helping him overcome a long-term addiction to drugs. After all, Scruffy needed him. And he needed Scruffy.

In 2011, the nine-month-old Scruffy cut herself on fencing and Daniel took her to the Arizona Humane Society veterinary clinic for treatment. Unable to immediately come up with four hundred dollars to pay for it, Daniel asked if they would accept his mother's credit card by telephone (she lived in a different state) or accept cash the following day when she was able to wire it to him. The Arizona Humane Society refused to do either. They told him that the only way they would treat Scruffy was if he signed over "ownership" to them. With a heavy heart but desperate for Scruffy to get the care she needed, Daniel agreed. But instead of treating Scruffy as promised, the Arizona Humane Society put her to death.

Over the next several weeks, Daniel tried to find out how Scruffy was doing, but could not get a straight answer. He repeatedly checked the Arizona Humane Society's shelter looking for Scruffy, but could not find her. Finally, after realizing he would not give up, they told him the terrible truth. She was killed the very day she came in. The Arizona Humane Society did not want to spend the money to treat her. Daniel became distraught: "Now I've got to think about how I failed that beautiful animal. I failed her... That's so wrong. There was no reason for her not to be treated."

The Arizona Humane Society says they "envision a world in which all people regard companion animals as lifelong, valued family members." Daniel already thought of Scruffy that way. In fact, he did what any family member would have done: he put his own desire aside, in order to do what he thought was best for the cat he loved. He gave her to an organization which promised it would treat her and whose proclaimed mission is "to

Daniel was asked to make a terrible choice—give up the most important thing in the world to him, his closest companion and dearest friend— because a "humane" society which takes in over 12 million dollars every year promising to help animals in just these situations couldn't wait one day to be paid.

The Arizona Humane Society failed to do the one thing they promised to do in exchange for Daniel giving up Scruffy and entrusting her into their care; they chose to kill her instead. Not only did they violate their most solemn duty in doing so, but they left Daniel with the guilt of believing he was the one who failed her, forcing him to carry a wound on his heart for the rest of his life.

improve the lives of animals, alleviate their suffering, and elevate their status in society. We safeguard, rescue, shelter, heal, adopt and advocate for animals in need, while inspiring community action and compassion on their behalf." Both their promise and their mission statement ring hollow.

In this case, Daniel was asked to make a terrible choice—give up the most important thing in the world to him, his closest companion and dearest friend—because a "humane" society which takes in over 12 million dollars every year promising to help animals in just these situations couldn't wait one day to be paid. They refused to accept a credit card over the telephone. And they refused to do charity, as they promised donors—and Daniel—that they would. And after making the heart wrenching decision that her health was more important than his happiness, he entrusted her to them so she could get the medical care she needed. Instead, the Arizona Humane Society betrayed them both.

Like their regressive counterparts across the country, AHS officials refused to acknowledge

the gravity of what they asked Daniel to do. And then, cavalierly—failing to do the one thing they promised to do in exchange for him giving up Scruffy and entrusting her into their care—they chose to kill her instead. Not only did they violate their most solemn duty in doing so, but they left Daniel with the guilt of believing he was the one who failed her, forcing him to carry a wound on his heart for the rest of his life.

When Scruffy's heartbreaking story made the local news, animal lovers were outraged. The Arizona Humane Society responded by explaining that they simply could not afford to treat Scruffy, despite revenues of over 12 million dollars a year, assets in excess of 30 million dollars and a surplus to expenses of several million per year, money which ostensibly sits in the bank. But when the fervor over Scruffy's killing did not subside, AHS brought in a public relations firm to quell the discontent. Their solution? Ask the community to donate even more money for animals they may or may not treat.

It's a crime.

IN BED WITH A MONSTER

MEET HSUS SPOKESPERSON MICHAEL VICK

WHEN NEWS of what had been uncovered at the home of football player Michael Vick first broke, it was an immediate media sensation. Twenty-four-hour news channels could not get enough, and images of Vick's house, his "Bad Newz Kennels" and dogs being seized by officials dominated television, newspapers, magazines and the internet. Americans were transfixed and then they were horrified. As the truth began to leak out about what Michael Vick had been doing to dogs, eyes welled up, stomachs turned and more than a few Americans likely had trouble sleeping at night, haunted as they were by images of the savage cruelty dogs suffered at the hands of Michael Vick. Yes, Michael Vick fought dogs, and that,

On numerous occasions, HSUS President Wayne Pacelle has refused to meet with the No Kill Advocacy Center, saying he doesn't "trust" those who have been critical of HSUS policies which favor killing. By contrast, Pacelle has toured the nation standing side by side with Michael Vick, the most notorious dog abuser of our time. Vick beat, drowned, electrocuted, hanged and shot dogs to death, burying some while they were still alive and laughing when they tore each other apart.

in and of itself, was horrible enough. In doing so, he caused dogs unimaginable pain, terror and untimely deaths, all while he laughed as they tore each other to shreds. But more than that, it was revealed that Vick was a sadist, a man who took perverse pleasure in killing dogs and doing so in ways that caused them the greatest possible suffering in the process. Michael Vick beat dogs to death. He drowned them. He electrocuted them. He stomped on them. He hung them. He shot them. He buried them alive. And when some of his co-conspirators wanted to give away dogs who would not fight rather than kill them, Vick refused. In one case, a dog Vick tried to hang by placing a nylon cord over a board that was nailed to two trees refused to die. Wearing a pair of overalls he donned so he would not get blood from the dogs on his expensive, tailored suits, Vick took the dog down and drowned him. In the annals of history, Michael Vick will be remembered as the most notorious dog abuser and dog killer of our generation. But he didn't stop doing those things because he realized they were wrong. In fact, he has never sincerely apologized for his crimes, claiming at one point that his "is a different kind of love" for dogs than most, and that he expressed that love in his own way—by hanging, drowning, electrocuting, beating to death and shooting them.

After the depths of Vick's depravity and the extent of his crimes were fully revealed, he was convicted by the federal courts, sent to prison, banned from the National Football League (NFL), bankrupted and despised by the American people. His public image in tatters, nothing but a miracle could bring him back.

Against reason, compassion and decency, that miracle was delivered to him by a person who should have remained his most vocal and outspoken critic: Wayne Pacelle, head of the

ON THE ROAD TOGETHER

nation's largest animal protection organization, the Humane Society of the United States. Pacelle would embrace the person he simply calls "Mike" and fight to rehabilitate his image by arguing publicly that he deserved a second chance, even as he fought to have each and every one of "Mike's" victims, the dogs who were still alive, killed. For Pacelle, Vick's victims did not deserve the second chance their abuser did. And after Pacelle lobbied the court to kill the dogs, he then began lobbying everyone else to forgive the monster who abused them.

"We're all sinners when it comes to animals," explained Pacelle. Pacelle agreed with Vick's statement that dog fighters express "a different kind of love" for dogs. And when Vick said he wanted to get another dog, which was against the terms of his parole, Pacelle agreed again, offering up the most stunning in a long line of stunning comments, "I have been around him a lot, and feel confident that he would do a good job as a pet owner."

After he was released from prison, Michael Vick began appearing at photo ops around the country with Wayne Pacelle right by his side. Pacelle and Vick toured the nation together, including many schools. And it worked. Michael Vick got his career back, the NFL reinstated him, Pacelle got the press coverage he coveted and HSUS was $50,000 dollars richer, thanks to a generous donation by a grateful Philadelphia Eagles franchise that was itself made richer by the presence of a quarterback who could win games. While little children across the country, who were once given the lesson that if you fight dogs and torture them for fun, what you have done is so wrong that you'll lose everything—you'll go to prison, you'll lose money, your career will end and you will be disdained by all decent and compassionate people—were taught that, in the end, dog fighting and killing animals are no big deal after all. Just find a way to line the pockets of an animal protection organization, go to a few schools and tell kids not to do what you did and you can move right back into your old life. Heck, you might even be allowed to have more animals to torture if HSUS has anything to say about it. Because, after all, they are only dogs.

When Vick was reinstated in the NFL, protests erupted nationwide. While Wayne Pacelle was holding Vick's hand and helping him reform his image, animal lovers from coast-to-coast demanded justice for his victims, the very dogs Pacelle lobbied to have killed.

Pacelle and Vick toured the nation's schools, undoing the lesson Vick's prison time, bankruptcy, lost career and public disdain taught our young people: torture dogs, lose everything. Here, Vick is presented with a school t-shirt and hat.

DEFINE "GOOD" MR. PACELLE

Wayne Pacelle says he feels "confident" that Michael Vick "would do a good job as a pet owner." Read the following account of one of the rescuers who was involved in the Vick case, and decide if you agree.

I just can't get myself away from the swimming pool in Vick's yard. I first learned about it while riding in the back seat of a federal agent's car that sweltering Tuesday back in Sept '07. The agent was assigned with escorting us to the various Virginia shelters so we could evaluate "the evidence" otherwise known as 49 pit bulls—now known as cherished family pets: Hector, Georgia, Sweet Jasmine and the rest. I'm not sure if sharing insider information with us was kosher, but you know how driving down long country roads can get you talking. I imagine she just needed to get some things off her chest. She said she was having trouble sleeping since the day they exhumed the bodies on the Moonlight Road property. She said that when she watched the investigators uncover the shallow graves, she was compelled to want to climb in and pick up the decomposing dogs and comfort and cradle them. She knew that was crazy talk, and she was grappling with trying to understand such a surprising impulse.

Her candor set the tone for this entire saga. Everyone we worked with was deeply affected by the case. The details that got to me then and stay with me today involve the swimming pool that was used to kill some of the dogs. Jumper cables were clipped onto the ears of underperforming dogs, then, just like with a car, the cables were connected to the terminals of car batteries before lifting and tossing the shamed dogs into the water. Most of Vick's dogs were small—40 lbs or so—so tossing them in would've been fast and easy work for thick athlete arms. We don't know how many suffered this premeditated murder, but the damage to the pool walls tells a story. It seems that while they were scrambling to escape, they scratched and clawed at the pool liner and bit at the dented aluminum sides like a hungry dog on a tin can.

I wear some pretty thick skin during our work with dogs, but I can't shake my minds-eye image of a little black dog splashing frantically in bloody water... screaming in pain and terror... brown eyes saucer-wide and tiny black white-toed feet clawing at anything, desperate to get a hold. This death did not come quickly. The rescuer in me keeps trying to think of a way to go back in time and somehow stop this torture and pull the little dog to safety. I think I'll be looking for ways to pull that dog out for the rest of my life.

On July 17, 2012, Michael Vick announced he will get a dog.

//// $$$$ //// $$$$

HSUS: KILL THE VICK-TIMS, AND SEND US MONEY

HELPING TO GET VICK reinstated in the NFL was not the only way HSUS betrayed Vick's victims or exploited the case for publicity and money. Pacelle lobbied to have all of the dogs killed, stating "Officials from our organization have examined some of these dogs and, generally speaking, they are some of the most aggressively trained pit bulls in the country." In truth, when an actual assessment of their temperaments was done, only two of the 51 dogs were determined to be beyond the hope of behavior rehabilitation. The rest were eventually placed in sanctuaries and loving homes where they are now cherished family members, treated with the gentleness and compassion they never knew before.

HSUS also fraudulently fundraised off of the Vick dogs, telling people that the dogs were in HSUS custody, when they were not. Shortly after the case broke, HSUS contacted the U.S. Attorney prosecuting Vick and asked if they could see the dogs,

Shortly after the Vick case broke, Wayne Pacelle began lobbying to have all of the dogs killed, stating "Officials from our organization have examined some of these dogs and, generally speaking, they are some of the most aggressively trained pit bulls in the country."

It was a lie.

then being held at six animal control shelters in Virginia. The U.S. Attorney agreed but only on condition that they take no photographs and not publicly talk about the dogs, citing fears of compromising the case, sensitivities involved in the prosecution and issues surrounding rules of evidence. HSUS agreed and then promptly violated that agreement. HSUS staffers took photographs of the dogs with people wearing HSUS shirts to make it appear that HSUS was directly involved in their care and then used these photographs to fundraise. Not only was that a lie, not only did they want the dogs dead, not only were they not going to use the money for the Vick dogs, but the U.S. Attorney's Office felt so betrayed that they did not want to work with any animal groups. If they had not been convinced otherwise, the dogs who eventually went to a sanctuary, rescue groups and loving homes would be dead right now, thanks to HSUS.

☑ **Yes! I want to make a special gift to help The Humane Society of the United States care for the dogs seized in the Michael Vick case and to support other vital animal protection programs.**

The HSUS has assisted federal authorities in the case against Michael Vick and his co-defendants, and is now overseeing the care of the 52 pit bulls seized from Vick's property in southwestern Virginia.

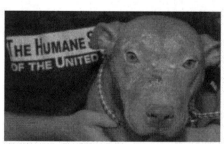

This dog was one of 52 pit bulls seized from Michael Vick's property -- dogs now being cared for by The HSUS in cooperation with shelters. ©The HSUS

We desperately need your help to care for these dogs while the case is pending. Please donate today by completing the fields below. Your gift will be put to use right away to care for these dogs and to support all our vital animal protection programs. Thank you!

This appeal sent out by HSUS encouraged animal lovers to donate to HSUS to help them care for the victims of Michael Vick. In reality, HSUS did not have custody nor did they provide care for the Vick dogs and were, in fact, lobbying to have them killed.

Dog Owners Can't Forgive Michael Vick

Quarterback shows greatness on the field, but evidence of former cruelty remains.

Mel

While Michael Vick was screaming toward the sky, a black pit bull named Mel was standing quietly by a door.

On this night, like many other nights, Mel was waiting for his owners to take him outside, but he couldn't alert them with a bark. He doesn't bark. He won't bark. The bark has been beaten out of him.

While Michael Vick was running for glory, Mel was cowering toward a wall.

Every time the 4-year-old dog meets a stranger, he goes into convulsions. He staggers back into a wall for protection. He lowers his face and tries to hide. New faces are not new friends, but old terrors.

While Michael Vick was officially outracing his past Monday night, one of the dogs he abused cannot.

"Some people wonder, are we ever going to let Michael Vick get beyond all this?" said Richard Hunter, who owns Mel. "I tell them, let's let Mel decide that. When he stops shaking, maybe then we can talk."

I know, I know, this is a cheap and easy column, right? One day after the Philadelphia Eagles' quarterback officially becomes an American hero again, just call the owner of one of the dogs who endured Vick's unspeakable abuse and let the shaming begin...

Cheap and easy, right? Not so fast. Vick's success is raising one of the most potentially costly and difficult perceptual questions in the history of American sports... If he continues playing this well, he could end up as the league's most valuable player... And yet a large percentage of the population will still think Michael Vick is a sociopath. Many people will never get over Vick's own admissions of unthinkable cruelty to his pit bulls—the strangling, the drowning, the electrocutions, the removal of all the teeth of female dogs who would fight back during mating.

Some believe that because Vick served his time in prison, he should be beyond reproach for his former actions. Many others believe that cruelty to animals isn't something somebody does, it's something somebody is.

Essentially, an ex-convict is dominating America's most popular sport while victims of his previous crime continue to live with the brutality of that crime, and has that ever happened before?

by Bill Plaschke
Los Angeles Times, November 16, 2010

SURVIVING VICK & HSUS

Despite HSUS' efforts to ensure that the 51 victims of Michael Vick were killed rather than given the lives and the love they deserved, the dogs were sent to rescue groups and all but two were saved. Here, some photographs of the dogs HSUS argued should be killed for aggression, living their new lives.

Where Are They Now?

They are enjoying the

Joy

Love

Kindness

Affection

Safety

and happy endings HSUS did not want them to have.

✓ REALITY CHECK
In Their Own Words

> *"I've put 70,000 dogs and cats to sleep... But I tell you one thing: I don't worry about one of those animals that were put to sleep... Being dead is not cruelty to animals."*

Phyllis Wright, HSUS Vice-President of Companion Animals, *HSUS News*, 1968

Over 40 years ago, the late-Phyllis Wright, the HSUS Vice-President of Companion Animals and the matriarch of today's "catch-and-kill" paradigm, wrote an essay in *HSUS News* called *"Why We Euthanize."* In it, she stated that she "put 70,000 dogs and cats to sleep... But I tell you one thing: I don't worry about one of those animals that were put to sleep." She then described how she does worry about the animals for whom she found homes. From that disturbing viewpoint, HSUS coined a maxim that says we should worry about saving lives but not about ending them and successfully propagated this idea to shelters across the country. *"Why We Euthanize"* could be found framed on the walls of animal shelters.

The essay not only created an emotionally acceptable pretext for killing, but it coined one of the biggest misnomers of them all: shelters were no longer killing animals, they were "putting them to sleep." Killing, Wright argued, is not only kindness, it is an imperative: no one wants to kill, but shelters have no choice in the matter. Although those propositions are false, they continue to be responsible for the extermination of millions of dogs and cats every year. In fact, every animal who enters a traditional shelter today faces the very real potential of being killed as a direct result of the shelter paradigm HSUS helped to create.

Barbara Cassidy, HSUS Director of Animal Sheltering and Control Division, July 13, 1990

There are thousands of rescue groups and No Kill shelters throughout the nation. Each animal they rescue is one less animal who enters—or if they are already there, faces a death sentence at—a killing shelter. Working with rescue groups frees up cage and kennel space at the shelter, reduces expenses for feeding, cleaning and killing, transfers the costs from taxpayers to private philanthropy and improves a community's rate of lifesaving.

Because millions of dogs and cats are killed in shelters annually, rare is the circumstance in which a qualified rescue group should be denied an animal. And yet, as they did with virtually every innovation of the No Kill Equation, HSUS bitterly opposed shelters working with such organizations. And they continue to oppose laws making such collaboration mandatory in order to save lives.

In fact, in 1998, California legislators were considering a law that would have made it illegal for shelters to kill animals if qualified rescue organizations were willing to save them, a law which HSUS also opposed. Over their objections, the legislature passed the bill and the Governor signed it into law. In just one California community, the number of animals sent to rescue groups rather than killed went from zero to roughly 4,000 per year. In 1997, before the law went into effect, only 12,526 dogs and cats were transferred to rescue groups rather than killed. In 2010, 58,939 were spared from death in California shelters because shelters were required by law to give them to rescue groups. That's an increase in lifesaving of 370 percent. Had HSUS had its way, over 46,000 additional animals would be needlessly losing their lives every year.

Apart from their longstanding policy that shelters should not work with rescue groups, even if the alternative for that animal was death, Cassidy also argued that shelters shouldn't give animals to other non-profit groups because an animal might find being placed on a leash or in a carrier and then moved from one location to another "stressful."

Essentially, she was arguing that animals are better off dead than going for a ride in a car. Taking her logic to its obvious conclusion, such a policy would prohibit taking animals to a veterinarian, a boarding facility or to daycare. It would prohibit taking a dog to a dog park. In fact, given that animals need to be driven home from a shelter after being adopted, this logic, faithfully applied, could be used to prohibit foster care and adoption as well.

Finally, Cassidy claimed that shelters should not work with rescue groups or other non-profits because those groups would take the more desirable animals, leaving a shelter with those she claimed no one would want, thereby destroying a shelter's public image. To HSUS, public impression is more important than the animals themselves. Worse, Cassidy believed that some animals were not desirable, placeable, lovable or worthy of compassion from the public.

"For feral cats, the traditional approach [killing] remains the only practical and humane solution. In comparison, neuter and release programs amount to nothing more than subsidized abandonment."

Mark Paulhus, HSUS Vice-President for Companion Animals, *Shelter Sense,* **May 1992**

On February 17, 1994, the cat lovers who made up the Outer Banks Spay/Neuter Fund in North Carolina met with officials of the Dare County Animal Control Advisory Board to ask for assistance. They were there to introduce themselves and demonstrate how the county could save money by investing in spay/neuter rather than continuing the local practice of impounding and killing the feral cats of the Outer Banks.

The Board suggested they present their plan to the Outer Banks SPCA. The SPCA director, however, told them not to bother. The SPCA had already declared "its total opposition to the spay/neuter of feral [cats]," preferring instead to kill them.

Members of the Outer Banks Spay/ Neuter Fund turned to HSUS for help. Since HSUS was the nation's largest companion animal and humane advocacy group—and one with significant influence over local shelters—leadership of the Outer Banks Spay/Neuter Fund expected their assistance in the struggle

to legitimize Trap-Neuter-Release (TNR) to the local shelter. The co-chair of the Fund explained:

We had thought HSUS would write a letter on our behalf. We thought that HSUS would encourage the Outer Banks SPCA to stop killing these cats since there was a non-lethal alternative. We felt that feeding and caring for these cats was in keeping with the humane mission of the Humane Society of the United States.

Instead, HSUS wrote to the Outer Banks SPCA calling TNR "inhumane" and "abhorrent," applauding the SPCA's opposition to the practice and encouraging the director to contact HSUS for assistance.

The SPCA did not have to take the initiative, however, because HSUS was not content to sit this one out; it wrote to the local criminal prosecutor and put plainly its "mission" when it came to feral cats and the people who care for them: feral cats should be taken to shelters and killed, and local feral cat caretakers should be subject to arrest and prosecution. The kind-hearted citizens who took it upon themselves to feed, neuter and care for the feral cats of the Outer Banks area were stunned.

According to HSUS, releasing feral cats after spay/neuter—even if the cats are fed, provided water and watched over daily as these particular cats were—amounted to animal abandonment, in violation of North Carolina anti-cruelty laws, an offense that carried both a fine and jail time. The cat lovers of the Outer Banks feared the worst—getting arrested and being jailed for feeding and caring for cats.

Thankfully, the prosecutor was not moved by HSUS' position. The North Carolina statute against abandoning pets, he stated, is,

> [D]irected at those people who dump their pets and those individuals who move from an area and leave their pets behind. If an animal is returned to the area where it is being fed, it would be a greater injustice to find that these animals had been abandoned so that no action to spay/neuter the animals would be taken by anyone.

The law, he said, was not intended to prevent animal lovers from feeding, altering, vaccinating and providing veterinary care to feral cats who do not live in a human home. Grateful that the local prosecutor employed common sense, as well as a dose of compassion for the cats and their caretakers, the Outer Banks Spay/Neuter Fund went back to work. They would continue to care for the cats, just as they had always done, but they did so without the naiveté that drove them straight into the arms of the enemy. Had they done a little research, however, the response by HSUS would not have surprised them.

Writing in *Shelter Sense* magazine, the primary device used by HSUS to influence policy among the nation's 3,000 or so shelters, Mark Paulhus, HSUS' Vice-President of Companion Animals, was very forthright about where the nation's "preeminent" animal organization stood on the issue. In May of 1992, in a column entitled *"Tough Choices About Feral Cats,"* Paulhus made the HSUS position crystal clear. Paulhus began by asking the rhetorical question of whether HSUS could support TNR for feral cats as an alternative to death at the pound. His response was emphatic: the "answers to these questions are still, and will always be, the same: no, no, and absolutely not!"

To HSUS, the answer was—and they asserted would always be—death. For many years that followed, HSUS would continue to promote the extermination of feral cats, calling mass slaughter in the nation's shelters, "the only practical and humane solution." HSUS went so far as to coin a phrase, "subsidized abandonment" to characterize efforts of cat lovers across the country who did TNR.

"*I no longer joke about those in the animal world who think it is their mission from God to bring down the successful, effective main stream agencies... [T]hese people operate under the same premise as those who ran airplanes into buildings. They simply do not care who gets hurt—not the animals, certainly not the people, and not the organizations which they see as mere buildings and symbols to be brought down... These people are small in number but are capable of huge destruction. Less than a dozen people brought down the World Trade Center and killed thousands. I guess you can say, someone has figuratively flown a piper cub into my building. The fight is on. We are looking to win, we intend to stop this evil.*"

Bill Garrett, Executive Director, Atlanta Humane Society, Member HSUS National Sheltering Committee, January 2002

During Bill Garrett's tenure, the Atlanta Humane Society ran Fulton County Animal Control. It did little more than kill animals. A small group of animal lovers began attending County Commission meetings in order to educate the community about the mass killing and move Fulton County, Georgia, toward greater lifesaving. Garrett, a darling of the Humane Society of the United States and a member of their national committee which helped shape HSUS policy on sheltering (and thus its staunch anti-No Kill rhetoric), likened the animal lovers wanting to reduce killing to 9/11 terrorists who brought down the World Trade Center. The name of this so-called "terrorist group"? *Kitty Village.*

It would be his undoing. A local rescue group was tapped to run animal control instead. The change was dramatic. According to its then-director, they,

> [T]ook over the horribly mismanaged Fulton County Animal Control from

Atlanta Humane Society (AHS) in 2003. This Fulton shelter which impounded 13,500 animals a year under AHS was the one that didn't allow adoptions, that killed every animal not reclaimed within 3 days (about a 90 percent [kill] rate), that didn't disinfect properly, had no vaccination protocol, had employees with horrible customer service, didn't work with rescue groups, it was a given that all puppies would contract parvovirus, had employees stealing animals, killing animals in horrific ways, etc. And wildlife was killed on intake, which meant that many reptiles and bats were stuck alive in a freezer to do so. We could go on and on with what we found when we arrived.

We have reduced the kill rate at the shelter from killing 11,500 animals a year to killing half that amount within the first year and now about 4,500 a year under our management. [And] we were able to accomplish all of this in an old, cramped, small animal shelter that was built in 1978 and is about [one-fourth] the size that we need for the volume of animals that we handle.

She further states, "Since we started on March 21, 2003—we have never, I repeat never, killed a healthy young puppy or kitten." In fact, animal lovers across the country celebrated after a photograph of a litter of kittens from Fulton County circulated online with the dramatic headline: *"The First Kittens to Leave Alive!"*

> *"We are taking their life, we are ending their life, we are giving them a good death. But we are not killing. And that is why I cannot stand the term 'No Kill Shelter.'"*

Penny Cistaro, HSUS Expo Conference Speaker on "Euthanasia," March 2006

"Expo" is the national animal shelter conference put on annually by HSUS. It draws animal shelter staff from all over the country and has historically been dominated by a killing orientation. Notable speakers have included Daphna Nachminovitch from PETA who told attendees that they should continue killing because No Kill is akin to a mental disease and causes great animal suffering; Sue Sternberg who claimed that all dogs labeled as "Pit Bulls" should be killed as a matter of policy, even if they are friendly, because they have a strong, swishing tail and opined, "The tail alone might cause bruising on a small child"; and Penny Cistaro, who they billed as the nation's foremost expert on "euthanasia" and who told attendees that there isn't a single shelter in America killing animals, a claim greeted by thunderous applause.

It is disturbing enough that national experts on killing healthy and treatable animals exist when the practice should be illegal. It is also disturbing that animal shelter staff from coast to coast applauded in agreement. And it is disturbing that the nation's killing expert is professing the Orwellian logic that killing is not killing. But most disturbing of all is the fact that when you deny any responsibility for the killing, when you deny that you are even killing when that is exactly what you are doing, the impetus to change your own behavior which would impact that killing disappears.

> *"Avoid contact with stray cats and do not let them in the house. Instead, notify your local animal shelter or animal control rather than take them in yourself."*

HSUS email alert, April 19, 2006

HSUS leadership often comes from animal control organizations that kill animals, and these individuals carry that mindset to HSUS even though it claims a different mission. And so they denigrate the animals they are supposed to protect and use HSUS to veil their reactionary animal control agendas under the cloak of "animal welfare."

During the height of the bird flu hysteria in 2006, the World Health Organization assured people that there was no risk of bird flu from cats. Yet, HSUS sent out an email to supporters recommending that people not try to help homeless cats themselves, but to call animal control instead, agencies with a history of mass slaughter, in order to protect themselves from bird flu.

Over the years, HSUS has also instructed shelters across the country to "document public health problems that relate to cats" in order to pass regressive laws which allow cats to be rounded up and killed. In their *"Guide to Cat Law," "Cat Care Basics"* and other publications, HSUS instructs animal control officers and others to "include diseases that are spread from cat to cat as well as those spread between cats and other animals," without regard for true risk analysis. These instructions reveal where the priorities of HSUS leadership truly lie, and they are not with the animals they are pledged to protect. They reveal an agenda to promote neither tolerance nor compassion for cats, but to sow unwarranted fear and suspicion of them—a far cry from the message of peaceful coexistence embodied in the HSUS motto, "It's Their World, Too."

> **"[HSUS] doesn't have a problem with humanely euthanizing a stray cat."**

John Snyder, HSUS Vice-President of Companion Animals, *Associated Press*, March 11, 2008

In 2008, the Town Council of Randolph, Iowa, offered five dollars to anyone who brought a cat to the pound to be put to death. While cat lovers cried foul and tried to stop the initiative, John Snyder, HSUS Vice-President of Companion Animals (who himself killed animals as the director of a pound in Florida), defended Randolph's killing, saying that HSUS doesn't have a problem with killing stray cats. He even suggested that the money allocated to the bounty would be better spent hiring someone who knows what he or she is doing.

> **"It's kind of like Monday morning quarterbacking: woulda, shoulda, coulda..."**

Tangipahoa, Louisiana Parish officials, August 2008

In August of 2008, the Parish President overseeing the pound in Hammond, Louisiana, ordered the killing of more than 170 dogs and cats, every single animal in their facility. A former employee of the pound says she'll never forget the image: "I did walk back there at one

What Would HENRY Do?

During the 19th century, children were paid 50 cents for every dog they brought to the New York City pound to be killed, leading to a profitable trade in dogs. Dogs were stolen from people's yards, from people's homes, even taken from the arms of their families so that they could be sold to the pound and ultimately drowned in the East River. Henry Bergh's answer was simple: the practice should be stopped. He succeeded in passing a law to make it illegal for anyone under the age of 18 to surrender dogs to the pound, thereby eliminating what he called "the thieving gangs of young dog catchers." Roughly 150 years later, officials in Randolph were working to establish a similar bounty for cats. HSUS' response: "[HSUS] doesn't have a problem with humanely euthanizing a stray cat."

point and they were all piled on top of each other, just lying there dead." The decision to exterminate the animals was made in response to a handful of dogs having shown signs of a mild virus that causes diarrhea but is self-limiting, meaning it resolves on its own without any medical intervention. It was also not contagious to cats. Nonetheless, every single dog—even those who were not sick—and every single cat—even though they were all immune—were put to death. While animal lovers protested, the pound's leadership dismissed their complaints: "It's kind of like Monday morning quarterbacking: woulda, shoulda, coulda..." In short, who cares?

Certainly not the Parish president who ordered the killing or Wayne Pacelle, the HSUS president, who defended it by blaming the killing on "pet overpopulation." In response to the killings, HSUS issued a statement that said, "The problem of pet homelessness is rampant throughout the nation and it is a challenge that shelters in virtually every community face." But animal lovers certainly cared. According to a former employee at the Louisiana shelter, "The [animals] didn't get the proper feedings, they didn't get the proper cleaning, they didn't get the proper exercise. I mean every issue about taking care of animals got jeopardized." And after getting dogs sick through its own mismanagement, and even though a veterinarian certified many animals as free of serious illness and rescue groups offered to help save the others, the pound added the ultimate injury (death) to insult (poor care that exposed them to disease) by killing each and every one. For shelter bureaucrats and their enablers like HSUS, none of this amounts to more than "woulda, coulda, shoulda."

"No-kill is a noble goal. But the sheer number of animals makes it almost unachievable."

Wayne Pacelle, HSUS President, *Newsweek,* **April 27, 2008**

While PETA was busy killing over 95 percent of the animals they took in, Wayne Pacelle defended them in *Newsweek* magazine by arguing that while No Kill might be noble, it was essentially impossible. But with cities and towns across the country having already achieved it, how could No Kill be "unachievable"? In fact, an HSUS-financed study proved that despite four million animals killed every year, the number of Americans looking to bring a new dog or cat into their homes topped 23 million. If there was an imbalance between supply and demand, Pacelle's own study showed it went in the other direction. But Pacelle has always seen his job as protecting poorly performing shelters and defending killing, calling his organization "the biggest cheerleader for shelters."

As he has always done, Wayne Pacelle refuses to condemn organizations that kill companion animals. In 2009, for example, the San Francisco Commission of Animal Control & Welfare held hearings on whether to enact shelter reform legislation mandating that shelters stop killing animals for being "too fat," "too old," "too playful," and "too shy," and adopt the lifesaving programs they were refusing to implement voluntarily. Pacelle himself wrote a letter insisting on the right of shelters to kill, arguing that pet overpopulation prevented more lifesaving and stating that shelters should not be regulated. As a result, the law was tabled and the Commission's No Kill reform effort was abandoned.

Pacelle does not even condemn shelters when they commit neglect and abuse. To the contrary, he came to the defense of Miami-Dade's regressive director (since forced to resign) after video surfaced showing abuse, with cats screaming in terror as they were put to death cruelly.

"Millions of people are bitten by dogs every year, many tens of thousands of children. I didn't want to add to that grisly statistic. Animals are important in our society and in my life, but I don't wish to make them quasi-religious objects of veneration."

Jon Katz, Interviewed in *Animal Sheltering*, January 1, 2008

At a time when No Kill proponents and Pit Bull advocates were gaining ground in their effort to overcome stereotypes of dog aggression and dog breeds (see pages 153-154), HSUS continued their long history of fear mongering about dog bites by publishing an article in their *Animal Sheltering* magazine entitled: *"I Chose a Child's Face Over My Dog."* Ignoring statistics that reveal that there is no dog bite epidemic in the United States, the article heightened the stereotypes and perpetuated the myths that have historically been used to justify the killing of dogs in shelters.

The article assumes the worst in dogs and the worst in people who don't want to see dogs killed. Dog lovers are pitted against children. It is the type of either-or, you-are-with-us-or-against-us, your-dog-or-your-child hysteria that those who love both dogs and children dismiss as irresponsible. According to the article:

- Killing dogs becomes unacceptable only when people inappropriately "humaniz[e] dogs";
- "Millions of people are bitten by dogs every year, many tens of thousands of children";
- If you do not believe in killing dogs, you have made them "quasi-religious objects of veneration";
- "[F]or every troubled or aggressive animal kept alive for months or years, healthy and adoptable animals go wanting for homes and often lose their lives";
- "Insurance companies are paying out billions of dollars to people bitten by dogs"; and,
- Adopting a "Pit Bull" appears to be more trouble than it is worth.

And yet, contrary to HSUS' claim that there is an epidemic of dog bites in the United States, the vast majority of dogs are in fact friendly and will never act aggressively toward people. If we take shelter dogs as a representative sampling of dogs in society, upwards of 98 percent are friendly to people. So where did the notion of an American dog bite epidemic come from? The numbers are simply flawed extrapolations from two outdated government studies which took poorly formulated and overly restrictive samples of the population (one reported six dog bites, the other 38) and then simply multiplied those numbers by how many people live in the United States. And although we are told in the HSUS article that, "Millions of Americans seek medical attention every year for animal bites or attacks," what they don't say is that over 92 percent of dog bites result in no injuries. And of those that do result in injury, 7.5 percent are minor. In fact, they are less severe than any other class of injury. In actuality, only ½ of one percent of all bites rank at "moderate or above."

Even if HSUS were correct that 4.7 million people are bitten by dogs each year, over 4.6 million people have no injuries and only 0.0002 percent die. You are five times more likely to be killed by lightning and four times more likely to be killed by a forklift, even though very few people have contact with forklifts. And yet in spite of this evidence, HSUS promotes public policy—and shelter standards—based not on thoughtful deliberation of the facts, but incendiary fanaticism that reduces the discussion to a meaningless debate about the value of dogs versus children, and thereby creates a less compassionate, less thoughtful society for all of us.

Instead of leading us to a more ethical future, HSUS fear mongering stands the HSUS mission on its head. Rather than advocate on behalf of dogs (and cats), HSUS fans the flames of misinformation that leads to their killing. And while HSUS may claim that "for every troubled or aggressive animal kept alive for months or years, healthy and adoptable animals go wanting for homes and often lose their lives," the truth once again is more sobering. "Healthy and adoptable animals" are killed in shelters because of regressive policies that allow shelters to do so—policies created and championed by HSUS itself.

> **HSUS promotes public policy—and shelter standards—based not on thoughtful deliberation of the facts, but incendiary fanaticism that reduces the discussion to a meaningless debate about the value of dogs versus children, and thereby creates a less compassionate, less thoughtful society for all of us.**

The TRUTH About "Pit Bulls"

THEY ARE THE VOICELESS VICTIMS of dog fighters. They are perpetually exploited by the media looking for a sensational story. Self-serving politicians pass legislation demanding their systematic destruction while wrapping themselves in the mantle of public safety. Some animal protection groups call for automatic death sentences for these dogs in shelters, while others promote policies that lead to killing by claiming that death is for the dogs' own good. Shelters use shoddy protocols to temperament test them literally to death, falsely claiming the vast majority are "unadoptable." And self-proclaimed "experts" advocate that even if they are friendly, they can't be trusted around children and other animals and should be killed anyway. Add poorly performing shelters that find killing easier than doing what is necessary to stop it, and the chances of dogs labeled as "Pit Bulls"* escaping regressive shelters alive are low.

> **prej·u·dice**
> [n., prej-uh-dis]
> A baseless and usually negative attitude toward members of a particular group. Common features of prejudice include negative feelings, stereotyped beliefs and a tendency to discriminate against members of that group.

---

* At one time, Pit Bull referred to the American Pit Bull Terrier. Today, it is a term used for any dog with a big head or muscular body. Moreover, shelters misidentify breeds as much as 75 percent of the time. As such, it makes little sense to talk about "Pit Bull" dogs or even "Pit Bull-type" dogs since there isn't a coherent group of dogs to apply the label to (see page 157).

In many of the shelters whose officers seek out dog fighters and abusers in order to "save" them, dogs labeled as "Pit Bulls" are relegated to locked and barren corridors away from public view. Ultimately, all of them—the healthy and friendly ones, side-by-side with the hopelessly sick or vicious—are put to death. In an Oregon county, dogs labeled as "Pit Bulls" are killed as a matter of policy by misusing temperament testing as a de facto ban on the breed. In Denver, Colorado, they are simply outlawed and executed. PETA calls for their full-scale slaughter. And HSUS led a coalition in Texas to defeat legislation which, among other things, would have banned breed discrimination by shelters. And yet roughly 95 to 98 percent of dogs entering shelters can be adopted safely, and that includes the dogs labeled as "Pit Bulls."

Thankfully, the view of dogs labeled as "Pit Bulls" is changing. When Ohio repealed its anti-Pit Bull law in 2012, the last statewide ban ended in the U.S. Many local cities in other states are following suit. And some states have gone further: outlawing breed discrimination altogether. Meanwhile, Pit Bull advocacy and rescue organizations are proliferating, working to undo years of misinformation, prejudice and intolerance by which such dogs have long suffered and died. They are educating the American public that, in the end, dogs labeled as "Pit Bulls" and even those dogs who might actually be an American Pit Bull Terrier are just like any other dog and we should treat them that way. That is what compassion and justice dictate. And that must be the first premise of advocacy on their behalf.

BREED BANS TEAR FAMILIES APART

In the summer of 2012, a 12-year disabled girl in Belfast (Northern Ireland) pleaded with authorities to return her dog who had never harmed anyone but had been seized after being labeled a "Pit Bull." Lennox was evaluated for aggression by authorities. During the evaluation, he repeatedly licked the face of the animal control official. She would lobby to have him killed anyway.

After battling in the courts for two years, Lennox was killed, simply because of his appearance. Protests by outraged animal lovers erupted worldwide.

FREE LENNOX

PLEASE **LET MY BEST FRIEND COME HOME**

Brooke, 12, pleads for pet locked in squalid cell as her health deteriorates

Sixty Minutes to Say Goodbye

BEAR & KOODA

When Australia banned "Pit Bulls" with the support of "animal welfare" organizations, the Australian Veterinary Association protested: "Not only will it fail to prevent dog bites, innocent dogs can clearly end up being scapegoats because of the way they look." They were right. Bear and Kooda, two beloved dogs, were seized from a couple by authorities. Even though neither Bear nor Kooda was a Pit Bull or Pit Bull-mix, an animal control officer testified that he believed they were. According to a local report, "These dogs were never accused of being unsocialized, uncared for or having ever shown any sign of aggression. It was never in doubt they were loved pets." In fact, court testimony showed that the dogs "wouldn't hurt anyone." It didn't matter. After losing a protracted legal battle, the court ordered them killed. The couple were given an hour's notice that the dogs would be killed and after racing to the pound where Bear and Kooda were being held, they were given just a few minutes to say goodbye. "They were just the kindest and best dogs. They were always playful, we loved them so much."

What Would HENRY Do?

In the late 1800s, New York City officials attempted to crack down on dogs by claiming that they were a public safety risk due to rabies ("hydrophobia"). First, they proposed a law requiring all dogs to be muzzled in public, followed by a proposed ban on the "Spitz,"* a type of dog which was erroneously believed to be particularly susceptible to rabies.

Recognizing that as an organization dedicated to advocating for animals, it was the duty of the ASPCA to speak out on the dogs' behalf; Bergh determined to set the record straight. He did a painstaking precinct-by-precinct search of rabies cases in New York City, finding only one possible case, which was not attributable to a dog bite. Because of intense ASPCA opposition, the proposed muzzling law failed to pass. While outlawed in many states and ordered killed on sight in others, the Spitz ran free in New York City.

The Spitz is a type of dog encompassing many breeds, is characterized by pointed ears and long, thick and often white fur and is related to the Akita, Husky, Malamute, Eskimo Dog and the Chow-Chow.

PIT BULL SAYS WHO?

A Frequent Case of Mistaken Identity

ANIMAL SHELTER
ANYTOWN USA
IMPERSONATING A PITBULL

What is a "Pit Bull"?

Historically, a "Pit Bull" referred to the American Pit Bull Terrier. Over time, the term was broadened to encompass two other breeds: the American Staffordshire Terrier and the Staffordshire Bull Terrier. But today, as used by shelters, law enforcement agencies and courts, the term does not apply to any particular breed. It is, according to a leading advocacy organization, "a catch-all term used to describe a continually expanding incoherent group of dogs, including pure-bred dogs and mixed-breed dogs. A 'Pit Bull' is any dog an animal control officer, shelter worker, dog trainer, politician, dog owner, police officer, newspaper reporter or anyone else says is a 'Pit Bull.'" In other words, calling a dog a "Pit Bull" is not only subjective and arbitrary; it creates the false impression that the label can predict the behavior of individual dogs, subjecting them to discrimination that can mean losing their homes and even their lives.

Not only are shelters killing the three breeds commonly referred to as "Pit Bulls" based on meaningless stereotypes, they are also killing dogs they mistakenly think are Pit Bulls because of how they look.

PIT BULLS

A CELEBRATED, FORGOTTEN PAST

In the first half of the 20th century, Pit Bulls were the most popular family dog in America, celebrated for their gentleness, loyalty and intelligence.

★ ★ ★

Advertisers, Hollywood producers and the U.S. government knew, to portray the Pit Bull was to convey America.

SERGEANT STUBBY

America's most decorated war dog was a Pit Bull who lived in the trenches with soldiers during the first World War.

Watchful-Waiting

The Germans have their "Wacht am Rhein," the English play "God Save the King," the Frenchmen sing their "Marseillaise," while Russians chant their National Hymn. Our Spirit shares this soul-like rock; peace breathes in what we proudly sing.

THE STAR SPANGLED BANNER

Curl long may it wave, o'er the land of the free and the home of the brave.

By these colors we stand ever true.

Three Cheers for the Red, White and Blue

The NANNY DOG

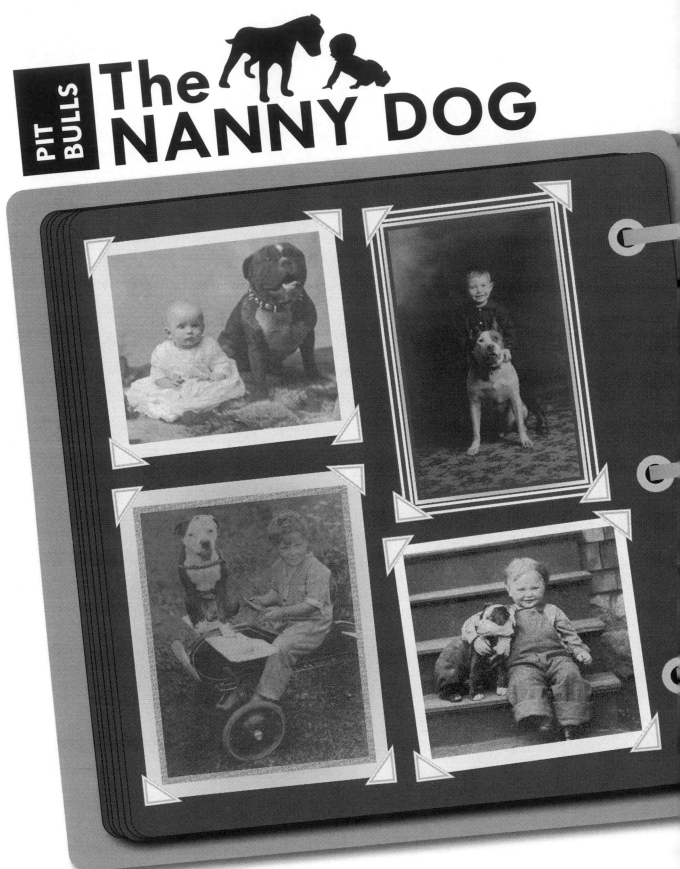

Today, Pit Bulls suffer from an unwarranted reputation as dangerous and untrustworthy. But there was a time in American history when they were known not for being vicious, scary or suspicious, but rather quite the opposite. They were known for being very good babysitters. A century ago, parents affectionately called the Pit Bull the "nanny" dog, and trusted these loyal and devoted animals to look out for their children, a job which Pit Bulls, given their careful attention and concern for the well-being of their family members, performed admirably and with great love.

AND THEN, THERE IS PETA

The Bizarre and Disturbing Truth About the Nation's Most Infamous "Animal Rights" Organization

IN MAY OF 2005, the bodies of dead dogs and cats began turning up in the trash bin of a supermarket in North Carolina. Local police conducted a stake out and eventually arrested two PETA staff members after a sting operation. The PETA van pulled up in front of the trash bin, and the two began filling it with garbage bags that contained the bodies of dead animals. Following is an account of the incident as reported in the *Roanoke News Herald* on January 24, 2007:

> [Ahoskie Police Detective Sgt. Jeremy] Roberts said he became involved in the case on May 19, 2005 after being dispatched to an area behind the Piggly Wiggly Supermarket in Ahoskie's New Market Shopping Center. There he was met by Kevin Wrenn of D&E Properties, a local firm that handles the maintenance of the shopping center. During his early morning rounds disposing of trash, Wrenn had discovered what appeared to be some sort of animal in a trash bag that was tossed in the dumpster behind Piggly Wiggly.
>
> "I immediately noticed a strong odor coming from the dumpster," Roberts said. Probing inside the dumpster, Roberts discovered 20, heavy duty trash bags. He eventually discovered a total of 21 dead dogs inside those bags.
>
> After using the Town of Ahoskie's help to bury the dogs at the town's old landfill, Roberts told [the District Attorney] he launched an investigation of how the dead dogs wound-up in an Ahoskie dumpster. He said he checked with the local animal hospitals and animal shelters to inquire of how they discarded of dead animals.
>
> Two weeks later (June 2, 2005) dead animals—17 dogs and three cats—were discovered within 20 bags in the same dumpster. Photographing the dead animals, Roberts took those photographs

to Bertie County Animal Control Officer Barry Anderson from whom Roberts had learned was working with PETA through an agreement to come to the Bertie shelter to collect unwanted, unclaimed animals. Anderson told Roberts he could not positively identify the animals by the photos.

Another report of dead animals found in the same dumpster came in on June 9. Eighteen bags containing 20 dead dogs were discovered...

After further investigation, two PETA employees, [Adria] Hinkle and [Andrew] Cook, became the subject of police surveillance. Detective Roberts further testified:

Upon picking-up and transporting an injured dog to the Ahoskie Animal Hospital (AAH), the PETA van in which Hinkle and Cook were traveling was followed by Bertie Sheriff's detectives Frank Timberlake and

Ahoskie Police Detective Sgt. Jeremy Roberts prepares to bury a puppy killed by PETA. This puppy and dozens of others animals including cats and kittens were found by police throughout June of 2005 after PETA employees dumped them in a garbage bin in North Carolina.

Marty Northcott. While at AAH, employees there, through a pre-arranged pick-up, released a mother cat and two kittens to Hinkle and Cook.

The van traveled back to the Bertie shelter where Hinkle and Cook took possession of several animals. At some point (PETA officials attending the trial said it occurred in the van while parked at the Bertie shelter), all of the animals were euthanized by Hinkle.

After leaving the shelter, the van was tailed as it made its way to Ahoskie. The van turned into New Market Shopping Center and headed behind Piggly Wiggly. There, according to Roberts, a female, later identified as Hinkle, was behind the wheel. She made a u-turn and parked the side doors of the van next to the door of the dumpster.

Roberts said while he and Bertie Sheriff's Detective Ed Pittman were approaching the van on foot from their surveillance locations behind the grocery store, he could hear the "thump, thump" of heavy objects striking the bottom of the empty dumpster.

Before the two lawmen could reach the van, it took off, heading out the same way it entered the back area of the grocery store. At that time he made contact with Timberlake who performed a traffic stop on the van while it was still in the New Market parking lot.

Meanwhile, Roberts performed a brief search of the dumpster, discovering the same type of trash bags found during the previous three weeks. At that point he placed Hinkle and Cook under arrest.

Dressed later in a hazmat suit, Roberts retrieved nine trash bags containing 16 dead dogs. Those animals, like their predecessors, were taken to the old landfill for burial. However, this time Anderson was at the burial site documenting the animals as they were removed from the bags. He confirmed they were the same animals picked-up earlier that day by Hinkle and Cook at the Bertie shelter.

A short while later as Roberts said he was preparing to inventory the van, held at the Ahoskie Police Department, he discovered another 12 bags containing eight dogs and 14 cats inside the van. Roberts confirmed that the mother cat and two kittens picked-up from AAH were among the dead animals.

Roberts also revealed during his testimony that he took into evidence several items found in the van. Included were boxes of trash bags, PETA manuals, doggie treats, cat food, animal toys, leashes and a tackle box containing syringes, needles and bottles of liquid substance, later determined by the SBI Lab in Raleigh as the drugs used to euthanize animals.

Testimony at the trial would show that some of the animals were in no danger of being killed before PETA took possession of them. Dr. Patrick Proctor, the veterinarian who gave PETA a mother cat and two kittens whom PETA promptly killed, said that PETA had promised him they would find the animals homes. "They came to the office last Wednesday and picked up the cat and two kittens.... They were just kittens we were trying to find homes for. PETA said they would do that..." said Proctor. "So imagine my surprise when I learned they allegedly dumped dead animals in a trash bin later that same day."

Proctor also stated that the animals "were in good health and were very adoptable, especially the kittens." And after Proctor was asked to examine one of the dead animals taken from the PETA crime scene, he told a local television station that, "The animal that I found was a very healthy six-month puppy that had

27,751 DEAD & COUNTING

KILLED BY PETA

This dead mother cat and her two dead kittens were given to PETA employees by a veterinarian after they assured him that they would find the animals homes. Instead, the PETA employees immediately killed the animals in the back of a van equipped with syringes and lethal drugs: a donor-funded PETA slaughterhouse on wheels.

years. PETA systematically seeks out, then kills, roughly 2,000 animals every year. Over 27,000 animals have died at the hands of PETA employees over the last decade alone. While communities across the country are ending the killing of healthy and treatable animals, with save rates as high as 98 percent, in 2011, PETA killed 96 percent of all dogs and cats and 93 percent of other companion animals such as rabbits that it took in, despite revenues of over 30 million dollars a year and millions of animal-loving members.

When PETA representatives have been questioned about this killing, they've argued that all of the animals they kill are "unadoptable." But this claim is a lie for numerous reasons. It is a lie because rescue groups and individuals have come forward stating that the animals they gave PETA were healthy and adoptable, as detailed above, and PETA insiders have admitted as much, one former intern reporting that he quit in disgust after witnessing perfectly healthy puppies and kittens in the kill room. It is a lie because there are over half a dozen shelters in Virginia where PETA is located which are now saving upwards of 90 percent of all animals they take in, while PETA, in that same state, is killing that many. It is a lie because Virginia shelters as a whole are saving 56 percent of the animals

been killed that day. It was a six-month-old lab mix and appeared to be in very good shape... and he had received some type of injection in his front right leg. PETA will never pick up another animal from my practice." Both Hinkle and Cook would themselves go on to describe some of the animals they killed as having been "perfect" and "adorable."* So why was PETA killing animals, sometimes within mere minutes of having promised that they would find the animals homes?

As surprising as the incidents described above may be, they in fact detail what has been business as usual by PETA employees for many

---

* Since PETA registers as a shelter in Virginia, the PETA employees were acquitted at trial and on appeal because it is not illegal for them to kill animals, another reason why shelter reform laws are needed across the country (see pages 214-217).

they take in, and many of those are doing so without even really trying. It is a lie because PETA refuses to provide its criteria for making the determination as to whether or not an animal is "unadoptable." It is a lie because according to a state inspector, the PETA facility where the animals are impounded was designed to house animals for no more than 24 hours. It is a lie because Newkirk herself admitted as much during a 2008 television interview: when asked whether or not PETA kills healthy animals, she responded, "Absolutely." And it is a lie because when asked what sort of effort PETA routinely makes to find adoptive homes for animals in its care, PETA responded that it had "no comment." Despite the public perception of PETA as a radical "animal rights" organization, in practice, the organization is itself the functional equivalent of a slaughterhouse.

PETA has long been one of the No Kill movement's most vociferous opponents. For years, PETA has advocated that feral cats and dogs labeled as "Pit Bulls" should be systematically put to death. They have been an outspoken advocate for killing shelters, even coming to their defense when they are cruel and neglectful, as they did in King County, Washington—a place where animals were not fed, were allowed to suffer with untreated injuries, and were neglected and even abused by staff. In that case, PETA wrote a letter to King County officials that referred to No Kill advocates as "radical," and urged the County not to give in to their efforts to reform the pound. In addition, PETA employees keep tabs on No Kill efforts nationwide so that they can undermine reformers by writing letters to the editor of local newspapers that equate No Kill with hoarding and animal abuse, and which lie about No Kill and its successes across the

country. And when it comes to working at PETA, employees who have expressed support for No Kill have been fired.

In some ways PETA's behavior towards the No Kill movement mirrors that of other large

FUELING POUND SEIZURE

While **PETA** claims to be against animal research, it championed a Pit Bull ban in Ontario, even though Ontario requires the pound to turn animals over for research. After 72 hours in a municipal pound, dogs can be sold for vivisection.

animal protection groups which likewise oppose it, and while PETA also wraps the killing that they do in the language of sheltering by blaming "pet overpopulation," PETA's killing and the positions they take are motivated by something far more nefarious than narrow self-interest and indifference. PETA does not perform animal control for the community in which they are located. They are not under any mandate—municipal or otherwise—to operate as a "shelter." PETA seeks out and takes in animals for primarily one purpose: to kill them.

Ingrid Newkirk founded PETA after a job working at the Washington Humane Society where she killed animals. It was a job she has admitted to doing with relish, explaining how she often came into work early to do it (see pages 178-179). She has stated that she does

DEFENDING ANIMAL CRUELTY AND NEGLECT

PETA has long been one of the No Kill movement's most vociferous opponents. For years, PETA has advocated that feral cats and dogs labeled as "Pit Bulls" should be put to death. And it has been an outspoken advocate for killing shelters, even coming to their defense when they are cruel and neglectful.

The right to life is an animal's most basic and fundamental right, without which, no other rights can be guaranteed. Because PETA employees seek out, then kill 2,000 animals every year, they are not an animal rights organization. And they would be the first to admit it. In fact, they already have.

not believe that animals have a right to live, and that, in fact, animals want to die, calling killing "a gift" (see pages 179-180). Perhaps most disturbing of all, she has recruited a legion of cult-like devotees who actively seek out then kill thousands of animals every year at her behest.

How has this been allowed to continue? Where is the outcry from animal rights leaders, from more of PETA's former employees? Tragically, leadership at other animal rights organizations have known for years that this is going on. They know PETA kills healthy animals and yet they all, collectively, look the other way and ignore it. In fact, in spite of this knowledge, one of the nation's oldest so-called animal rights organizations, Farm Animal Reform Movement, has even inducted Newkirk into their "Animal Rights Hall of Fame."

It is not clear whether all PETA employees participate in the killing or just a select few who have been handpicked by Newkirk (although the silence and complicity of every PETA employee makes them as much to blame for the killing as those who actually inject the animals with poison). This fact, combined with

CHAMPIONING EXTERMINATION AND THE ORPHANING OF KITTENS

When Georgetown University announced plans to kill all of the feral cats living on campus, cat advocates pleaded with them to implement a non-lethal TNR program instead. They refused, citing PETA's support for their plan. Unweaned kittens, left to starve to death when their mothers had been trapped through the PETA-endorsed extermination campaign, were found throughout the campus.

the climate of fear and intimidation for which Newkirk is infamous—routinely sending letters threatening legal action to any animal lover who publicly condemns PETA's killing (see page 171) and firing employees who support No Kill—may explain why few have come forward to provide more details.

But of this much we are certain: approximately 2,000 animals cross PETA's threshold every year, and very few make it out alive. The vast majority—96 percent in 2011—exit the facility dead when Pet Cremation Services of Tidewater stops by on their regular visits to pick up their remains. Between these visits, the

bodies are stored in the giant walk-in freezer PETA installed for this very purpose. It is a freezer that cost $9,370 and, like the company which incinerates the bodies of PETA's victims, was paid for with the donations of animal lovers who could never have imagined that the money they donated to help animals would be used to end their lives instead.

PETA'S KILLING: BY THE NUMBERS

Over the last 10 years, PETA has killed 27,751 animals. That's an average of seven animals a day, every day, for a decade. Here are statistics for the last three years, as reported by PETA to the Virginia Department of Agriculture.

2009

ACQUIRED: 2,366
ADOPTED: 8
SENT TO KILL SHELTER
(FATE UNKNOWN): 31
KILLED: 2,301

97%
KILL RATE

2010

ACQUIRED: 2,345
ADOPTED: 44
SENT TO KILL SHELTER
(FATE UNKNOWN): 65
KILLED: 2,200

94%
KILL RATE

2011

ACQUIRED: 1,992
ADOPTED: 24
SENT TO KILL SHELTER
(FATE UNKNOWN): 44
KILLED: 1,911

96%
KILL RATE

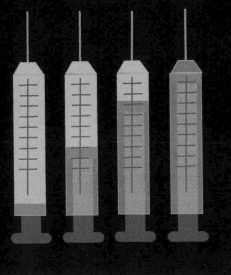

The vast majority of animals who enter the front door of PETA's headquarters in Norfolk, Virginia go out the back door—in a body bag.

Fund the Killing of Animals and the Intimidation of Animal Activists:
DONATE TO PETA

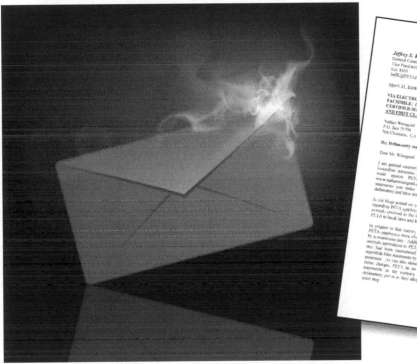

Many animal lovers who have publicly condemned PETA for their killing have received a letter from the PETA legal department, threatening a lawsuit. However, because a lawsuit would allow for subpoenas of PETA employees past and present—leading to testimonies under oath about the grisly reality of what has gone on and continues to go on at PETA headquarters—it is unlikely that PETA would ever follow-through with these empty threats.

Their donor-funded attorneys rattle their sabers, but know they have a lot more to fear from the public disclosure that would result from a lawsuit than the activists who are truthfully—and, given PETA's threats and intimidation, bravely—reporting on PETA's atrocities against animals in the hope of bringing them to an end.

P E T A

A CULT-URE OF KILLING

WHY? Why does PETA kill animals? Why does PETA call for more killing even in the face of alternatives? Why do they fight efforts to save animals when they are supposed to be an organization that helps them? And why do they embrace even abusive shelters when community activists try to reform them? These behaviors seem truly baffling until possible psychological causes are considered.

Case history reveals that nurses who kill their patients often show no remorse for their killing, arguing that their actions were motivated by mercy and compassion and that their patients, desperate to be relieved of their suffering, wanted to die. PETA's language about "overburdened" shelter workers, and about giving animals what Ingrid Newkirk, PETA's founder, calls "the gift of euthanasia," and how "it was the best gift they've ever had," is eerily similar. In her case, she also believes she is the hero and those who try to stop her are betraying the animals. She once blasted a No Kill supporter by stating: "How dare you pretend to help animals and turn your back on those who want an exit from an uncaring world!" Indeed, Newkirk-through-PETA has stated that blaming shelters for killing animals is like blaming hospitals for killing patients. Is Newkirk trying to tell us something?

Unfortunately, with no formal psychological evaluation to support a diagnosis, we are left with pure conjecture. But given the similarity of language and the acts themselves: the killing,

the death squads, the indoctrination against and hateful denunciation of No Kill and the proactive efforts to stop communities from embracing No Kill principles, this may be as close as we ever come to understanding the motivations of PETA's President. Yet even absent a definitive diagnosis, this much is clear: PETA's killing has claimed the lives of more than 27,000 animals in just the last decade, and this number includes healthy, adoptable puppies and kittens. And when asked by a reporter what efforts they make to find animals homes, PETA replied that they had "no comment." The truthful answer in the vast majority of cases— "none"—would have been more damning.

Not only does PETA's registration with the State of Virginia as a shelter give PETA the ability to acquire the controlled substance sodium pentobarbital which they use to poison animals, but being registered as a shelter allows them to mislead people into believing that the killing that they do is consistent with that being done by shelters, a form of killing which, tragically, has long been tolerated even by people who claim to love animals. Were Ingrid Newkirk to independently—without a staff and organization to back her—seek out thousands of animals a year after saying she will try to find them homes, by taking them from rescue groups and shelters, gathering animals through trapping or acquiring those displaced by natural disasters, only to inject them with poison and kill them—most people would opine that she was a deeply disturbed person inflicting death upon animals in obedience to dark impulses. Unfortunately, her association with PETA and its claim that they are a "shelter of last resort" obscures the issue for many people.

Because it is widely regarded as an organization dedicated to protecting rather than harming animals, PETA provides Newkirk not only the perfect cover for her agenda, but, paradoxically, the perfect place to recruit others to participate in it as well. With the stamp of legitimacy her association with PETA affords her, Newkirk has not only been granted the unrestricted ability to kill without the scrutiny or condemnation of many so-called "animal rights" activists who grant her absolution, but it has given her access to naïve and easily manipulated young people who arrive on PETA's doorstep starry-eyed. And somehow, the details of which are a mystery, Newkirk manages to transform at least some of these people into dangerous, mindless drones incapable of critical thinking, people who not only defend the right to kill animals with the same, deadly language that she does, but who also seek out, then kill animals themselves, such

as the PETA staff who were caught tossing garbage bags filled with dead animals into the supermarket dumpster—or the three PETA employees who approached Nathan after a lecture he gave at UCLA Law School in March of 2012. The views these young people expressed revealed that PETA followers are not just parroting Ingrid Newkirk for a paycheck; but are, in fact, fully indoctrinated true believers—immune to logic and reason—in the belief that animals want to die and should be killed.

During a discussion that spanned various topics, including feral cats, open admission No Kill shelters, the myth of pet overpopulation and adoption incentives by shelters, the conversation invariably ended at the same deadly destination—with the PETA employees insisting that it is okay to kill animals to spare them any future suffering and that no matter what the circumstances, killing by lethal injection is not unethical because it is just like being put under anesthesia for spay/neuter, with the only difference being that the animal never wakes up. Moreover, whenever Nathan attempted to

IS PETA A CULT?

Political cults are terrifying because they often endorse campaigns of extermination. Could PETA—which not only actively seeks out and then poisons thousands of animals a year, but which works to undermine lifesaving efforts across the country in order to ensure that shelters keep killing animals—be just such a cult?

discuss the logical implications of their viewpoint—including the fact that their assertions decimated the philosophical underpinning of the entire animal rights movement and veganism—they would have none of it, simply repeating that killing animals is okay because they might someday suffer, and killing is okay because it's just like going to sleep and never waking up. What could possibly explain such bizarre assertions?

Experts on cults report that they come in many varieties. There are religious cults like those founded by David Koresh and Jim Jones. There are commercial cults that recruit members to sell their products, thereby enriching their leaders. There are self-help cults which manipulate the emotionally vulnerable. And then there are political cults which, according to one organization which tracks cults, don't appear to be cults at all; having, as their outer façade, "a slick well-rehearsed Public Relations front which hides what the group is really like. You will hear how they help the poor, or support research, or peace, or the environment." And yet many of these cults are particularly scary because the harm they inflict is not limited simply to their membership.

As with all cults, members of political cults become victims of emotional and psychological manipulation. They often live in desperate need for the approval of their charismatic leader. But what makes political cults so particularly terrifying is that they often promote philosophies that endorse campaigns of extermination. Could PETA, which not only actively seeks out and then poisons thousands of animals a year, but which works to undermine lifesaving efforts across the country in order to ensure that shelters keep killing animals, be just such a cult?

> **The PETA employees insisted that it is okay to kill animals to spare them any future suffering and that no matter what the circumstances, killing by lethal injection is not unethical because it is just like being put under anesthesia for spay/neuter, with the only difference being that the animal never wakes up.**

Indeed, No Kill activists have often been baffled as to why PETA does not attempt to modulate its message in defense of killing in light of the No Kill movement's evolving success, continually hammering home, as they do, tired clichés and disproven dogmas that many savvy animal lovers are now too informed to accept. Yet information about how cults actually work sheds some light on why that might be: In a cult, any information from outside the cult is considered evil, especially if it is opposing the cult. Cults train their members to reject any critical information given to them, and to not even entertain the thought that the information might be true.

As the employees Nathan spoke to demonstrated, although they had just sat through a 2½ hour presentation debunking all their justifications for killing, the message had fallen on deaf ears that were incapable of comprehending anything that contradicted the story line that PETA perpetuates and continually disseminates, including the myth that open admission shelters cannot be No Kill, the myth of too many animals and not enough homes, the notion that feral cats are suffering horribly, that

The more shelters are brought into the 21st century, the more difficult it will become for PETA to stave off scrutiny and accountability for their actions by cloaking it in the excuses that have been historically used to justify the killing of companion animals in shelters. A nation where No Kill animal shelters are the norm—where animals are given both good quality care and the loving, new homes they deserve—will further reveal how senseless and cruel PETA's own killing is. The leadership at PETA would no longer find safety in numbers, which may explain why they won't let that happen without a fight.

any attempt to find more homes would put animals in the hands of abusers, and the most absurd of these absurdities, that killing is kindness, a gift.

For every time Nathan had attempted to break down for the PETA employees exactly where their information or logic was incorrect or flawed—their insistence that open admission shelters cannot be no kill, for example, by citing numerous animal control shelters nationwide that are, in fact, No Kill *and* open admission— or that pet overpopulation is a myth by showing that the number of homes that become available for animals every year vastly exceeds the number of animals being killed in shelters—the information simply did not penetrate. It was as though he was speaking a foreign language they could not understand; and in response, they simply kept repeating the same mantras over and over again: animals are suffering, killing is okay and killing is a gift. In short, they were entirely beyond the reach of reason.

There is much we do not know about PETA. Admittedly, we lack details to confirm the diagnosis of what, exactly, ails the leadership

of PETA and the people who go to work there. Is Ingrid Newkirk mentally ill? Is PETA a cleverly disguised cult, using proven mind control techniques to manipulate people into accepting and participating in a deadly and nefarious campaign for the extermination of animals? At this time in history, we do not yet know the answers to these dark and disturbing questions. Yet even if we can merely speculate about the why and the how 2,000 animals die at the hands of PETA employees each and every year, ethics compel every animal lover to see beyond the façade PETA has created to mask the ugly and sordid truth about what that organization really is. Because for all we do not know, this much is certain: PETA is letting loose upon the world individuals who not only maniacally believe that killing is a good thing and that the living want to die, but who are legally armed with lethal drugs which they have already proven—27,751 times in the last ten years—that they are not adverse to using.

✓REALITY CHECK
In Their Own Words

> "We do not advocate 'right to life' for animals."

Ingrid Newkirk, PETA President, December 1994

When Nathan wrote Ingrid Newkirk to ask her how, as an animal rights organization, PETA could oppose non-lethal programs for feral cats in shelters, and why her organization advocates that they be rounded up and killed, Newkirk wrote back that PETA is not an animal rights organization, stating in no uncertain terms: "We do not advocate 'right to life' for animals."

NOTE: Newkirk's statement that "There are always exceptions" addresses an unrelated question and is not a qualifier to her belief that animals do not have a "right to life."

> "Most people have no idea that at many animal shelters across the country, any pit bull that comes through the front door doesn't go out the back door alive. From San Jose to Schenectady, many shelters have enacted policies requiring the automatic destruction of the huge and ever-growing number of 'pits' they encounter. This news shocks and outrages the compassionate dog-lover... Here's another shocker: People for the Ethical Treatment of Animals, the very organization that is trying to get you

to denounce the killing of chickens for the table, foxes for fur or frogs for dissection, supports the shelters' pit-bull policy... People who genuinely care about dogs won't be affected by a ban on pits."

Ingrid Newkirk, PETA President,
San Francisco Examiner, **1999**

There are no dogs in America more abused, maligned and misrepresented than those who are classified by shelters as "Pit Bulls." There are no shelter dogs more in need of the humane movement's compassion, in need of a call to arms on their behalf and in need of what should be the full force of a shelter's sanctuary and protection. Many shelters and animal protection organizations, however, have determined that these dogs are not worthy of their help. And no one has been more emphatic and unapologetic than Ingrid Newkirk in promoting this unfair and deadly double standard—along with the idea that those who care about animals needn't concern themselves with the fate of these particular dogs.

"I would go to work early, before anyone got there, and I would just kill the animals myself... I must have killed a thousand of them, sometimes dozens every day."

Ingrid Newkirk, PETA President,
The New Yorker, **April 14, 2003**

We are told no one wants to kill. But Ingrid Newkirk, the founder of PETA, not only began her career in "animal welfare" killing animals at the Washington Humane Society, a shelter with regressive policies at the time, she went into work early to perform the job: "a thousand of them, sometimes dozens every day."

It is an understatement to say that killing animals should be regarded as a deeply disturbing experience. Not only is the person doing the killing cruelly robbing an animal of his or her life, but it is not uncommon for an animal who is being killed to experience fear, disorientation, nausea and, at times, even struggle against it.

A dog who is skittish, for example, is made even more fearful by the smells and surroundings of an animal shelter. He doesn't understand why he is there and perhaps away from the only family he has ever loved. For this dog to be killed, animal shelters may use a catch pole. These dogs often struggle to free themselves from the grip, which results in more fear and pain when they realize they cannot. They sometimes urinate and defecate on themselves, unsure of what is occurring. Often the head is held hard to the ground or against the wall so that another staff member can enter the kennel and inject him with a sedative. While the catch pole is left tied around the neck, the dog struggles to maintain his balance, dragging the pole, until he slumps to the ground. Slowly—fearful, often soiled in his own waste, confused—he tries to stand, but his legs give way. He goes limp and then unconscious. That is when staff administers the fatal dose.

And yet in spite of this, Newkirk admitted to not only killing sometimes dozens of animals a day, but to actually going into work early in order to do so. What are we to conclude about a person who opts to go into work early to do their job when that job is killing animals?

> *"The animals… got the gift of euthanasia, and to them it was the best gift they've ever had. How dare you pretend to help animals and turn your back on those who want an exit from an uncaring world!"*

Ingrid Newkirk, PETA President, 2006

To PETA, killing is not a moral issue: "It's just like spaying an animal, the only difference is they never wake up." It doesn't matter to them that the animal could be adopted into a loving home. It doesn't matter that the animals have an immediate place to go with rescue groups. It's not the fact that animals are being killed that matters. To PETA, the only thing that matters is how they are killed: so long as they are killed by poisoning with an overdose of barbiturates, killing is "a gift." And yet PETA's position that animals can and should be killed subverts the entire foundation upon which all social justice movements are inherently based: the right to life.

The right to life is a fundamental right because it is a necessary condition for the enjoyment of all other rights. In what many consider to be the cornerstone of the human rights movement—our own Declaration of Independence—there is a reason the Founding Fathers began the list of "unalienable" rights to which everyone is entitled with "life." Without life, the rights to liberty and the pursuit of happiness become meaningless—for one can be neither free nor happy when they are dead. How can one

guarantee that animals be treated kindly, be given fresh food and water and even love, when all those things can be taken away at someone else's discretion by killing?

PETA's position—so at odds with the philosophy of animal rights—not only condones the slaughter of millions of companion animals every year, but it undermines protections for other animals as well. It is the relationship between Americans and their animal companions that can open the door to larger animal rights issues. In their daily interactions with their dogs and cats, people experience an animal's personality, emotions and capacity both for great joy and great suffering. They learn empathy for animals. Someone who is

compassionate—and passionate—about their companion animals can over time and with the right information become supportive of efforts to help animals on farms, in circuses, in research facilities and elsewhere. Right now, however, PETA is actively working to ensure that doesn't happen—by not only arguing that dogs and cats do not have the right to life, but that killing them is an act of kindness, and therefore a moral imperative.

And though the need to refute the views expressed by Newkirk is a tragic necessity due to the credibility her association with PETA affords her, in truth, to substantively address them is to grant unwarranted credibility to a position that is so irrational and inhumane that it is simply beyond the reach of reasoned discourse. For although the result of the opposition to No Kill by shelter directors

and others is anything but mundane, the motivation behind their resistance is ultimately attributable to pedestrian flaws of human nature: primarily uncaring, greed and narrow self-interest. But Ingrid Newkirk is different. She opposes No Kill because the No Kill movement represents the antithesis of her definition of animal activism. To her, killing *is* the goal because she believes that life itself is suffering and therefore animals want to die. It is a view that is not only perverse and in obvious opposition to every creature's instinctual will to live, it is also terrifying when considered in light of her success at manipulating others to share and act upon her views, her legal access to lethal drugs and the ongoing and mortal threat to thousands of animals every year which she and PETA pose.

"The dangerous, unrealistic policies and procedures pushed on the council by this small but fanatical constituency is part of a national movement to target, harass, and vilify open admission shelters and their staff in an effort to mislead the public into believing that 'no kill' is as easy as simply not euthanizing animals... [Quoting HSUS:] 'There are no municipal shelters in the country that operate as 'no-kill.' A few have tried, but have quickly turned back due to overcrowding, inability to manage services, and staff outcry. It is the municipality's job to accept all animals and conduct responsible adoptions. The reality is there are not enough homes for all animals...' The goals of reducing overpopulation and euthanasia do not get accomplished by limiting yourself to the category of 'no-kill.' It is an unattainable goal that will set you up for failure."

Daphna Nachminovitch, PETA Vice-President, Cruelty Investigations Department, Letter to the Mayor of Norfolk, Virginia, February 23, 2012

PETA is an organization that publicly claims to represent the best interest of animals—indeed their "ethical treatment"—while at the same time engages in a campaign to exterminate them and to prolong the ability of others to do the same. They call companion animals slaves and argue that sharing one's life and home with an animal subjects that animal to bondage and oppression: "Let us allow the dog to disappear from our brick and concrete jungles—from our firesides, from the leather nooses and metal chains by which we enslave it." And they are an organization whose infamous antics ranging from the absurd to the obscene alienate rather than educate the American public.

Yet this organization—with views about killing dogs and cats that are so extreme as to defy credulity—refers to those laboring to bring an end to their unnecessary killing through simple, common sense alternatives such as foster care, adoption, working with rescue groups and TNR, as dangerous "slow-kill hoarders" who want to put animals in "hellholes." This is the very definition of ironic.

In defense of shelters, PETA has told legislators not to listen to "fanatical" and "radical" reformers who have asked for less killing and more lifesaving in communities where those very shelters have abused animals: allowed them to go days without food, allowed them to slowly die due to lack of care, drowned puppies in trench drains, physically abused them and cruelly killed them.

So not only are statements like these (made to city and county officials across the country) a classic case of the pot calling the kettle black, but they are made in a manner than defends animal abusers and killers and denigrates those working to stop such practices. Moreover, their claims are also dishonest. There are, in fact, dozens of communities across the country that have ended the systematic killing of healthy and treatable animals, some of which have been No Kill for over a decade. Calling something "unattainable" when it already exists is a lie.

REPORTED ON AUGUST 14, 2012

Shelby County Animal Shelter Threatens to Kill Animals

WLKY.com
SHELBY COUNTY, Kentucky:
"It's maintained a no-kill status for four years, but starting next month, the Shelby County Animal Shelter will change its policies. The Shelby County animal shelter will begin euthanizing some cats and dogs who are not adopted or fostered by Sept. 1..."

DELIVERED TO SHELBY COUNTY OFFICIALS ON AUGUST 17, 2012

The accompanying card read:
"Thank you for doing the right thing for animals. The PETA Staff"

IN 2011, the Shelby County, Kentucky shelter finished with a save rate of 98% for cats and 94% for dogs. It was their fourth No Kill year. But Shelby County officials stated that they would start killing again on September 1, 2012 because they claimed that they had a large number of animals in the shelter. Once again, as they have done so many times before, Shelby County No Kill Mission (SCNKM), a private organization both responsible for and dedicated to ensuring that Shelby County remains No Kill, went to work and the "crisis" was averted through rescue, foster and adoption.

Shelby County No Kill Mission wasn't the only group to reach out to shelter officials when the story broke. PETA did also. Unlike SCNKM and despite over 30 million dollars in revenues and millions of animal loving supporters, they didn't offer to help foster animals, adopt animals, or spread the word across Kentucky that animals were in need of help.

Instead, PETA sent Shelby County government and shelter officials a gift basket, with a note thanking them for their decision to start

killing again. Before the first cat was poisoned with an overdose of barbiturates, the PETA staff had begun to celebrate the proposed killing. Instead, the animals were saved. They were adopted. They were fostered. They were placed under the protective embrace of rescuers.

Thank you for doing the right thing for animals, though we know it can be the hardest thing for you. Anyone who criticizes your move to ensure the health and welfare of animals in your custody has simply never been in your shoes. We have, and we commend you for putting the animals first.

With admiration,

The PETA Staff

PETA also sent Shelby County officials this card, which arrived on August 21, 2012.

A BLANK CHECK TO
K I L L

WHENEVER NO KILL ADVOCATES expose the many ways in which HSUS, the ASPCA or PETA undermine efforts to save lives, betray the mission they ostensibly exist to promote, kill or cause animals to be killed, there are invariably those who come to their defense by stating that these organizations should not be criticized because they "do so much good for animals." It is a tragically commonplace argument, but no less indefensible because of it. In effect, they are arguing that because some of the money donated to these organizations may actually be used for its intended purpose, that they have earned the right to cause harm to other animals themselves—terrible, irreversible, life-ending harm.

The fact that those who most commonly make these arguments are people who support these organizations because of their professed missions and would therefore likely self-identify as "animal lovers" is as troubling and paradoxical as the argument itself. Sadly, for such people, a misplaced trust and need to identify with such groups or the people who work at them at some point became more important than the professed values that presumably led them to support these organizations in the first place. The ideals that animals have rights and interests independent of humans—including the right to be free of suffering and the right to live—are casually discarded so long as those causing the suffering

or death are self-proclaimed members of the animal protection movement.

Indeed, this argument is problematic precisely because it promotes the harmful idea that under the right circumstances, animal abuse or killing are acceptable. That is, as long as the harm is being done by the right people or balanced by a counterweight of good, there is no harm that is in and of itself inherently wrong or unacceptable, effectively eviscerating the philosophical foundation of the cause. Moreover, by arguing that we should ignore or overlook certain forms of animal abuse or killing as "payment" for some perceived "good," the door is opened to condone all

For although those who defend these organizations seemingly lack the vision or passion for the cause necessary to imagine a future in which animal protection organizations are authentic and unadulterated forces for good, we do not need to accept or tolerate some harm of animals in one sphere in order to promote their well-being in another.

WHERE DO *YOU* DRAW THE LINE?

THE BANK OF DEATH

1000

11/19/11

Pay to the order of *PETA*

DEATHS

FOR *Congratulations! You've earned it!* **Your name here?**

1:00 000 000 :: 000 000 00 1000

Even if it were true that these groups do "so many good things" for animals, it does not entitle them to a blank check to call for the killing of two-week old puppies or to fight a bill that would have ended the cruel, painful gas chamber as HSUS did. It does not entitle them to send kittens to their deaths as the ASPCA does or to kill dogs who have a place to go. It does not entitle them to seek out and kill 2,000 animals a year as PETA does. And yet that is the argument some make on behalf of those organizations. If you are one of those people, how much killing is acceptable to you? How many deaths are you willing to allow them before you draw the line? We'll start: zero. First, do no harm.

manner of animal cruelty and exploitation. By this same logic, were a slaughterhouse owner to donate a percentage of his profits to a vegan advocacy organization, or a dog fighter to donate some of his winnings to a companion animal rescue group, the killing and cruelty they inflict upon animals would therefore be rendered acceptable, the harm being cancelled out by the good. Though an obvious absurdity, time and again self-professed animal lovers and animal rights activists postulate this exact scenario, but in the reverse.

And not only does this argument capriciously surrender the welfare of animals and the principles which should guide all advocacy on their behalf, but it also hinders the cause by setting the bar for these organizations at a dismally low—in fact, counterproductive—level. In condoning behavior that is the antithesis of the cause such organizations are supposed to be advocating, this argument promotes the defeatist mentality that we have no right to expect or demand that our animal protection organizations be what they claim to be in practice as well as rhetoric, when of course we absolutely do. For although those who make this argument seemingly lack the vision or passion for the cause necessary to imagine a future in which animal protection organizations are authentic and unadulterated forces for good, we do not need to accept or tolerate some harm of animals in one sphere in order to promote their well-being in another. The corruption at these organizations is neither inherent, nor inevitable. It has been fostered by various historical, financial and sociological factors that the leadership of these groups would be forced to address and overcome if animal lovers stopped making excuses for the betrayals and funding them with their donations. *Some* animal suffering and *some* animal killing are not and never have been the price we must pay to end other animal suffering and killing. In fact, as the faulty logic of that statement clearly demonstrates, to believe so is to surrender to a self-defeating, hopeless tautology that can never succeed in eliminating that which it simultaneously perpetuates.

The Animal Rights Movement That Wasn't

IN FEBRUARY OF 2012, an important animal protection bill was pending in the Florida Legislature: the Florida Animal Rescue Act. This bill was designed to protect animals by making it illegal for shelters to kill animals when qualified rescue groups were willing to save them. Like the successful California bill after which it was modeled, this bill had the potential to save thousands of shelter animals every year.

A survey of Florida rescue groups revealed that 63 percent have been turned away from shelters, which then killed the very animals those rescue groups offered to save. Yet Florida legislators received roughly 1,000 calls and emails from people who would most likely identify themselves as "animal lovers," urging them to oppose the bill. Who were these people? Why were they arguing that a bill designed to stop animals from being killed when someone wants to save them was a bad idea? They were "animal rights activists," following the dictates of a PETA action alert asking their members to help them defeat what in truth was one of the most vital animal protection laws ever introduced in that state. And in blind faith and allegiance, they obediently did so and the bill was defeated.

Stop almost any American on the street, and chances are pretty good that within just a few seconds of striking up a conversation about PETA's killing—that once the person you are talking to overcame their initial disbelief that PETA routinely kills animals—she or he would be quick to condemn it. Yet strike up the same conversation with self-professed "animal rights activists" and you are likely to get a litany of excuses that condone and defend it.

> **A deadly and hypocritical double standard emerged within the animal rights movement that exists to this very day, one that says dogs and cats are unworthy of rights advocated for other species.**

Unfortunately, those who should be the first and loudest to condemn PETA's actions and fight for No Kill policies in our nation's shelters are the least likely people to actually do so. To animal rights activists, animals have a right to life up until the moment they cross the threshold of either PETA headquarters or one of our nation's shelters and then they no longer do.

Who and what is to blame for this unlikely and tragic juxtaposition? A look at the history of the animal rights movement and its early founders provides the answer.

THE NO KILL MOVEMENT VS. THE ANIMAL RIGHTS MOVEMENT: AN ACCIDENT OF HISTORY, A CONSPIRACY OF SILENCE

Although the last decade has seen the No Kill movement make unprecedented progress solving a crisis responsible for the deaths of millions of animals every year, there continues to be a deep bias against and ignorance about the No Kill movement within the animal rights community today. And while there are thankfully a growing number of animal rights activists who are making the leap to supporting No Kill, overall they remain the exception. Of course, PETA's anti-No Kill propaganda is to blame for some of this confusion. The fact that PETA continuously equates No Kill with hoarding and animal suffering while lying to their followers about the "necessity" of killing cats and dogs is the primary factor contributing to this troubling paradox. But it is not the only one.

Like Ingrid Newkirk, many of the founders and employees working at our nation's animal rights organizations came to animal rights by way of sheltering. This meant that they not only brought to the cause the historical excuses used to justify the killing of animals in shelters, but having had many animals die at their very hands, they needed a way to justify their own untoward behavior in light of their competing beliefs. To champion a cause that claims that animals have rights while at the same time having killed thousands of animals themselves required them to adopt an inconsistent philosophy to reconcile what in reality are diametrically opposing values. This view became firmly cemented within the animal rights movement when other animal right leaders, deferring to the "expertise" of their friends and colleagues who had worked in shelters, bought into the rationalizations and failed to challenge them. And so a deadly philosophical dichotomy emerged within the animal rights movement: one that held that all animals have a right to life, except those who enter shelters. This killing, it was argued, was necessary where the other kinds were not and those doing the killing were not to blame, but rather unsung heroes courageously performing the public's dirty work.

In fact, efforts that focus on dogs and cats are often viewed with disdain and somehow "less animal rights" than other issues. Many animal rights activists erroneously believe the thousands of shelters across this country are in fact meeting the needs of these animals who therefore require no further advocacy or attention on their part. And they believe this because the people and organizations they trust to keep them informed about important issues affecting animals refuse to do so when the victims are not on farms or in laboratories, but inside our nation's animal shelters.

Today, healthy debate within the animal rights movement is discouraged in favor of "movement unity" and deference to the agendas promoted by large, powerful organizations. It is a top-heavy movement—and therefore intolerant of dissent, suspicious of change and prone to censorship. While many animal rights activists, lacking a sophisticated understanding of the pressing need for No Kill reform, underestimate and dismiss the cause as a mere "animal welfare" issue, leadership of animal rights organizations are not so naive

and are far more calculating. They willfully ignore the No Kill movement and fail to champion its more widespread implementation precisely because it challenges the historical narrative they have used to explain and excuse shelter killing since the movement's inception. In the animal rights movement today, innovations that threaten the prevailing paradigm are rejected in favor of the status quo.

There is no mention of No Kill in the newsletters of large animal rights organizations. It is unlikely to be found on their websites, on their Facebook pages, or any of the other ways these organizations regularly communicate with their members, except—in the case of PETA— to denigrate it. Because the guidelines of animal rights conferences mandate that speakers not criticize other animal protection organizations—even when doing so is required to expose their actions which harm animals and deny them their rights—No Kill advocates are

Today, healthy debate within the animal rights movement is discouraged in favor of "movement unity" and deference to the agendas promoted by large, powerful organizations. It is a top-heavy movement—and therefore intolerant of dissent, suspicious of change and prone to censorship.

ANIMAL WELFARE VS. ANIMAL RIGHTS: A FALSE DEBATE

The distinction between "animal welfare" and "animal rights" is a fabrication used to justify exploitation and killing. Where there is no respect for life, there is no regard for welfare.

under a gag order that prevents them from sharing the true causes of shelter killing as well as its proven cure—rejecting old philosophies and those who embody them. Within the animal rights community today, it is not *what* is right that matters, but *who* is right—even when they are clearly wrong. As a result, many animal rights activists continue to parrot the charade that the killing of innocent dogs and cats is acceptable, consistent with their beliefs that one should never kill pigs, cows or chickens.

This conspiracy of silence combined with an historical embrace of both the excuses used to rationalize the killing and those who promote them have coalesced to render the No Kill movement essentially invisible to most animal rights activists, except when it is being bashed and misrepresented by PETA. The so-called

> NO KILL
>
> A conspiracy of silence combined with an historical embrace of both the excuses used to rationalize the killing and those who promote them have coalesced to render the No Kill movement essentially invisible to most animal rights activists.

leaders of the animal rights movement keep grassroots activists ignorant and impotent, denying them the information necessary to see through PETA's nefarious agenda and the tools they could use to assure lifesaving success at the shelters in their own communities. And while dogs and cats may come away as the most obvious losers, they are by no means the only ones.

For it is the public's love and compassion for companion animals that could create profound social and legal precedents that would benefit all animals, such as laws making it illegal to kill them. A recent survey revealed that three out of four Americans already believe that shelters should not be allowed to kill healthy animals. Were such laws to be introduced, their passage would provide an important framework for future animal advocacy. History and the human rights movement predict that such a door, once opened, will, with time, be pushed ever wider to accommodate other species of animals currently being exploited or killed in other contexts. Yet the nation's largest animal rights groups work to ensure that this door remains firmly shut, not only leaving vast potential that would benefit all animals lying untapped, but sacrificing their most fundamental ideals for the reputations of those who defend the killing and have schooled an entire generation of animal rights activists to do the same.

The BANALITY of *EVIL*

Many people guilty of perpetrating atrocities in history seemed, to those who actually met them, like perfectly normal people. They could be polite, funny, even charming. Why? Because in the real world, people who have done horrible things do not bear horns on their heads and carry pitchforks. On the contrary, they look and seem to be just like everyone else, a phenomenon author Hannah Arendt called "The Banality of Evil." It is a phenomenon that works to the advantage of those guilty of cruelty by disarming and dissuading those who should be holding them accountable for their behavior. In the animal protection world, where those doing the killing often mingle socially with those who should be doing the protecting and much of the harm committed against animals in shelters is immoral but not yet illegal, the attenuating power of this phenomenon is especially pervasive and detrimental.

IT IS EASY TO BE CRITICAL of people who have done horrible things if we have never met them. It is harder to publicly decry people we know, especially when they appear nice, normal, soft-spoken and accommodating. As difficult as it may be to understand the disconnect, this phenomenon is not uncommon.

And so it was not surprising when a bestselling author visited an urban shelter recently sued for killing animals in violation of law, for allowing animals to languish and die with no medical care, and for other inhumane conditions and came away with a very different view of it. Here was a shelter overseen by people who allowed the most atrocious conditions; a shelter that was filthy; that hired thugs who were abusive to the animals; that kept cages empty to reduce their workload which meant more killing; that allowed animals to die of starvation; that dragged injured animals across hot asphalt by way of a tight, hard-wire noose wrapped around their necks; and that even killed them cruelly. But after spending time with one of the managers, a manager who was considerate, charming and accommodating to him, he could not square it with the reports of rescuers, volunteers and shelter reformers, complete with data, photographs, even video of some of the most heart-wrenching cruelty and needless killing going on under the manager's watch. The manager was not evil at all, according to the account. He was... nice. And so nice, he concluded, that the killing could not possibly be the manager's fault. How was that possible?

The answer is found in the 1963 classic of political science, Hannah Arendt's *"Eichmann in Jerusalem: A Report on the Banality of Evil."* This isn't about cheap "Nazi" analogies. The book itself was a misinformed view of Adolf Eichmann's trial and his role in helping turn the world into a graveyard, but Arendt got one thing right: You do not have to be a raving monster to do horrible things. "The trouble with Eichmann," she wrote, "was precisely that so many were like him, and that the many were neither perverted nor sadistic, that they were, and still are, terribly and terrifyingly normal."

This is something with which William Wilberforce, the great crusader against the British slave trade, struggled. Wilberforce was a unique figure in history because he was a reformer who was also a member of the establishment. He was a wealthy English

For all the talk of paradigm shifts, infrastructure improvements, the programs and services of the No Kill Equation, the No Kill movement is, in the end, a fight against individual people who hold the power over life and death.

gentleman, a Member of Parliament and a college friend of a future Prime Minister. And that meant that his efforts to abolish the British slave trade affected his friends and colleagues. As the wealthy owners of British sugar plantations in the Caribbean, Wilberforce's peers in and out of Parliament relied on the slave trade to provide them with a constant supply of new slaves because not only were slaves so brutally treated that they often died young, but many of them were too ill and malnourished to bear children.

What was shocking to Wilberforce, what he could not wrap his mind around, was that the face of so much obscene barbarity, killing and cruelty was not the face of the devil incarnate. The face of all that violence was, in many cases, an English gentleman, a man seemingly committed to civility and good manners. These individuals owned plantations halfway around the world run by overseers who, at their behest, brutalized, tortured and killed other human beings. Yet, these very same gentlemen welcomed people like Wilberforce into their homes with graciousness and gentility and then dedicated themselves to their guest's comfort and well-being. They didn't seem like monsters; in fact, quite the opposite. They seemed like normal, considerate people.

Yes, it is easy to be critical of people who have done horrible things if we have never met them. But it can be much harder to publicly decry those we know, especially when those people—like the manager of the large, urban shelter—appear normal. It can seem harder because we have trouble reconciling the two. And it can seem harder still because we are afraid decision makers will dismiss us. But No Kill advocates do not have a choice and ethics compel them to find the courage and determination to do it anyway.

Because for all the talk of paradigm shifts, infrastructure improvements, the programs and services of the No Kill Equation, the No Kill movement is, in the end, a fight against individual people who hold the power over life and death. And despite their outward appearance, they have proven that they are not equal to the task before them. They have proven that they are people who do not treat animals with the kindness and compassion the animals deserve. In short, they are people who must be called to account no matter how "nice" they might appear.

The primary obstacle to success in communities which were once steeped in killing but are now No Kill was, in the vast majority of cases, the shelter's director. The obstacle to success wherever there is killing today is also the shelter's director. If No Kill is to succeed, these individuals must be replaced. If No Kill is to prevail, they must be judged by the decisions they make and the actions that result from those decisions, decisions that are often accompanied by cruel and lethal consequences.

Across the nation, individual people are collectively putting to death millions of animals every year and often allowing their staff to neglect and abuse them in the process. They are then going home to their friends and families who embrace them with open arms. It is hard for some to reconcile this. But change won't happen if we ignore the fact that the difference between lifesaving success and the status quo of killing comes down to the choices made by individual people running the shelters and those working at our nation's animal protection groups who continually enable and/or legitimize them when the choices they make are the wrong ones. They must be judged and held accountable to those very weighty choices and not by any other criteria.

In the final analysis, animals in shelters are not being killed because there are too many of them, because there are too few homes or because the public is irresponsible. Animals in shelters are dying for primarily one reason: because people in shelters are killing them—people who appear "terribly and terrifyingly normal."

ANIMAL SHELTERING IN AMERICA
MEET ACE

MEET ACE. In 2011, an emaciated dog wandered into an Ace Hardware store in Detroit, Michigan looking for food, warmth and a caring hand. Ace had either been starved or been a stray for a long time. He also had dried blood around his neck from what appeared to be an embedded collar. The owner of the hardware store opened up his heart to Ace. Thinking he was doing the right thing, he called the local shelter. Like many Americans, he believed that shelters were places that help animals in need and that Ace would receive the care he needed and the loving new home he deserved. He also, however, called one of his staff, a rescuer, on her day off. Unfortunately, the shelter got there first. When the owner informed them that he no longer needed them because a rescuer was en route, they took Ace anyway. Unfortunately, Ace entered a typical and traditional shelter in the U.S. Because Detroit Animal Control labeled him a "Pit Bull," city officials announced that Ace would be put to death.

When word spread of Ace's plight, the people of Detroit demanded that Ace be allowed to live. Rescue groups offered to take him, but the leadership of the health department which oversees the shelter refused. In response, activists filed a lawsuit and a court order was issued prohibiting the shelter from killing Ace.

They killed him anyway. And while the shelter claimed they did not get the court order in time, there is evidence to suggest otherwise. We may never know the truth. But regardless of whether they had or had not received the court order, there was simply no reason to kill Ace—he had an immediate place to go, to the rescue groups who offered the veterinary care and the loving home that was his birthright.

A shelter bureaucrat defended his position by arguing that if he allowed Ace to be rescued, rescuers would want to save other dogs, too. That the vast majority of people would consider this a good thing was something to which he could simply not relate. Yet shelter directors with precisely this attitude—an attitude deeply out of touch with how most people feel about dogs and cats—are the rule rather than the exception in American shelters today. The prevalence of small-minded bureaucrats who find killing easier than doing the minimum amount necessary to stop it, including letting others save animals they plan to kill, is the real "overpopulation" problem that is to blame for the killing in American shelters today. And they have no business leading the very institutions that are supposed to give meaning to the American love affair with companion animals.

The hardware store owner who called the shelter that ultimately killed Ace was plagued by sorrow and regret and wrote the following tribute to him:

Dear Ace,

You came into my lobby, crouched behind my door and stared blankly at the wall, shaking... I fed you, warmed you and you rewarded me by finally looking into my eyes, and for a moment, we shared your pain. I reached for the phone, thinking that I could find you a better life... Instead I sent you to your death. Please forgive me. You did not die in vain, nor will you be forgotten. This I promise you.

Your last but far from only friend.

3 out of 4

Americans believe it should be illegal for shelters to kill healthy animals

Nasty, Brutish & Short?

THE LIFE OF A WILD CAT

NO

THE LAW WOULD HAVE BEEN SIMPLE. Senate Bill 359, a bill pending in the Virginia legislature in 2012, would have clarified that neutering and releasing feral cats back to their habitats was not illegal, allowing cat advocates to continue doing so without fear of prosecution. But PETA successfully led the effort to oppose the law, joining kill shelters throughout the state and the Virginia Animal Control Association in defeating it.

While cats as a whole face a roughly 60 percent chance of being killed in shelters, when those cats are "unsocial," the percentage becomes nearly 100 percent. At shelters across the country, without TNR, every unsocial cat is put to death. And groups like PETA believe this is as it should be. According to these and other groups, cats belong in homes or they should be killed. To these organizations, the practice of TNR is setting the cats up for a lifetime of suffering, a claim which they and others use to round up and exterminate thousands of healthy and happy cats every year in communities across the country.

But is it true? In fact, it is not. Several studies confirm that from the cat's perspective, the great outdoors really is great. A comprehensive 11-year study of outdoor cats found that they had similar baselines in health, disease rates and longevity as indoor cats. A subsequent study gave feral cats "A+" grades across a wide range of physical and health characteristics. In yet another study, less than one percent of over 100,000 feral cats admitted to seven major TNR programs across the United States were killed for debilitating conditions; while a fourth survey across 132 colonies of cats in north central Florida showed that 96 percent of the cats had a "good" or "great" quality of life.

The idea that cats belong indoors is contrary to the natural history of the species, which evolved and then flourished outside for over 100,000 years. Several studies confirm that from the cat's perspective, the great outdoors really is great.

And yet, even if it were true that these cats were disproportionately suffering outdoors, it would not change what the ethical response should be. It is never okay to kill an *individual* cat based on a group dynamic. If we were to postulate, for the sake of argument, that most feral cats die prematurely due to disease or injury, it would still be unethical to kill any individual cat because not only do that cat's inherent rights ethically prohibit it, but we would never know if that particular cat will ever succumb to such a fate, let alone when.

Moreover, even if we did, even if we knew that a cat would get hit by a car two years from now, it isn't ethical to rob him of those two years by killing him now. In the end, the answer from opponents of TNR programs—that we should stop cats from being killed by killing the cats ourselves—is a hopeless contradiction. But the contradiction goes even deeper.

"[T]he most compassionate choice [is] to euthanize feral cats. You can ask your veterinarian to do this or, if your local animal shelter uses an injection of sodium pentobarbital, take the cats there."

- PETA

While traditional shelters argue that all cats are the same, need the same things (namely, an indoor home), and should be treated the same because they cannot live outside, they themselves hold feral cats to a different standard. Once in the shelter, a "friendly" cat may be deemed suitable for adoption, while an "unfriendly" cat, by contrast, is killed outright, in some cases within minutes of arriving because they conclude such cats are "unadoptable" or unsuited for life inside a human home.

BIOLOGICAL XENOPHOBIA

While some groups oppose allowing feral cats to live out their lives by arguing it is "for their own good," others do so because they argue that cats are decimating bird populations and therefore deserve to die. Not only does the science contradict these claims,* but the idea that some animals have more value than others comes from a troubling belief that lineage determines the value of an individual animal. This belief is part of a growing and disturbing movement called "Invasion Biology." The notion that "native" species have more value than "non-native" ones finds its roots historically in 1940s Germany, where the notion of a garden with native plants was founded on nationalistic and racist ideas cloaked in scientific jargon. This is not surprising. The types of arguments made for biological purity of people are exactly the same as those made for purity among animals and plants.

In the United States, Invasion Biologists believe that certain plants or animals should be valued more than others if they were at a particular location "first," although the exact starting point varies, is difficult to ascertain and, in many

---

* For an in-depth discussion, see the chapter called "Witch Hunt" in Nathan's Redemption: The Myth of Pet Overpopulation & the No Kill Revolution in America (2nd Ed., Almaden Books: 2009).

Feral cats are not "homeless." The outdoors *is* their home. Killing feral cats isn't an act of love; it's an act of violence.

THE FLAWS & FOLLY OF NATIVISM

Nature cannot be frozen in time or returned to a particular past, nor is there a compelling reason why it should be. To claim that "native" species are somehow preferable than "introduced" species equally or better adapted to a changing environment ignores the inevitable forces of migration and natural selection.

cases, is wholly arbitrary. Indeed, all plants and animals were introduced (by wind, humans, migration or other animals) at some point in time. But regardless of which arbitrary measure is used, Invasion Biologists ultimately make the same, unethical assertions that "introduced" or "non-native" species are not worthy of life or compassion. They conclude that these species should be eradicated in order to "restore" an area to some fixed point in the past.

Nature, however, cannot be frozen in time or returned to a particular past, nor is there a compelling reason why it should be. To claim that "native" species are somehow preferable than "introduced" species equally or better adapted to a changing environment ignores the inevitable forces of migration and natural selection. All animals have a right to live, regardless of how and when they arrived or were "introduced." Their rights as individuals supersede our own human-centric preferences,

which are often based on arbitrary biases, subjective aesthetics or narrow commercial interests.

Moreover, no matter how many so-called "non-native" animals (and plants) are killed, the goal of total eradication can never be reached because, quite simply, nature is not static, nor is it possible to force it to become so. To advocate for the eradication of feral cats is not only cruel and unethical, it is to propose a massacre with no hope of success and no conceivable end.

Equally inconsistent in the philosophy of Invasion Biology is its position—or, more accurately, lack of a coherent position—on humans. If one accepts the logic that only native plants and animals have value, human beings are the biggest non-native intruders in the United States. With over 300 million of us altering the landscape and causing virtually all of the environmental and species decimation through habitat destruction and pollution, shouldn't Invasion Biologists demand that non-native people leave the continent? Of course, non-profit organizations that advocate nativist positions would never dare say so, or donations to their causes would dry up. Instead, they engage in a great hypocrisy of doing that which they claim to abhor and blame "non-native" species for doing: preying on those who cannot defend themselves.

In addition, it is not "predation" that Invasion Biologists actually object to. Animals prey on other animals all the time without their objection. In fact, they themselves prey on some birds by eating them, and they prey on animals they label "non-native" by eradicating them. For Invasion Biologists, predation is unacceptable only when it involves an animal they do not like. And when it comes to animals they do not like, animals who do not pass their narrow litmus test of who is worthy to live and who should die, the cat stands at the top as "Public Enemy No. 1."

TEACHING TOLERANCE, RESPECTING DIVERSITY
The ultimate goal of the environmental movement is to create a peaceful and harmonious relationship between humans and the environment. To be authentic, this goal must include respect for other species who share our planet. And yet, given its alarming embrace of Invasion Biology, the environmental movement has violated this ethic by targeting species for eradication because their existence conflicts with the world as some humans would like it to be. Condemning animals to death because they violate a preferred sense of order does not reject human interference in the natural world as they claim; it reaffirms it. And in championing such views, the movement paradoxically supports the use of traps, poisons, fire and hunting, all of which cause great harm, suffering and environmental degradation—the very things they ostensibly exist to oppose.

Over the last 250 years, the story of humanity has been the story of the human rights movement—of overcoming our darker natures by learning tolerance for the foreign and respect for the diverse. In the early 21st century, these are the cherished ideals to which humanity aspires in our treatment of one another. And yet when it comes to our relationship with other species, these values are turned on their head, and environmentalists—the very people who should be promoting tolerance and compassion for all Earthlings regardless of their antecedents—are instead teaching

There is no such thing as an invasive species.

On a tiny planet surrounded by the infinite emptiness of space, in a universe in which the anomaly of life renders every blade of grass, every insect that crawls and every animal on Earth an exquisite, wondrous rarity, it is breathtakingly myopic and quite simply inaccurate to label any living thing found anywhere on the planet which gave it life as "alien" or "non-native." There is no such thing as an "invasive" species.

disdain for some, leading the charge to kill them and turning our beautiful, natural places into war zones and battlefields. We need a different, more humane and more responsible way of seeing the world and our place in it.

For in the end, not only is it wrong to label any species an "alien" on its own planet and to target that species for extermination, but it is also breathtakingly myopic. On a tiny planet surrounded by the infinite emptiness of space, in a universe in which the anomaly of life renders every blade of grass, every insect that crawls and every animal on Earth an exquisite, wondrous rarity, it is quite simply inaccurate to label any living thing found anywhere on the planet which gave it life as "alien" or "non-native." There is no such thing as an "invasive" species.

We must turn our attention away from the futile and pointless effort to return our environment to the past toward the meaningful goal of ensuring that every life that appears on this Earth is welcomed and respected as the glorious, cosmic miracle it actually is.

TNR TRAP, NEUTER, RELEASE

A Free-Living Cat's Ticket Back Home

FOR MOST OF THE HISTORY of animal sheltering in the United States, feral cats who ended up in shelters faced an almost certain death sentence. Without a human address, there was no one to reclaim these animals. Fearful of humans, they were not considered candidates for traditional adoption and were not afforded the opportunity. Combined with the misconception that they disproportionately suffer without human caretakers because they belong in homes, the tragic result has been the execution of virtually all healthy and self-sufficient unsocial cats in shelters across the nation. Such killing was the status quo until roughly

30 years ago, when cat lovers finally said "Enough!" and began advocating for the alternative of neutering and releasing them back into their habitats, a program called TNR.

In a TNR program—an essential component of the No Kill Equation—any feral cats who end up in the shelter are neutered and released back into their habitats. The shelter also works with local feral cat caregivers who trap community cats for spay/neuter. Sometimes, these cats have human caretakers who watch over them and feed them. But often, feral cats who end up in shelters are like other "wild" animals, thoroughly unsocialized to humans, surviving on their own through instinct and wit and no worse off because of it.

Many shelters argue that since cats are "domestic," the unsocial cat without a human home is better off taken to a shelter and killed. These groups argue that a free living cat's life is a series of brutal experiences and shelters need to protect the cat from continued and future suffering. Not only does this fly in the face of actual experience and virtually all scientific analysis, even if it were true, the reality is that all animals living in the wild may face some hardship—and wild cats are no exception. But they also experience the joys of such a life, as well. Life, by its very definition, is a mixture of happy and sad, easy and hard. Since animal groups do not support the trapping and killing of other wild animals— raccoons, mice, fox—why do they reserve this fate for feral cats?

If feral cats are genetically identical to wild animals, and they survive in the wild like wild animals, and they are unsocial to humans like wild animals and if they can and do live in the wild like wild animals, shouldn't they be treated like wild animals—with animal protection groups advocating on their behalf, pushing for their right to life and respecting and protecting their habitats? And, more importantly, why should any of them be condemned to death because of the sloppy logic that some may face hardship?

Of course, this inevitably begs the question, if feral cats are wild animals, why the special treatment? Why alter them? Why vaccinate? In such circumstances, sterilization and vaccination against rabies is necessary for several reasons. Not only does it eliminate the chance of future offspring ending up in the shelter, but because feral cats often live in close proximity to humans, it also eliminates behaviors associated with mating that have the potential to cause friction and intolerance. This is important given that the historic solution to such conflicts has been to trap and kill the cats. Moreover, because of decades of unsubstantiated fear mongering by animal protection organizations about the health risks associated with feral cats, vaccination is a way of addressing any perceived concerns of local health departments or regressive shelter directors, which exist even though feral cats pose virtually no health or safety risk to humans. Finally, once in the shelter, TNR is the functional equivalent of adoption. Spay/neuter isn't the most important variable. The most important part of the TNR equation is the "R."

Through TNR, cat advocates have found a life-affirming way to address the dogmas which the animal protection movement itself created and expounded for decades that have been responsible for the mass slaughter of unsocial cats. Right now, TNR is the most humane option for feral cats because it assures their safety and buys them a ticket back home.

CAUGHT BETWEEN TWO WORLDS

Whether categorized as "domestic" or "wild," feral cats face man-made dangers that threaten their well-being and their right to live.

Cats can live happily and healthily in homes and they can thrive outdoors. According to a cat advocacy organization, "This ability to adapt and re-adapt is a central characteristic of this species... The notion that cats belong only indoors as an 'owned' pet is contrary to the natural history of the species, a species that has flourished outdoors for [tens of thousands of] years." But just as cats occupy a unique niche between wild and domestic, they also occupy a gray zone in the law.

For many cats, their status as "domestic" animals means certain death in shelters. But wild animals tend to fare little better. In those states where it is allowed, wildlife is subjected to trapping, poisoning and hunting, particularly if they are an unprotected species. Feral cats, in essence, are caught between two anachronistic views. If they are legally domestic, they are subject to mass slaughter in shelters. If they are legally wild, they are subject to killing by hunting, trapping and poisoning. The feral cat, in this case, is a grim reminder of how far we have yet to go—as a humane movement and as a society.

What's In a Name?

A Closer Look at State "Humane" Organizations

As No Kill advocates seek to pass progressive shelter reform legislation in communities and states throughout the country, time and again their fiercest opponents are organizations with names that allow them to masquerade as something they are not.

THE NEW YORK STATE HUMANE ASSOCIATION. The Florida Animal Control Association. The Texas Humane Legislation Network. Organizations with such names exist in virtually every state. They often weigh in on local and state issues pertaining to animals, particularly legislation. And their names command instant respect from the media and legislators, conveying as they do, the idea that they have expertise in the field of animal welfare and sheltering policy in particular. But is it true? What, exactly, are these organizations? Who staffs them? Whose interests do they truly represent? And, most importantly, what are their credentials?

In 2010, shelter reform legislation was pending in New York State. The law was projected to save roughly 25,000 animals a year at no cost to taxpayers. And despite overwhelming support for the legislation from rescue groups and New York animal lovers, what finally killed the bill, dooming to death tens of thousands of animals every year whom rescue groups statewide were ready and willing to save, was

the opposition of groups like the New York State Humane Association (NYSHA).

Despite over 20,000 emails, telephone calls and letters from New Yorkers, the bill was tabled and animals who have an immediate place to go continue to be killed. In fact, since the first of many bills of this kind was introduced and subsequently defeated, as of August 2012, the number of animals killed who could and would have been saved has topped 55,000. It is not easy to conceptualize 55,000 dead animals. But if you were driving along the road and each was lined up end to end, that monumental trail of dead bodies would stretch over 15 miles long. Put another way, they would fill more than all of the seats at Yankee stadium.

The "Legislative Chair" of the NYSHA expressed her opposition to legislators, making several false claims about its mandates based on a bungled reading of the law, calling basic, common sense measures such as not killing a savable animal when there is an empty cage "unreasonable" and suggesting that asking shelters to do what they have been entrusted by taxpayers to do is too "burdensome." She also claimed that the law would lead to hoarding and that the animals were better off dead, 11 years after those arguments were proven false when similar legislation was passed in California.

What gave this woman and her organization the experience and authority to make these claims? Her move to the NYSHA came by way of HSUS, where, as program coordinator, she made a career out of defending the "right" of pounds to kill animals. In 2002, she defended the New York City pound, despite documented animal neglect and abuse. Despite seven out of 10 animals being put to death, she called those statistics "useless."

In 2003, she supported the pound in Rockland County, New York, even after an auditor substantiated allegations of high rates of shelter killing and other deficiencies that were not corrected after a year. In her letter to the Rockland County Executive on behalf of HSUS, she underscored her commitment to killing, arguing against a No Kill orientation. Although the County Executive was inclined to turn operations over to a No Kill group, her efforts succeeded in swaying the decision in favor of retaining a traditional kill-oriented facility. Her intervention harmed the potential for animals to receive the care of a No Kill service provider, just as it would later kill the chances of thousands of New York animals making it out of shelters alive.

She is a woman who refuses to admit problems in shelters exist or to have standards and benchmarks that would hold them accountable. In other words, although she feigns an expertise in sheltering, she has willfully failed to keep pace with the dynamic and innovative changes in the field as a result of the No Kill movement, choosing instead to fight those changes. And yet she and her organization and others like it

When legislation is introduced to expand the power and authority of animal control, even when that power will lead to greater killing, they support it. When legislation seeks to limit the power or discretion of animal control, to hold shelters to higher standards and greater lifesaving, they predictably oppose it.

in every state in the country, with relatively small memberships composed mainly of both past and present directors of kill shelters, often control the debate regarding shelter policy in our state capitols. When legislation is introduced to expand the power and authority of animal control, even when that power will lead to greater killing, they support it. When legislation seeks to limit the power or discretion of animal control, to hold shelters to higher standards and greater lifesaving, they predictably oppose it.

As No Kill advocates seek to pass progressive shelter reform legislation in communities and states throughout the country, time and again their fiercest opponents are organizations with names that allow them to masquerade as something they are not. In 2011, for example, shelter reform legislation in Texas was defeated by a coalition which included a group calling itself the Texas Humane Legislation Network (THLN). As No Kill advocates and everyday animal lovers rejoiced at the introduction of a bill which would have banned the gas chamber, ended convenience killing and mandated collaboration—flooding the Texas State House with thousands of calls and letters of support—THLN released a statement of opposition and worked with HSUS to successfully defeat it. The Virginia Animal Control Association, the Florida Animal Control Association, and similar groups in Georgia, Rhode Island and West Virginia did the same in their respective states in 2012.

Those who embrace a brighter future, those who seek to finally bring some accountability to a field that has lacked it, have found they must work to overcome the false perceptions the public, legislators and the media have regarding these individuals and the groups with

> **In the end, these individuals, with views so out of touch with the majority of people, succeed in defeating legislation that would mandate reasonable, common sense provisions that almost every American would be stunned to learn have not already been voluntarily implemented.**

which they are associated, simply because they have the names "humane" or "animal" in their titles. People believe these organizations speak for the animals, even though they protect incompetence and fight innovation of any kind. They believe the organizations are run by "experts," despite having no experience creating No Kill communities nor reforming those plagued with regressive, high-kill shelters. And in the end, these individuals, with views so out of touch with the majority of people, succeed in defeating legislation that would mandate reasonable, common sense provisions that almost every American would be stunned to learn have not already been voluntarily implemented.

DEMYSTIFYING THE ENIGMATIC NAYSAYER

ANIMAL LOVER OR ANIMAL ABUSE ENABLER?

Although they publicly wear the mantle of animal lover, Enigmatic Naysayers vehemently oppose No Kill and any effort to reform animal control, no matter how dysfunctional the department or how cruel local practices are.

THEY CLAIM TO BE ANIMAL ADVOCATES but they are promoters of death. They cannot be swayed by logic, facts or alternative points of view. They seek out that which fits their beliefs and reject everything else to the point of taking facts out of context—and in many cases, making up "facts"—to fit the story. Fighting the No Kill efforts of others in their community, the "Enigmatic Naysayer" has a predetermined agenda of support for animal control, regardless of how many animals the local shelter kills.

Every community has at least one, but more commonly a small number of

FIGHTING NO KILL LOCALLY

individuals who fit this description. Because they sometimes belong to spay/neuter organizations or "Friends of the Shelter" groups and because they are often politically active (testifying at City Council meetings for more funding for animal control or for mandatory spay/neuter legislation), they are perceived as "animal activists." Consequently, their opposition to No Kill and shelter reform sows seeds of doubt where none should be among local politicians and the media. Moreover, because they exist in every community, their pervasiveness and predictability suggest shared psychological profiles. A better understanding of what motivates such individuals is the key to hindering, if not eliminating, their destructive power and influence.

What identifies these naysayers is that they are champions of continued killing, defenders of draconian animal shelters and purveyors of punishment through misguided legislative efforts such as pet limit laws, leash laws and feeding bans, even when community after community has shown that such efforts kill animals (see pages 212-213). Yet they stubbornly refuse to acknowledge these facts, continue to blame the public, continue to fight for more and tougher laws that empower animal control to kill even more animals, all while vehemently fighting No Kill reformers by claiming that their community is different, that their situation is unique, that local citizens are particularly—or peculiarly—irresponsible.

While they claim to be motivated by saving lives, there is something much more powerful driving them: the desire to punish the public.

While they claim to be motivated by saving lives, there is something much more powerful driving them: *the desire to punish.* An activist truly focused on lifesaving, who subsequently learns that punitive legislation is not only a dismal failure, but that it has the opposite result (more impounds, more killing), would end their support of such methods and begin to push for the programs and services of the No Kill Equation.

By contrast, the naysayers are willing to ignore all the evidence about legislation's true results or about how to truly save lives and instead empower animal control to kill animals in the process, which animal control is generally more than willing to do. In the end, these activists become that which they claim to most despise—people whose actions result in the impound and killing of animals. They become the "irresponsible public."

> **Naysayers fight No Kill advocates in their demands for change and their call for the replacement of poorly performing staff because they are friends with the staff and therefore have a privileged relationship with the shelter—a relationship which would be upended if those reform efforts were to succeed.**

Unfortunately, naysayers nationwide have internalized the viewpoint that the public, rather than the shelter, is to blame for the volume of killing. Since the very "solution" they propose makes the goal impossible, they seek more power for animal control departments, more officers, more sweeps of animals, more citations written, more animals impounded and more animals killed, broadening the divide between the shelter and the public and moving further from true lifesaving with each piece of punitive legislation.

Their promotion of punitive legislation diverts focus from establishing vital programs such as offsite adoptions, TNR and foster care in favor of traditional enforcement. They also feed the backyard breeder market as people who surrender their animals to avoid citation turn around and purchase other unaltered animals. That individuals who claim to be concerned with high levels of shelter killing actually seek legislation to empower dysfunctional animal control bureaucracies to impound—and kill—even more animals, is conveniently ignored.

In 2008, while California mandatory spay/neuter proponents attended a legislative hearing with shelter directors whose facilities were infamous for poor, hostile and even abusive treatment of animals, a Senator asked one of the law's chief proponents: "This bill doesn't even pretend to be about saving animals, does it?" In a moment of candor, the shelter director responded: "No, Senator, this is not about saving dogs and cats." For shelter directors, it is about increasing the power of animal control. It is about getting more money for enforcement. It is about diverting focus from their own failures to save lives by getting activists who might challenge them to focus on a straw man: the "common enemy." It is about control, not compassion. And for the enigmatic naysayer, it is also about being special.

Naysayers fight No Kill advocates in their demands for change and their call for the replacement of poorly performing staff because they are friends with the staff and therefore have a privileged relationship with the shelter—a relationship which would be upended if those reform efforts were to succeed.

Moreover, to embrace No Kill is to admit that they are not superior to the masses, as the emerging success of the No Kill movement proves that while some people are irresponsible, most people do care. Most people find killing abhorrent. Most people pass on their own needs during difficult economic times to provide what their animals need. Most people would do the right thing if given the information they need to make good choices and the help to see it through. Most people are not only part of the solution; they are the key to it. And that, according to these naysayers, is unacceptable. Because if it was, they aren't so "special" anymore. Most people are not only as committed to animals as these "animal advocates" claim to be, they are more so because they oppose killing, too. And this is something the enigmatic naysayers cannot accept. So they block it out, because what else do they have? Who else are they? To recognize the truth is to lose their identity as "saviors"— these addicts of being "special" at the expense of the animals.

The strategy to overcome these people is simple: Because they can never be convinced to change their point-of-view, true animal lovers working to reform their local shelters must remove any legitimacy these naysayers have,

Since such individuals can never be convinced to change their point-of-view, true animal lovers working to reform their local shelters must remove any legitimacy these naysayers have, by isolating and exposing them for who and what they really are.

by isolating and exposing them for who and what they really are. No Kill advocates must demonstrate that such people are not motivated by "saving dogs and cats," but are in fact emperors who have no clothes, disingenuous and misanthropic in their elitist disdain for other people and heartless in their lack of true commitment to what is in the best interests of animals. In the end, they are nothing more than bullies. And because the only way to stop a bully is to stand up to a bully, No Kill advocates must give up the notion of working collaboratively with such individuals and simply fight back.

The Deadly Siren Song of Mandatory Spay/Neuter Legislation

ALTHOUGH NO KILL ADVOCATES encourage and promote incentives for spay/neuter, many oppose the mandatory spay/neuter laws the naysayers champion. That is neither a contradiction nor a philosophical position. If these laws worked, No Kill advocates would support them. But if one is goal oriented, and if the goal is reducing shelter intakes and shelter deaths, support for mandatory spay/neuter laws does not follow the belief in the importance of spay/neuter.

Over and over, mandatory spay/neuter legislation is pushed as a quick solution to high rates of shelter killing. "If only we had a spay/neuter law" the argument goes, "all the bad, irresponsible people would have to take care of their pets properly, and shelters wouldn't have to kill so many animals." If this were true, given the proliferation of such punitive mandates nationwide, these laws

would have already created many No Kill communities. That there are none as a result of mandatory spay/neuter laws proves that such legislation does not work. In fact, it often has the opposite effect. Communities that have passed such laws are not only far from No Kill; they are moving in the opposite direction.

Mandatory spay/neuter laws are a distraction not just because they fail to target the true cause of killing—the failure of a shelter to implement lifesaving alternatives—but because they don't even succeed in forcing the behavior they theoretically exist to encourage. Studies show that people who do not spay/neuter are at the lowest rungs of the economic ladder— and that the vast majority would have their companion animals sterilized if it was affordable.

Instead, mandatory spay/neuter laws divert funding from true lifesaving programs—such as providing low-cost spay/neuter—and empower

Mandatory spay/neuter laws target low-income households for enforcement: subjecting them to citation and the round-up and killing of their companion animals. Not only do they fail to remove the primary barrier preventing people from sterilizing their animals—cost—but because the shelters make no effort to implement alternatives to killing, the increased number of animals impounded for being in violation of the law are simply killed.

animal control officers to cite people with unaltered animals—people who often simply surrender the animals to avoid citation or the costs of sterilization. And because many of these communities do not offer an affordable alternative to the high fees charged by veterinarians, low-income people with animals cannot comply, while the laws may also empower these officers to forcibly impound those animals for not being sterilized. When the City of Los Angeles passed a mandatory spay/neuter law, not only did impound and killing of animals increase dramatically for the first time in a decade, but private practice veterinarians raised their prices because they now had a captive market required to sterilize their animals. And because the pound made no effort to build the infrastructure to save those lives once they entered, more animals were killed—an all-too-common occurrence across the country.

LIVES IN THE BALANCE

The Importance of Legislation in the Fight for a No Kill Nation

With the number of No Kill communities multiplying and a public that is increasingly savvy about the true causes of shelter killing, there is no doubt that the No Kill movement is coming into its own. The "adopt some and kill the rest" paradigm which has dominated the country is being upended and with it, the call for new leaders to replace regressive ones. But to fully destroy it, to ensure a more humane future for all posterity, we need more than individual leaders passionate about saving lives. We need more than additional directors willing to implement the No Kill Equation. The goal is to permanently build a more compassionate society for animals, to end their killing in shelters now and forever.

Today shelters are permitted to kill most animals who come through their doors. It doesn't matter if they are healthy or sick, young or old, friendly, scared or traumatized, the choice is up to the people running those shelters. With some small exceptions, if the animal was surrendered by a family, he or she can be killed within minutes of arriving. Not even a meager holding period. No chance at adoption. No food, water or shelter, just a trip from the front counter to the gas chamber or to be poisoned with an overdose of barbiturates.

If the animal came in as a stray, he or she will be held from 48 hours to one week depending on the state, and then that animal can also be put to death with no opportunity or chance for adoption—just a one-way ticket to the morgue. In the communities which have embraced the No Kill philosophy, they'll be held until they find a home, but that is the exception. Nationally, shelters will find homes for only about half of all animals. In some communities, it is less than 10 percent. And it all depends on who is in charge, on how much they care, on how committed they are.

LEGISLATING JUSTICE

The aim of every social movement in our nation's history has been legislation to gain and then protect the rights of those who are the focus of its efforts, a legacy which reaches back to the very founding of our Republic. It is a legacy that is at the core of who we are and how we effect change: a government of the people, by the people, for the people.

The No Kill movement has made tremendous progress, to be sure. But in too many communities, we still have this:

I tried to adopt from my local shelter, but they weren't open on the weekend, it was almost impossible to reach them on the telephone and when I did, I was treated rudely. Nonetheless, I raced down there one day after work, and the place was so dirty. It made me cry to look into the faces of all those animals I knew would be killed. But I found this scared, skinny cat hiding in the back of his cage and I filled out an application. I was turned down because I didn't turn in the paperwork on time, which meant a half hour before closing, but I couldn't get there from work in time to do that. I tried to leave work early the next day, but I called and found out they had already killed the poor cat. I will never go back.

> *"In framing a system which we wish to last for ages, we should not lose sight of the changes which ages will produce."*
>
> JAMES MADISON

We can end this. The aim of every social movement in our nation's history has been legislation to gain and then protect the rights of its members or the focus of its efforts, a legacy which reaches back to the very founding of our Republic: a more compassionate society, a democracy, the ability to end injustice through self-rule as codified in law. It is a legacy that is at the core of who we are and how we effect change: a government of the people, by the people, for the people. Our system of government was designed not only to solidify the ideals of the American Revolution, but to change with the changing times, a flexibility envisioned by James Madison, the Father of the Constitution, who stated, "In framing a system which we wish to last for ages, we should not lose sight of the changes which ages will produce."

No matter what the issue: the fight for democracy as epitomized by Madison, Benjamin Franklin and John Adams; the abolition of slavery as epitomized by William Lloyd Garrison, Harriet Tubman, Sojourner Truth and Frederick Douglass; the struggle for women's suffrage as epitomized by Susan B. Anthony, Elizabeth Cady Stanton and the great Alice Paul; an end to child labor as epitomized by Lewis Hine; civil rights as epitomized by Dr. Martin Luther King Jr. and Harvey Milk; or disability rights as epitomized by Justin Whitlock Dart, Jr. and Richard Pimentel; all these movements culminated in the passing of laws.

The goal was never mere promises that we would strive to do better as a society. The focus was always on changing the law to eliminate the ability to do otherwise. The suffrage movement did not seek discretionary permission from election officials to vote, an ability that could be taken away. Its goal was winning the right to vote, a right guaranteed in law. The civil rights movement did not seek the discretionary ability to sit at the front of the bus or to eat at the same lunch counters. Its goal was winning the right to do so, a right guaranteed in law. Without legal rights, one's fate is contingent on who the election official is, who the restaurant owner is, who the mayor is and in the case of animals entering shelters, who the director is.

For No Kill success to be widespread and long lasting, we must focus on institutionalizing No Kill by giving shelter animals rights and protections afforded by law.

While the ideal animal law would ban the killing of animals in shelters, given that local and state governments may not pass such sweeping laws at this time in history, advocates must begin by seeking legislation that forces shelter leadership to operate their shelters in a progressive, life-affirming way. With rigorous and comprehensive mandates codified in law comes accountability. And with accountability comes an end to the tragic killing of millions of animals each and every year. When shelter directors no longer have discretion to neglect and then kill animals, the era of the status quo will be over.

The Companion Animal Protection Act

A comprehensive shelter reform law, the Companion Animal Protection Act codifies the programs and services of the No Kill Equation, increasing lifesaving by:

1 Establishing the shelter's primary role as saving the lives of animals;

2 Protecting all species of shelter animals;

3 Making it illegal for a shelter to kill animals rescue groups are willing to save;

4 Requiring shelters to provide animals with fresh food, fresh water, cleanliness, environmental enrichment, regular exercise and veterinary care;

5 Requiring shelters to have fully functioning adoption programs including offsite adoptions, use of the internet and operating hours when the public is available;

6 Prohibiting shelters from killing animals based on arbitrary criteria such as breed bias;

7 Ending the practice of "convenience killing" when there are empty cages, animals can share kennels or when the animals are candidates for foster care;

8 Requiring shelters to allow volunteers to help with fostering, socializing and assisting with adoptions; and,

9 Requiring shelters to be truthful about how many animals they kill and adopt by making statistics public.

MODEL LEGISLATION & AN ACTIVIST'S GUIDE TO PASSING LEGISLATION ARE AVAILABLE FOR FREE AT:
NOKILLADVOCACYCENTER.ORG

How Our Nation's Sheltering Crisis Hurts People, Too

IN 1998, CALIFORNIA LEGISLATORS held hearings on whether to make it illegal for shelters to kill animals when non-profit organizations were offering to save them. Some legislators were confused, asking why shelters would want to kill animals who have an immediate place to go. The answer, of course, was *power*. The legislation threatened to open up shelter killing and other atrocities to public scrutiny. As frequent visitors to the shelters, rescuers saw systemic problems and inhumane treatment, but their access to animals was tenuous and many times hinged on not publicly disclosing concerns. Under the pending legislation, their right to rescue would no longer be legally premised on silence as to inhumane shelter practices. The

law, in effect, would create a desperately needed whistleblower provision and allow rescuers to go public without fears of retribution, as evidenced by what one rescuer faced before the law went into effect:

I went to the shelter because I was told they had a mother cat and four kittens that they had scheduled to be killed even though they were healthy. When I arrived to pick up the cat and kittens, the shelter manager asked to see me. She told me that a member of our rescue group wrote a letter complaining about the shelter to the Board of Supervisors and that they didn't appreciate it. She told me I could therefore only have one kitten. I begged her to let me take them all, but she said that I couldn't. She told me to pick one and she was going to euthanize the rest, including the mother cat. I didn't know what to do. And so I picked. My hand was shaking as I filled out the paper work. After I got the kitten, I went outside and sat in the car. Then I threw up all over myself.

Had the California law which has since saved hundreds of thousands of lives been in effect when this rescuer arrived at the shelter she described, its manager would not have been allowed to deny her the right to adopt those animals nor would she have had the ability to emotionally torment the rescuer by forcing her to make a choice that would haunt her for the rest of her life. Stories like these are, in reality, tragically commonplace. When rescue access legislation was pending in New York and Florida, studies found that roughly half of all rescuers routinely look the other way at animal neglect and abuse in shelters for fear of losing their ability to rescue should they ever express their concerns. Other rescuers who did go public told of shelter employees retaliating by killing animals they had offered to save.

These actions were intended to wound people who have expressed concern for the animal victims of shelter neglect, abuse and killing. Day in and day out, these rescuers show tremendous courage and compassion—visiting a place that is hard for animal lovers to go: their local shelter. And yet they go back, again and again. They endure the hostile treatment. They endure the heartbreak of seeing the animals destined for the needle. They endure having to jump through unnecessary and arbitrary hurdles set by shelter directors who are holding hostage the animals they want to save. They endure having to look the other way

at abuse of other animals, because if they don't, if they speak out, they will be barred from saving *any* animals. And yet efforts to protect rescuers, to empower them to save animals, remain the exception nationwide and many recent efforts to pass legislation mandating rescue access rights have been defeated.

Of course, it is the animals who pay the ultimate price when cruel and vindictive shelter workers retaliate against rescuers, but they are not the only ones who suffer. Retaliatory killing of animals is an effective punishment of rescuers because it hits them where it hurts the most. Rescuers do what they do out of sheer love and concern for the well-being of animals. When a particular animal a rescuer has requested is needlessly killed, it can take a heavy emotional toll on that rescuer, leading to feelings of anger, helplessness and despair. And not only does retaliatory killing deny the rescuer what he or she wants—to save a particular animal—the rescuer is often haunted by guilt, left to contemplate whether in singling out a particular animal or openly criticizing the shelter for neglect or abuse, they are somehow culpable in that animal's death.

When, under Nathan's leadership, Tompkins County, New York, became the first No Kill community in U.S. history, much of his initial work involved repairing that agency's broken trust with the community it served, particularly its volunteers. For years, volunteers at that shelter had complained to an inattentive Board of Directors about poor care, dirty facilities and rampant killing only to have those complaints dismissed and ignored. For years, volunteers had to endure the knowledge that animals in their community shelter were being routinely neglected, needlessly killed and at the mercy of a shelter manager so lacking in compassion that she once killed a puppy with muddy paws who jumped up to greet her and soiled her skirt. Another volunteer told of how she had stopped volunteering after two motherless kittens whom she had fostered for the shelter were killed when she returned them to be adopted. Although she had tenderly cared for each of the kittens over the course of several weeks, and though she had told the shelter to let her know if they were ever in any danger so that she could take them back, they were killed without anyone ever calling her:

> I checked the logbook to see when they were adopted. Instead, I was stunned to learn that two of them had been killed. I never even received a telephone call or an email asking that I take them back. They had been perfectly healthy and loved and wanted, and they had a place to go if the shelter ran out of room. I felt sick. The room began spinning. I was in tears. I'll never forget the looks of shock on the faces of the other volunteers. The staff didn't budge. One other volunteer was concerned and tried to stop me from leaving, but I fled the building and somehow managed to bike the several miles home, even though I could barely see for crying.

Nor was her experience out of the ordinary. Many of the volunteers at the shelter were forced to endure emotional hardship in order to help animals. Although these were individuals who volunteered their free time out of love, they were treated with neither gratitude nor respect, but rather resentment and contempt. While lazy, uncaring employees smoked cigarettes and socialized, it was the volunteers who cleaned the cages, fed the animals, counseled potential adopters and, when staff members who had forbidden them to enter the isolation ward weren't looking, administered medication to sick animals who otherwise would have never received it. With their expectation that animals should be kept in clean cages, be given fresh food and water, be socialized, walked, given every opportunity to find a home and be otherwise well-cared for, volunteers found themselves at odds with an organization that resented their "interference."

Retaliatory killing of animals is an effective punishment of rescuers because it hits where it hurts them the most: straight through the heart.

These attitudes expressed themselves through petty vindictiveness and arbitrary displays of power that not only caused needless animal suffering, but created a climate of fear and intimidation that caused volunteers stress and anxiety not just for the animals, but for themselves and each other as well. "Volunteers are more trouble than they are worth," said the shelter manager to Nathan shortly after he arrived (a shelter manager he would soon terminate), even though it was the volunteers who did the lion's share of the work that she and her lazy, uncaring staff refused to. And all of this abuse—to animals, to people and to the citizens of every community whose tax dollars fund local shelters that are run neither humanely nor professionally—comes down to

Although the shelter volunteer had tenderly cared for these four orphaned kittens for several weeks, and though she told shelter employees to let her know if they were ever in any danger so that she could take them back, two of them were killed without anyone ever calling her. She was devastated.

one root cause: corruption fostered by an imbalance of power.

Right now, shelters are the fiefdoms of their directors who can kill almost any animal, almost any time and for any reason. They can exclude members of the community from volunteering. They can prevent other non-profits, such as rescue groups and other shelters, from saving the lives of animals in their custody. And when volunteers or rescuers go public with their concerns, they are terminated. It doesn't have to be this way.

As a society, we owe a particular debt of gratitude to people who voluntarily offer a helping hand to the needy and that includes our nation's homeless animals. Animal rescuers and shelter volunteers are compassionate people who open their hearts and homes to provide a safety-net for animals others may have abandoned and whom our dysfunctional shelters betray even further by killing. And yet those who should be celebrating them as heroes—our nation's animal protection groups—instead denigrate and malign them, paradoxically equating them with some of the cruelest people there are—hoarders and dog fighters—in order to fight legislation that would empower them to overcome shelter directors in community after community who make it impossible to do what should be simple and straightforward—partnering with others to save lives.

Rescue rights and shelter reform laws not only save lives, they foster fairness, respect and consideration for people who both need and deserve it. Animal rescuers and shelter volunteers are already donating their time, their energy, their resources and their love to make our world a better place. They shouldn't have to sacrifice their emotional well-being, too.

THE TACTICS OF NO KILL OPPONENTS

Stifling Innovation & Reform with Fear Mongering & Dishonesty

BULLIES

"We can never be No Kill as long as the public is irresponsible."

"There are simply too many animals and not enough homes for them all."

"Requiring shelters to give animals to rescue groups means putting animals into the hands of hoarders and dog fighters."

"No Kill is very expensive. Our community cannot afford it."

FIFTEEN YEARS AGO, No Kill opponents argued that No Kill was simply impossible. They called it a "hoax," a "marketing ploy" and nothing more than "smoke and mirrors." With No Kill success throughout the nation, these claims have lost traction. With an increasingly informed public and the pressure for reform mounting across the country, those who defend killing have evolved their tactics in several ways.

Some of them are adopting the language of No Kill, but not the programs and services that make it possible. Prior to the achievement of No Kill communities across the country, virtually all shelter administrators openly admitted killing for reasons such as lack of space, antipathy to certain breeds, because the cats were feral, the animals had (highly treatable) illnesses like upper respiratory infection and kennel cough, or because the director claimed there were too many black dogs or cats in the shelter. Some shelter directors today would never be so blatant, so unapologetic for the slaughter. They still kill at an alarming rate, but many are now doing it with a difference. They are falsely claiming they too are No Kill—or very nearly there—and the only animals they kill are "unadoptable." When King County's notoriously abusive shelter claimed to embrace the No Kill philosophy, the death rate did not decline; the number of animals they claimed were "unadoptable" merely skyrocketed. No Kill is not achieved by recategorizing animals; No Kill is achieved by actually saving their lives. Others deflect blame, misrepresent what No Kill is, or tell outright lies.

As animal lovers work to overcome the crisis of cruelty and uncaring endemic to animal shelters, the entrenched opposition—both shelter directors themselves and their allies at animal protection organizations—invariably respond to demands for reform with the excuses highlighted on the following pages.

"We can't be No Kill because we can't adopt out animals who might injure someone, especially a child."

"We have all the No Kill programs but it just doesn't work."

"No Kill advocates are radical extremists."

"No Kill means animals living their entire lives in cages."

"No Kill causes animal suffering."

THE ANIMAL LOVER'S PLAYBOOK

Overcoming the Predictable & Recurring Excuses of the Entrenched Shelter Director

OPPONENT'S MANEUVER: DEFLECT BLAME

Play #1: *"It's pet overpopulation."*
RESPONSE: Pet overpopulation is a myth. Every year, over 23 million people add a new dog or cat to their household, but only three million are killed in shelters for lack of a home.

Play #2: *"It's the irresponsible public's fault."*
RESPONSE: There is still a "public" in No Kill communities. The public did not change, the shelter did. In communities which have ended the killing of savable animals, it is the public which has made the difference in terms of adoptions, volunteerism, donations, foster care and other community support.

Play #3: *"It's too expensive."*
RESPONSE: Not only is there no correlation between a shelter's budget and its save rate, but the programs of the No Kill Equation are more cost-effective than killing: killing costs money; adoptions bring in revenue.

Play #4: *"No Kill threatens public safety."*
RESPONSE: Because the No Kill philosophy does not mandate that vicious dogs be made available for adoption, it is consistent with public safety.

Play #5: *"We tried No Kill. It doesn't work."*
RESPONSE: Half-hearted efforts are not enough. The programs of the No Kill Equation have to be implemented comprehensively so that they completely replace killing.

OPPONENT'S MANEUVER: NO KILL HARMS ANIMALS

Play #6: *"No Kill leads to warehousing."*
RESPONSE: No Kill is about valuing animals, which means not only saving their lives but also giving them good, quality care. It means vaccination on intake, nutritious food, daily socialization and exercise, clean water, medical care and programs to find them all loving, new homes.

Play #7: *"Animal rescuers are dog fighters and hoarders in disguise."*
RESPONSE: Rescuers do not harm animals, they seek to deliver them from it. By contrast, the first time most animals experience neglect or abuse is at the very place that is supposed to protect them from it: the shelter itself.

OPPONENT'S MANEUVER: LIE

Play #8: *"Shelter reformers are seeking outrageous and unreasonable standards for shelters."*
RESPONSE: The programs of the No Kill Equation are reasonable and common sense provisions which most Americans would be shocked to learn are not already followed by every shelter.

Play #9: *"No Kill advocates are extremists and terrorists and working to undermine the humane movement."*
RESPONSE: No Kill activists are regular people from all walks of life, working to expose the hypocrisy between the animal protection movement's professed values and its actions which cause suffering and death. In so doing, they are working to strengthen the cause of animal protection, not weaken it.

IT'S PET OVERPOPULATION

THINK THERE ARE "TOO MANY ANIMALS AND NOT ENOUGH HOMES"?

THINK AGAIN...

Until very recently, the notion that pet overpopulation was to blame for the killing of animals in shelters was undisputed, taken for the gospel truth within the animal protection movement. Why? Because it seemed to provide a logical explanation for the killing: generally, shelters impounded far more animals than they adopted, and this was regarded as the result of an imbalance between supply and demand that could only be addressed by decreasing the supply through spay and neuter programs. But what was conveniently ignored all those years were the facts: in reality, there are many more people looking to bring an animal into their home every year than there are animals being killed in shelters. The problem is not too many animals or too few homes; it is failure to compete effectively for the market share of those homes. Rather than adopting from shelters, people are getting their animals from pet stores, breeders, newspaper ads, friends and other places. In other words, the challenge is in getting those potential homes to adopt shelter animals through comprehensively implemented adoption programs and, it is now understood, forcing shelters to keep animals alive long enough to find new homes.

About eight million animals enter shelters every year. Can shelters find homes for that many animals? The good news is that they don't have to. Some animals need adoption, but others do not. Some animals, like feral cats, need neuter and release. Others will be reclaimed by their families. Some animals will go to rescue groups. Others are irremediably suffering or hopelessly ill and need hospice care or sanctuary. And many can be kept out of the shelter through a comprehensive pet retention effort. While about four million will be killed in pounds and shelters, only three million will be killed for lack of a new home. Can we find homes for those animals? Yes we can.

Statistics show that shelters should be able to find homes for about nine million animals a year with reasonable effort, three times the

> **In the United States, there are 23 million people looking to bring a cat or dog into their home every year, while three million animals are killed in our nation's shelters but for a home. There are many reasons why animals are being killed in shelters. But pet overpopulation is not one of them. It simply does not exist.**

number being killed for lack of a home. In fact, it is more than total impounds. But the news gets even better. There are over 23 million people who are going to get an animal next year. Some are already committed to adopting from a shelter and will already do so. Some are already committed to getting one from a breeder or other commercial source. But 17 million have not decided where that animal will come from and research shows they can be influenced to adopt from a shelter—that's 17 million people potentially vying for roughly three million animals. So even if 80 percent of those people got their animal from somewhere other than a shelter, we could still end the killing.

Not only does the data prove it, but so does the success of the dozens of No Kill communities that now exist throughout the nation, including communities which take in 20 times the per capita intake rate as large metropolitan areas like New York City.

So if there is no pet overpopulation, WHY DO SHELTERS KILL?

There are many reasons why shelters kill animals at this point in time, but pet overpopulation is not one of them. In the case of a small percentage of animals, the animals may be hopelessly sick or injured, or the dogs are so aggressive that placing them would put potential adopters at risk.* Aside from this relatively small number of cases (less than five percent at this time in history and even that is being pushed lower and lower by innovative No Kill shelters), shelters also kill—and mostly kill—for other reasons.

They kill because they make animals sick through sloppy cleaning and poor handling. They kill because they do not want to care for sick animals. They kill because they do not effectively use the internet and the media to promote adoptions. They kill because they think volunteers are more trouble than they are worth, even though those volunteers would help to eliminate the perceived "need" for killing.

They kill because they don't want a foster care program. They kill because they are only open for adoption when people are at work and families have their children in school. They kill because they discourage visitors with their poor customer service. They kill because they do not help people overcome problems that can increase impounds. They kill because they refuse to work with rescue groups. They kill because they haven't embraced TNR for feral cats. They kill because they don't walk or socialize the dogs which make them so highly stressed that they become "cage crazy" and then they kill them for being "cage crazy." They kill because their shoddy temperament tests allow them to claim the animals are "unadoptable." They kill because their draconian laws empower them to kill.

Some kill because they are steeped in a culture of defeatism or because they are under the thumb of regressive health or police

---

* Even this killing is being challenged by the growing sanctuary and hospice care movements. Compassion must be embraced in all its forms, especially when it ensures an animal's right to live.

department oversight. But they still kill. They never say, "We kill because we have accepted killing in lieu of having to put in place foster care, pet retention, volunteer, TNR, public relations and other programs." In short, they kill because they have failed to do what is necessary to stop killing.

THE POWER OF ONE

Seagoville, Texas, had a typical and traditional American shelter. It not only killed dogs and cats, it also did so cruelly by gassing them. In 2011, a new director took over. His first act on his first day was to abolish the gas chamber. He also brought the killing of healthy and treatable animals to an immediate end. Seagoville finished the year with a 97 percent save rate—killing fewer animals all year than used to be killed in a single week.

PLAY #2 IT'S THE IRRESPONSIBLE PUBLIC'S FAULT

We have been told that the public is irresponsible and to blame for the killing. But is it true? Even while virtually all other sectors of the economy plummet, purchases for our companion animals increase every year and increased again in 2011 to over 50 billion dollars. On top of the billions spent on their own animals, Americans also give hundreds of millions more to animal related charities. They miss work when their animals get sick and they cut back on their own needs to meet the needs of their animal companions. Evidence of this caring is all around us, but even rescuers too often dismiss it as the "exception"—even when they are constantly seeing so-called "exceptions." They get letters from people who adopt animals they rescued sharing how much they love their pets. They see people at the dog park or on their morning dog walks. They fail to recognize caring at the veterinarian's office—the waiting rooms always full, the faces of scared people wondering what is wrong, the tears as they emerge from the exam rooms after saying goodbye for the last time. They don't see that books about animals who have touched people's lives are not only being written in ever-increasing numbers but are often bestsellers because people do care, and the stories touch them very deeply and very personally. They don't see that the success of movies about animals is also a reflection of the love people have for them. And, more importantly, they fail to recognize that No Kill success throughout the country is a result of people—*people who care deeply*. Caring is not the exception; it is the rule.

There are now No Kill communities nationwide. Some of these communities are in the North, some in the South. Some are urban, some rural. Some are public shelters; some are private. Some are in what we call "blue" or left-leaning states and some are in very conservative parts of the country—at least one is in the reddest part of the reddest state. No matter the

In communities that have achieved No Kill success, the public didn't change, the shelter's own policies and procedures did.

location, no matter the particular demographics of a community, No Kill success nationwide proves that there is enough love and compassion for animals in every community to overcome the irresponsibility of the few.

Existing No Kill successes prove that there is enough love and compassion in every community to overcome the irresponsibility of the few.

Moreover, in those communities which have ended the killing, it is the public which has made the difference: in terms of adoptions, volunteerism, donations, foster care and other community support. So defenders of killing need to put to bed, once and for all, the idea that dogs and cats—animals most Americans now consider cherished members of their families—need to die in U.S. shelters because people are irresponsible and don't care enough about them.

IT'S THEIR JOB

Animal shelters are supposed to provide a safety net, just like other social service agencies which deal with the effects of human irresponsibility. The difference? The others don't use "public irresponsibility" as an excuse to avoid their obligation to put into place the necessary programs to respond humanely and effectively. Imagine if Child Protective Services took in abused, abandoned and unwanted children and then killed them. We should no more tolerate it for animals.

PLAY #3 IT'S TOO EXPENSIVE

With municipalities facing financial pressures across the nation and, as a result, cutting programs and services to their communities, arguing that No Kill is too expensive is a common tactic employed by regressive shelter directors to defray criticism and decrease lifesaving expectations. Yet thankfully, many of the programs identified as key components of saving lives are more cost-effective than impounding, warehousing and then killing animals. Some rely on private philanthropy, as in the use of rescue groups, which shift costs of care from public taxpayers to private individuals and groups. Others, such as the use of volunteers, augment paid human resources. Still others, such as adoptions, bring in revenue. And, finally, some, such as neutering rather than killing feral cats, are simply less expensive both immediately and in the long-term, with exponential savings in terms of reducing births.

In addition, a multi-state study found no correlation between per capita funding for animal control and save rates. One community saved 90 percent of the animals, while another saved only 40 percent despite four times the per capita rate of spending on animal control. One community has seen killing rates increase over 30 percent despite one of the best-funded shelter systems in the nation. Another has caused death rates to drop by 50 percent despite cutting spending.

Moreover, as most shelter costs are fixed, keeping additional animals alive does not dramatically increase costs. Since it takes roughly the same amount of time to clean a kennel as it does to kill an animal, staff increases often prove unnecessary, with the added financial benefit that cleaning requires less-skilled, less-expensive labor and can be augmented through unpaid volunteer support. Not only do the cost-effective programs that make No Kill possible benefit a municipality's bottom line, they can be enhanced with the free support of nonprofit organizations and volunteers. In San Francisco during the 1990s, volunteers spent over 110,000 hours at the shelter each year. Assuming the then-prevailing hourly wage, it would have cost the agency over one million dollars to provide those services.

All too often, however, volunteers and rescuers are prevented from assisting by regressive policies in shelters across the country. Even in those communities that allow them, traditional shelters find it difficult to retain volunteers who do not want to work in an environment of killing. By adopting the No Kill philosophy, shelter volunteer rates increase dramatically. In Reno, Nevada, the local humane society increased the number of volunteers from 30 to nearly 8,000 after launching its No Kill initiative. In addition, the number of foster homes increased from a handful to almost 2,500, all of whom help save lives at little cost to the shelter. The services volunteers provide reduce expenses, while increasing capacity and the animals they save are then adopted out, bringing in additional adoption revenue to the shelter.

NO KILL MAKES DOLLARS & SENSE

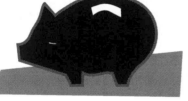

Many of the programs identified as key components of saving lives are more cost-effective than impounding, warehousing and then killing animals. Some shift costs to private philanthropy. Others bring in revenue. Still others are simply less expensive or foster exponential savings over the long-term.

Before Reno's No Kill initiative, the shelter adopted out fewer than 5,000 dogs and cats every year. The rest were put to death at great cost to taxpayers and donors. In 2010, as death rates declined, the number of animals adopted doubled to just under 10,000. In

Dedication Matters More Than Money

A multi-state study found that there was no correlation between rates of lifesaving and per capita spending on animal control. The difference between those shelters that succeeded at saving lives and those that failed was not the size of the budget, but the commitment of their directors to implementing alternatives to killing.

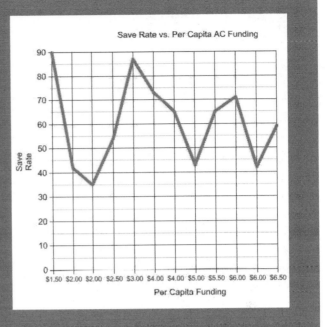

addition to a cost savings of roughly $200,000 associated with killing, adoption fees brought in almost $250,000 in additional revenues. Moreover, the positive impact of economic spending by adopters on those animals to community businesses totaled over 12 million dollars in annual sales. With an average lifespan of roughly 10 years per animal, the total revenues to community businesses over the life of those pets could potentially top 120 million dollars.

The number is substantially higher given that those impacts are exponential (in year two, businesses would benefit from two years worth of adoptions; in year three, they would benefit from three years of adoptions). In addition, not only do those businesses then employ people who turn around and spend even more, all these activities also bring in badly needed tax revenues. At an average six percent rate, adoptions over a 10-year period could potentially bring in over 20 million dollars in sales tax alone.

While many of these economic benefits will be realized even if people acquire their animals from commercial sources like breeders, cost savings and other revenues will not be.* For one, the animals will not be sterilized before adoption, requiring the shelter to absorb the costs of taking in the offspring of some of those animals. Moreover, the municipality will not benefit from the decreased costs and increased revenue associated with adopting the animals to those homes. Finally, a successful adoption marketing program not only results in citizens who are more likely to adopt from a shelter, but it can increase the number of available homes as well by inspiring local citizens to feel like valued allies in the shelter's lifesaving mission, thereby encouraging them to open their homes to additional animals.

* In addition to the fact that animals are under the constant threat of a death sentence in many shelters, some commercially-sourced animals come from mills which contribute to animal cruelty.

NO KILL THREATENS PUBLIC SAFETY

When No Kill advocates were trying to reform their local shelter in Illinois, the shelter's director replied that, "We can't be No Kill because we can't adopt out vicious dogs who might injure someone, especially a child." The fear mongering had its intended effect. Local politicians claimed that though they loved animals, they had to put the welfare and safety of people, especially children, first. It was, they claimed, irresponsible to suggest otherwise. But no one was and the shelter's regressive director knew it.

A No Kill community is one where no healthy or treatable animals are killed. Unfortunately, there are some animals who are hopelessly ill or injured, irremediably suffering or in the case of dogs, aggressive with a poor prognosis for rehabilitation. These animals are often not adoption candidates and, at this time in history, are killed, unless shelters also embrace hospice and sanctuary care. And while many shelters

are having great success placing animals many would have considered "unadoptable" in years past and those efforts will continue and accelerate in the coming years with greater innovation in veterinary and behavior medicine, because the No Kill philosophy does not mandate that vicious dogs be made available for adoption, it is consistent with public safety.

WE TRIED NO KILL, IT DIDN'T WORK

Killing is a choice. It is a choice made by the person who runs a shelter to take the easy, uncaring and inhumane way out. No Kill is also a choice. It is a choice made by the person who runs the shelter to replace that killing with alternatives. Its success is therefore directly proportional to the commitment that is made to it. A shelter director who claims to have tried "No Kill," but who then sent one litter of motherless kittens into a foster home and the other litter into the kill room, has failed to make

the necessary level of commitment required to replace killing entirely. In such circumstances, No Kill has not failed. It offered an alternative, a choice—in this case, foster care—that the director willfully chose to disregard in favor of killing. Likewise, a shelter committed to No Kill does not neuter and release some feral cats while killing others. Other than not allowing them to enter shelters in the first place as some communities have done, TNR becomes the primary lifesaving option for feral cats. A

CHOICE

Shelter killing is not an inevitability imposed onto shelters by outside forces. Whether animals entering shelters live or die comes down to one thing: the choices made by the people who run them.

shelter committed to No Kill does not merely allow rescue groups access to animals "some of the time," but every time a rescue group is willing to take over care and custody of an animal. Indeed, a No Kill shelter actively seeks these groups out.

Unfortunately, many shelters claim they have tried No Kill but that it did not work. This claim is based on the fact that they may have implemented some or all of the programs, but not enough of them or not to the point that they

replace killing. In 2004, for example, one SPCA in a city of 1.5 million people conducted roughly 150 free spay/neuter surgeries for the companion animals of the community's low-income population. The shelter's director boasted of a low-cost and free spay/neuter program, but such a token level of surgeries in a large city where one in four people fall below the federal poverty line, will not impact the number of animals entering city shelters. By contrast, another SPCA, in a city with roughly half the population, performed over 9,000 surgeries a year, 84 percent of them for free.

Similarly, animal control in another community allowed only employees to participate in its foster care program. The shelter claimed it was already implementing the programs and services of the No Kill Equation, but it was excluding thousands of animal lovers from participating in the lifesaving effort, seriously limiting how many lives they saved. And a municipal shelter in yet another community boasted of an offsite adoption program, of which they do two a year, less than a No Kill shelter which does seven offsite locations each and every day.

At a well managed No Kill shelter, the size and scope of programs are determined by one thing alone: *need*. Convenience and traditional sheltering dogma that excuse and condone killing are abandoned in favor of both proven solutions that don't, and the flexibility and imagination to respond to extraordinary circumstances with similarly extraordinary determination. Successful No Kill shelter

WHEN LIFE GIVES YOU ORANGES...

The Great Orange Cat Rescue

September 18 - October 18

Adoptions $10 for Adult Orange Cats
6 months or older

2825 Longley Lane, Reno, NV 89502
www.nevadahumanesociety.org
775 856 2000

In 2007, the Nevada Humane Society took in 54 orange cats from an alleged hoarder. At a traditional shelter, animals from such households are often killed, while the shelter director claims that there is simply no choice because there are too many animals for the too few homes available. Thankfully, NHS is not a "traditional" shelter. As with the 11 other hoarding cases the shelter has handled since it embraced the No Kill philosophy, creative outreach to the public resulted in loving, new homes for all the animals. None were killed. Moreover, the shelter reaped the rewards from a grateful public, too. The people of Reno were so touched by "The Great Orange Cat Rescue" that the shelter quickly raised all the money it needed to cover medical care for the cats—and most of it from individuals who had never donated to the shelter before. One man who loved orange cats was so moved by their response that he sent them a $5,000 donation just to say, "Thank you."

If a shelter does good things for animals, tells people about it and then asks for their help, people will give it.

directors maintain a commitment to No Kill even in times of crisis or unanticipated circumstances (such as a dog fighting, hoarding or animal cruelty case that might result in a large influx of animals) with creative alternatives to killing that harness the power of the public's love and compassion for animals. In short, they turn challenges into opportunities, rather than use those challenges as an excuse to kill.

To achieve No Kill success, therefore, a shelter must implement the programs and services of the No Kill Equation not in a piecemeal or in a limited manner, but comprehensively. Shelters must take killing off the table for all savable animals, and utilize the No Kill Equation not sometimes, not merely when it is convenient or politically expedient to do so, but for every single animal, every single time.

PLAY #6 NO KILL LEADS TO WAREHOUSING

In February 2007, a Las Vegas, Nevada, shelter that claimed to be "No Kill" was closed down due to filthy conditions and inhumane treatment of animals. According to reports, disease was rampant and sick animals were left to die in their cages. The animals were not vaccinated on intake, healthy animals subsequently grew sick and there was a complete breakdown of animal care. The Las Vegas shelter's story is one of incompetent leadership, a Board of Directors that failed in its oversight mandate and a director who refused to put in place programs that actually save the lives of animals. What happened in Las Vegas is a tragic example of uncaring rampant in our broken animal shelter system.

Another example of institutionalized uncaring are shelters that recklessly kill the vast majority of animals in their care in the face of alternatives: in other words, run-of-the-mill high-kill shelters such as those that can be found across America. While the mechanics are different, the underlying dynamic is the same: both types of shelters are run by people who do not truly care about animals. The Las Vegas shelter's "No Kill" claim is irrelevant. In the final analysis, it had more in common with its killing counterparts and the leadership and staff who run them, than those running truly successful and compassionate No Kill shelters.

Conditions at the Las Vegas animal shelter— rampant disease, filth, neglect and animal suffering—do not represent the No Kill movement. No Kill does not mean poor care and abusive treatment, and warehousing animals minus the intentional killing. It means

The "No Kill leads to warehousing" argument is a cynicism which has only one purpose: to shield those who fail to save lives from public criticism and public accountability by painting a picture of the alternative as even darker.

WHERE WOULD *YOU* RATHER BE?

A NO KILL SHELTER

Animals in true No Kill shelters are not in filthy, cramped cages nor do they wait months or years to be adopted. On the contrary, at a well-run No Kill shelter the animals are housed in clean, well-lighted environments, are fed nutritious food, receive good quality medical care, and are socialized daily by volunteers while they wait for a good home, one that the vast majority of animals find quickly. Contrast the following images from No Kill shelters with those from traditional, high-kill shelters. If you were an animal, where would you rather be?

(ABOVE) Dogs wait for adoption at this spacious No Kill shelter in Minnesota. The physical shelter is reflective of how caring the programs and staff are.

(ABOVE) Cats lounge about and enjoy the sun and fresh air in this cat colony room in a clean, caring, comfortable No Kill shelter in Nevada.

(LEFT) A cat begs for food in King County's abusive pound. Cats were not fed at the shelter during a long holiday weekend. An employee who came forward as a whistleblower was threatened with violence by other staff. PETA told the County Council not to listen to "radicals" who wanted to improve conditions.

(RIGHT) A dog and her puppies at a Texas animal control shelter. Diarrhea is all over the cage, floor and in the water bowl.

(LEFT) At the same shelter, a suffering puppy is left in a cold metal cage with no blanket or towel on which to lie. She can barely keep her head up and urinates all over herself. At this shelter, staff has drowned puppies, not fed kittens and one employee beat a dog but was not fired. Employees who scored the lowest on city aptitude tests were placed in animal control. PETA has also defended this shelter, urging city officials not to listen to reformers.

OR A KILL SHELTER

modernizing shelter operations so that animals are well cared for and kept moving efficiently and effectively through the shelter and into homes. The No Kill movement puts action behind the words of every shelter's mission statement: "All life is precious." No Kill is about valuing animals, which means not only saving their lives but also giving them good quality care.

Predictably, HSUS seized upon the tragedy in Las Vegas to promote their own agenda of defending an antiquated model of sheltering based on archaic notions of "adoptability," regressive practices and the premise that animal life is cheap and expendable. They used the Las Vegas shelter to denounce the No Kill paradigm by intimating that the Las Vegas example is the natural outcome of trying to end the killing of savable dogs and cats in shelters today, and they use the "No Kill equals warehousing" argument to undermine shelter reform efforts nationwide.

In fact, roughly 1,000 animals lost their lives at the hands of the HSUS team that came in, needles blazing, to "help" the animals in Las Vegas. To HSUS, helping animals meant putting them to death. Today, by following HSUS policies that favor killing, that Las Vegas shelter kills many animals without offering them for adoption.

> **Roughly 1,000 animals lost their lives at the hands of the HSUS team that came in, needles blazing, to "help" the animals in Las Vegas. To HSUS, helping animals meant putting them to death.**

HSUS is not alone in using the No Kill equals warehousing tactic to fight No Kill. Both the ASPCA and the National Animal Control Association have also equated No Kill shelters with hoarding. According to one article from NACA,

> Dogs and cats linger for weeks, sometime months, in tiny, cramped cages with barely room to move... dogs are rarely walked. They may sit in their own waste because overworked kennel workers hardly have time to clean more than once a day. Cats face a similar fate. Shelter managers can boast of decreased euthanasia rates, yet from the animal's point of view, is their suffering worth it?

The article ends by asking the question whether it "is compassionate to force dogs and cats to live their lives in small, confined spaces for weeks or months at a time when their chances for adoption are slim to none?"

The calculus, however, is far from "slim to none." First, it would be far preferable for an animal to endure a few "weeks or months" in a shelter before moving on to a loving, new home than to be killed out of convenience. Second, these animals are not in filthy, cramped cages at true No Kill shelters. At well-run No Kill shelters, the animals are housed in clean, well-lighted environments, are fed nutritious food, receive good quality medical care, and are socialized daily by volunteers who walk them, groom them, pet them and play with them while they wait for a good home. And they are not waiting weeks or months or even years. At one open admission No Kill shelter, the average length of stay was only eight days and no animal ever celebrated an anniversary there. At another, it is 14 days, roughly the same amount of time as an average stay for animals at a boarding kennel while their families are on vacation.

By denigrating the movement to end shelter killing as akin to warehousing and abuse, and by ignoring the protocols of shelters which have truly achieved No Kill and are clean, well-run and successful, these naysayers embrace a nation of shelters grounded in killing—a defeatist mentality, inherently unethical and antithetical to animal welfare.

ANIMAL RESCUERS ARE HOARDERS & DOG FIGHTERS

Right now, the goals of the No Kill movement are two-fold: to save the lives of animals by reforming our nation's broken animal sheltering system, and until we achieve that goal, to get animals facing death in these shelters immediately out of harm's way. To do the former, some animal advocates focus on political advocacy to force implementation of the No Kill Equation at their local shelter or by seeking shelter reform legislation. To achieve the latter, other advocates focus their energy on rescue, saving animals from death row at their local shelter and finding them homes through organizations founded for this purpose.

Unfortunately, too many shelters are unwilling to voluntarily give animals to rescue groups. In 2010, the president of the ASPCA vowed to defeat rescue access legislation in New York. To do so, the ASPCA argued that allowing animal rescue groups to save animals on death row in New York State shelters would mean placing them in the hands of dog fighters and hoarders. It was an argument that the HSUS-led opposition to shelter reform bills in other states used the following year to dissuade legislators. And in Minnesota, it was the main claim made by the Animal Humane Society which parroted HSUS and the ASPCA when it coordinated opposition to that state's shelter reform bill, even going so far as to spend donor funds to

Rescuers are animal lovers, many of whom have started their organizations after volunteering at their local shelter and realizing that if the shelter wasn't going to do what was necessary to save lives, *they* would.

hire a public relations firm to promulgate this view. In Virginia, Florida, Georgia and elsewhere, efforts to empower rescue groups to save the animals shelters are intent on killing have been defeated using the same arguments.

ANIMAL SHELTERING IN AMERICA
MEET KAPONE

MEET KAPONE. In June of 2011, Kapone and another dog escaped from their yard near Memphis, Tennessee. A neighbor reported seeing the dogs picked up by a Memphis Animal Control Officer, and records show that, indeed, the officer picked up two dogs, but only one made it to the shelter. What happened to Kapone?

For months, Kapone's family demanded an answer to this question from Memphis Animal Services but was never given one. Kapone was considered a "Pit Bull," and there was great concern that employees at MAS had sold their dog to dog fighters. They were right to be concerned, because not only was the Animal Control Officer who picked up Kapone a convicted felon (knowledge MAS had when she was hired), but when the Memphis Police Department busted a dog fighting ring and took the animals to MAS at an earlier date, the

dogs mysteriously disappeared shortly thereafter. Becuase there were no signs of forced entry, it was suspected to be an inside job. In fact, a later audit of the organization revealed a broadly held suspicion that MAS employees have ties to dog fighting.

Kapone's family didn't give up, and because the case received a lot of publicity, a Crime Stoppers' tip ultimately revealed Kapone's whereabouts, and he was found under suspicious circumstances in a backyard in another state with other (neglected) "Pit Bulls." When animal protection organizations fear monger that giving animals in animal control shelters to non-profit rescue organizations would place them in harm's way, remember Kapone and who it was that delivered him to that very fate.

Kapone, back home and playing with his boy.

Logic and fairness—both to rescuers and the animals—demand that altruistic people who devote their time and energy to helping shelter animals stop being equated with mentally ill people who cause them harm.

Animal hoarding, however, is the result of mental illness and is not as common as many animal protection organizations would have us believe. Psychologists estimate that only two percent of the population suffers from hoarding, and of those, not all of them "collect" animals—many collect inanimate objects. And only four percent of animals in shelters are there because of abuse or dog fighting. By contrast, an animal at an "average" shelter has a 50 percent chance of being killed. In places like Montgomery County, North Carolina the odds are more extreme: 99 percent of animals are killed. And because rescue groups generally only save those animals scheduled to be killed, there is a 100 percent chance the animal will die without them.

To suggest that we must protect animals from rescuers is backward thinking. If we care about saving animals, we must save them from *shelters* by putting them in the hands of *rescuers*. Moreover, logic and fairness—both to rescuers and the animals—demand that altruistic people who devote their time and energy to helping shelter animals stop being equated with mentally ill people who cause them harm.

Shelter killing is the leading cause of death for healthy dogs and cats in the United States.

In the end, it is not hoarders or dog fighters or cruel people who are responsible for the greatest harm to befall healthy dogs and cats in this country. The number one cause of death for these animals is the local shelter. To truly protect animals, the mandate is clear: *get them out of shelters.*

THE HOARDING CARD

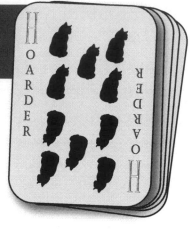

THERE IS NO QUESTION that the effects of hoarding are tragic: animals live in their own waste, are denied food and water for long periods of time, do not get necessary veterinary care, are sometimes crammed into crowded cages and do not receive walks or regular exercise, all of which result in tremendous suffering and often death. Hoarding is cruel, painful and abhorrent. But what does it have to do with giving rescuers the legal right to save animals scheduled to be killed in shelters? The answer is nothing. Nonetheless, it is a card those opposed to such laws like to play as part of their fear mongering to defeat them. Their real concern is not the animals (if it was, they wouldn't be neglecting and abusing the animals themselves or putting them under the constant threat of a death sentence). Instead, they are opposed to empowering rescuers who would be protected as whistleblowers if the laws were passed. And so they demonize animal rescuers in the hopes of confusing the issue and thereby defeating such laws.

Unfortunately, when hoarding cases are brought to the attention of authorities and these cases make the news, some hoarders claim to be "No Kill shelters" or "animal rescuers" as a means of escaping culpability. And the groups opposed to rescue rights laws exploit that. In reality, hoarders have nothing in common with true animal rescuers, individuals who have founded non-profit organizations, who must report annually to the Internal Revenue Service, their state's Attorney General and often a State Department of Charities. They have a Board of Directors which oversees them, they maintain a network of volunteer foster homes and make animals available for adoption to the public, unlike hoarders who refuse to let their animals go. Non-profit rescue organizations seek to provide animals with care that is the *opposite* of that inflicted on animals by hoarders; and often inflicted by shelters themselves, which are rife with neglect, abuse and killing as well.

HELPING ANIMALS BY HELPING PEOPLE

One morning after Tompkins County became a No Kill community, a woman brought in a stray cat she had found. She explained to Nathan how this was the first time she had ever brought an animal into a shelter. In the past, whenever she found a lost, sick or stray animal, she took the animal home. She explained how she often felt overwhelmed by the amount of animals she had to care for, but she didn't have a choice because the shelter would have killed any cats she found and brought in, something she would never allow to happen. She then expressed her relief and gratitude that Tompkins County was now No Kill, and therefore an agency she could turn to for help.

Although animal protection organizations and regressive shelters like to fear monger that "No Kill equals hoarding," in reality, it is the traditional model of animal sheltering that increases the chances of people becoming overwhelmed with large numbers of animals. In communities where shelters are killing, people rationalize that they have no choice but to keep animals they find because the shelter will only kill them. Moreover, when the directors of killing shelters go on the news after a large seizure only to condemn "hoarders" and claim they had no choice but to kill all the animals, other people in the community with more animals than they can adequately care for will not come forward for help. In fact, in one community which guarantees they will not kill any medically and behaviorally savable animals, they have helped 11 alleged "hoarders" empty their homes, without a single animal losing his life. Some of these people came forward for help on their own.

ANIMAL SHELTERING IN AMERICA
MEET THE ST. ANTHONY CATS

Meet the St. Anthony cats. In 2009, the Animal Humane Society (AHS) in Minnesota seized over 100 cats from a mobile home in St. Anthony, Minnesota. A No Kill shelter and rescue groups offered to take the cats in order to ensure their safety, but AHS, for years an ardent adversary of No Kill, refused. Within just 48 hours of seizing the cats, they killed them all.

To prevent this sort of senseless tragedy from recurring, a legislator introduced the Minnesota Companion Animal Protection Act (CAPA), which—among other things—would have mandated rescue access. This law would have leveled the playing field between Minnesota's large non-profit animal protection organizations like AHS and their smaller counterparts which are prevented from fulfilling

their mission—saving the lives of animals.

Predictably, AHS opposed this legislation. In a letter sent to their donors, they argued that the law would force them to give animals to hoarders, which would lead to animal suffering. In fact, these types of laws require no such thing. Despite the fact that killing in shelters is so common and hoarding so rare, the various bills have plenty of safeguards.

These laws—of which Minnesota CAPA was no exception—exclude organizations which have a volunteer, staff member, director and/or officer with a conviction for animal neglect, cruelty and/or dog fighting and suspend the organization while such charges are pending. In addition, the bills require the rescue group to be a not-for-profit organization, recognized under Internal Revenue Code Section 501(c)(3). As a result, they must register with the federal government and with several state agencies, providing a number of checks and balances.

In fact, surveys in other states have found that over 90 percent of respondents who rescued animals but were not 501(c)(3) organizations would become so if such a law passed in their state, effectively *increasing* oversight of rescue organizations. Moreover, some of these laws specifically allow shelters to charge an adoption fee for animals they send to rescue groups, which would further protect animals from being placed in hoarding situations. Finally, nothing in these laws require shelters to work with specific rescue groups. They are free to work with other rescue organizations if they choose and they are also free to adopt out the animals themselves. What they cannot do, what they should not be permitted to do, is to kill animals when those animals have a place to go.

In addition to lying to donors about the bill, AHS ignored the fact that far from putting animals at risk, it was written to protect animals from harm—the kind of harm caused by shelters like AHS. When AHS killed over 100 cats from an alleged hoarder in St. Anthony, it was AHS itself that inflicted the greatest harm that ever befell those cats: death. They killed them, even when they could have cared for them themselves or allowed others to do so.

<table>
<tr><td>PLAY
#8</td><td>SHELTER REFORM EFFORTS ARE UNREASONABLE</td></tr>
</table>

Shelter reform laws mandating the No Kill Equation already exist, in part, in states such as California and Delaware, in local communities such as Austin, Texas, and have been introduced in Virginia, Florida, Minnesota, Rhode Island, Texas, Georgia, New York and elsewhere. One of the key tools No Kill opponents use to defeat such laws is to lie about what the bills require.

No Kill opponents work to defeat shelter reform and rescue access laws by lying about their requirements. Their goal is to make these important laws which mandate simple, common sense procedures appear unreasonable and a threat both to public safety and the animals themselves.

Their goal is to make such laws appear unreasonable and a threat both to public safety and the animals themselves.

Although in places where these laws are already in effect, lifesaving has increased and none of the predicted fears have come to pass, that has not stopped the opposition from repeating their lies over and over again. In New York, a rescue rights law was opposed on the grounds that it would have threatened public safety by mandating the release of dangerous animals, even though the legislation specifically excluded dogs who have been deemed dangerous or had a history of vicious behavior. Although the bill specifically excluded people who have been convicted of animal cruelty to qualify for rescue and allowed inspections of rescue groups, they stated that the law would have forced shelters to give animals to animal abusers.

One shelter director opposed to shelter reform legislation in Florida went so far as to claim that the bill pending in that state was unfair to rescue groups because it required those rescue groups to take animals from shelters at their own expense even if they did not want to. Of course, the legislation did no such thing. Such a law would be unconstitutional and illegal. But these lies had their intended effect, and in both cases (and others), legislators—even well-meaning legislators who love animals and thought they were doing the right thing because these groups, in their minds, represented the best interests of animals—listened to these "experts," believed their lies and opposed the laws.

STEP RIGHT UP AND LIE

In January 2012, when the Florida Senate held hearings on the Florida Animal Rescue Act, an animal law attorney and former law professor described the opposition at the first hearing:

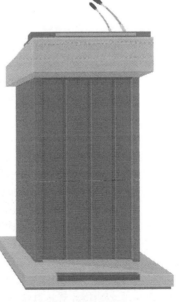

"[I]t was abundantly clear that all of these groups have one goal, and that is to protect the status quo. They are so hell bent on doing that that they stood before a legislative body and disseminated false and misleading information, and they did it in a concerted, organized fashion... Afterward they all huddled as a group in the hallway laughing and slapping each other on their backs at their 'success' of getting this bill tabled. It was nauseating to think that their celebration was at the cost of the lives of innocent companion animals who deserve so much better."

NO KILL REFORMERS ARE EXTREMISTS

It is an age-old story: if you can't attack the message, attack the messenger. When animal lovers try to reform their local shelters, these shelters—and the animal protection groups which defend them—often create a distraction by arguing that No Kill activists themselves are harming animals by criticizing the groups which help them. HSUS has a history of referring to people who want to reform deplorable sheltering practices as "divisive" and asserting that such people hurt animals by creating strife and fostering discontent within the animal protection movement. PETA tells their followers that No Kill activists are not really animal lovers at all, but people with a hidden, secret agenda to destroy the animal rights movement.

SMEAR THE MESSENGER

These groups, as well as shelter directors under scrutiny in their own communities, frequently respond to concerns about their own sordid actions by arguing that everyone should work together to defeat "our common enemy"— those who exploit animals. What this argument conveniently ignores, however, is that in causing the needless killing and suffering of animals in shelters, *they* are the enemy. To fail to take them to task, therefore, is to abandon the cause of No Kill itself. It is to admit and accept defeat and to condone the unending slaughter of innocent animals who can and should be saved.

Moreover, their argument ignores that movements for social justice are not about organizations or the individuals who work at them. They are, first and foremost, about ideals. Authentic and effective advocates are duty-bound to recognize that it is not *who* is right,

but *what* is right and orient their advocacy accordingly, regardless of what label an organization may claim: SPCA, humane society, shelter or animal rights group. Indeed, standing up to those who claim to be "friends" of animals—the very shelters and animal protection organizations that kill, defend the killing and are working to thwart the reform that would end it—is the only way the No Kill movement can ever hope to fully succeed, and the only way the animal protection movement as a whole can ever reach its fullest potential.

For in practicing and condoning shelter killing, the animal protection movement opens itself up to valid censure for its own hypocrisy. Right now, there is a double standard within the animal protection movement, one that (rightfully) condemns the abuse and killing of animals, except (wrongfully) when that abuse and killing occurs in our nation's shelters. This position weakens the movement's credibility and gives those who exploit or kill animals in other

> **It is not *who* is right, but *what* is right that matters. Standing up to those who claim to be "friends" of animals but in reality defend their killing and work to thwart the reform that would end it is the only way the animal protection movement can ever reach its fullest potential.**

contexts a convenient means of deflecting criticism. Moreover, it blinds activists to the important gains that could be easily made for all animals through No Kill if only the animal protection movement stopped getting in its own way.

Today, not only do we have a solution to shelter killing, but we also have an American public ready and willing to make it happen. Through the No Kill movement, we can create a country in which it is illegal to kill animals who enter shelters. We can create a country in which children are raised with higher expectations for the treatment of animals—and an understanding and acceptance that animals have legal rights. And we can establish powerful advocates for the well-being of animals in every community by reclaiming the thousands of shelters across our nation, and reorienting them away from killing and back to their founding missions: to advocate for and save animals.

In failing to fully exploit this stunning potential, we are failing all animals who would benefit from the powerful legal, philosophical and societal precedents the animal protection

movement could realize through the achievement of a No Kill nation. Yet we are prevented from harvesting this low-hanging fruit by the very groups who should be leading the charge to reap it.

In the end, those who defend the paradigm of killing are betraying not just animals in shelters, but the entire animal protection movement and by extension, all animals in need of effective advocacy. They are the ones harming the animal protection movement, not those who are seeking ethical and philosophical consistency and all the benefits that would come of it.

Is 5 a Magic Number?

IN 2003, surrounded by fanfare and what would eventually amount to tens of millions of dollars flowing into their coffers, the Mayor's Alliance for New York City's Animals announced a plan to make New York City shelters No Kill by 2008. This was not the first time it had been promised. Earlier, New Yorkers had been promised a No Kill city by 2005. Within a few years, the Mayor's Alliance realized they were failing. Publicly, they assured everyone they were "on track" to achieve it.

In 2007, they announced a new five-year plan, promising No Kill by 2012. And, yet again, despite public assurances they were "on track," in 2010—as if the previous five-year plans were never announced—they rebranded the current one as a "ten-year" plan, promising No Kill in New York City by 2015. Once again, they claim to be "on track" to achieve it, even while the New York City municipal shelter system was then and is now a den of rampant neglect, abuse and systematic killing—one of the worst in the nation.

Anyone familiar with the systematic culture of failure of the New York City pound system, and the callous indifference of groups like the Mayor's Alliance and the ASPCA, knows that 2015 will also come and go, and far from achieving No Kill, the groups will announce a new five-year No Kill plan. And whatever the results, the private acknowledgment of failure will be ignored in favor of the public claims that they will be "on track" to achieve it at some new date in the future. No matter. With resources coming into groups like the Mayor's Alliance and the ASPCA from ever-willing-to-help, animal-loving New Yorkers, there is no downside.

In fact, while the Mayor's Alliance is taking in millions by claiming a serial string of five-year plans, other animal protection groups are also realizing that claiming a five-year plan to No Kill will not only fend off criticism about killing today—kicking the can of accountability into the future—but is also very lucrative. As a result, they are announcing five-year plans of their own, promising the public that the light is at the end of the five-year tunnel, if the public just digs deeper and donates more.

Maddie's Fund, a national foundation that is funding the New York City "No Kill" initiative, is also claiming—as part of its own cycle of fail-to-deliver five-year plans—that the whole nation will magically become No Kill by 2015; that every single shelter in every single community in every single state will have ended

"Come back in five years when we will magically pull No Kill out of this hat!"

Five-year No Kill plans don't work because they are not supposed to. They are not sincere, but rather a means of stifling criticism or raising money by creating the impression that plans are underway that will someday—in the future—finally bring the killing to an end. Meanwhile, the actions necessary to actually make No Kill happen—instituting alternatives to killing and reforming the shelter—are never taken. And so the five years come and go, and the killing continues unabated.

It doesn't take five years to implement alternatives to killing. It doesn't take five years to set up a foster program, to recruit volunteers, or to set up offsite adoption venues. All of these things can be done in a matter of weeks or even days—whatever need dictates to prevent killing. No Kill requires action, not endless planning.

the killing of healthy and treatable animals by achieving save rates of roughly 95 percent, even as No Kill advocates nationwide battle hostile and entrenched shelter directors backed by the nation's largest animal protection groups.

In New York City (as well as Contra Costa County in California, the entire state of Utah, Maricopa County in Arizona and everywhere else that the public has been promised a five-year plan to No Kill by Maddie's Fund), it didn't happen and it won't happen—at least under the current leadership. It won't happen nationally by 2015. That is because it has *never*

happened when it's been promised as part of a five-year plan to No Kill.

Five-year No Kill plans don't work because they are not supposed to. Those who promise them aren't really interested in delivering success because their priorities lie elsewhere. Five-year plans are a means of stifling criticism or raising money by creating the impression that plans are underway that will someday bring the killing to an end.

Meanwhile, the action necessary to actually make No Kill happen—*reforming the shelter*—is never undertaken. People are asked to spay/neuter more, to adopt more and—here's the rub—to donate a lot more, but the shelter is let off the hook. In fact, as part of the five-year collaboration, No Kill advocates are not allowed to ask for policy, program or personnel changes at the local shelter, because even though this is the very place where the needless killing occurs, they are told that the shelter is a "partner" in the five-year No Kill plan.

And so the five years come and go and the killing continues because no one did what was really necessary to stop it; while those in charge keep their fingers crossed that everyone has forgotten the empty promises that made them very rich, so they can start the whole process over again and make even more money.

The truth is it doesn't take five years to implement alternatives to killing. It doesn't take five years to set up a foster program, to recruit volunteers or to set up offsite adoption venues. All of these things can be done in a matter of weeks, or even days; whatever need dictates to prevent killing. No Kill requires action, not endless planning and five years of fundraising.

In fact, the communities across the country that have ended the killing of healthy and treatable animals did so virtually overnight.

In Austin, City Council members gave shelter leadership a maximum of two years, removed the director who was the primary roadblock to No Kill success and unanimously embraced a shelter reform plan to mandate the No Kill Equation. It took a few short months to achieve a better than 90 percent save rate. Not five years. Not even the two years allotted by the City Council. A great thing happens when you remove a regressive director and appoint new leadership that immediately and comprehensively implements alternatives to killing: the killing stops.

By contrast, Los Angeles recently announced its third five-year No Kill plan, this one spearheaded by Best Friends Animal Society. Los Angeles has a per capita intake rate that is one-fourth that of Washoe County, Nevada, which achieved No Kill within a year of its initiative. New York, with its endless parade of failed five-year plans, has still not achieved it despite having the single largest adoption

market in the nation and a per capita intake rate one-tenth that of Washoe County. Unlike New York, Washoe County is not a center of our nation's wealth. It does not have organizations taking in tens of millions of dollars per year. But New York does. And so does Los Angeles. Like New York, Los Angeles is home to tremendous wealth and resources.

With 9,452 dogs killed and 13,467 cats killed in 2011 in a city of 3.8 million people, a No Kill Los Angeles should be achieved *this year*. In fact, comparing adoption rates with Washoe County and adjusting for population, Los Angeles city shelters should be adopting out 87,000 animals a year, more than total impounds. So why should it take five times as long with a fraction of the problem?

Because five years is a mighty long time—just long enough for memories of bold promises of No Kill to fade and be forgotten—and just long enough for the needless body count of animals to sow such despair that another promised five-year plan will be greeted with enthusiasm and support, enthusiasm and support that will result in lots of donations.

WHAT DO WE WANT? NO KILL
WHEN DO WE WANT IT? NOW!

What About Other Animals Entering Shelters?

NO KILL 2.0

WHEN SAN FRANCISCO launched the No Kill revolution in America, becoming the first community in the nation to end the killing of dogs and cats then defined as "healthy" or "adoptable," the news spread across the country like a wildfire. When Tompkins County ended the killing of all but irremediably suffering animals and vicious dogs—93 percent of all intakes—becoming the first No Kill community in U.S. history, the revolution had crossed the Rubicon. Since that time, the number of communities saving over 90 percent of dogs and cats has grown—communities with even higher save rates than Tompkins County. Some of these communities are reaching save rates as high as 98 percent, saving all dogs and cats but those who are truly beyond our current medical or behavioral ability to rehabilitate. Unfortunately, while San Francisco was pushing

the envelope on dogs and cats in the 1990s, it was ignoring the killing of rabbits, guinea pigs, hamsters, pigeons, bats and other animals. The city shelter continued to put roughly half of them to death. When Tompkins County extended the lifesaving guarantee to sick and injured animals, it did not make the same mistake. The lifesaving guarantee included all species of shelter animals, but this fact seems to have been forgotten or conveniently ignored by other shelters emulating its success.

While the focus on dogs and cats has preoccupied the movement (after all, they make up the majority of animals killed), there are other species of sheltered animals still being killed, even in some communities that boast No Kill-level save rates for dogs and cats. Those communities are certainly not No Kill

from the standpoint of other animals such as rabbits, reptiles and guinea pigs.

Of course, we must have a language for progress and we should celebrate the dozens of communities nationwide saving all healthy and treatable dogs and cats. Just over a decade ago, we had none. They have much to be proud of and much to celebrate, especially given how far they've come. In 2011, Austin, Texas, had the highest save rate of any large, metropolitan area in the United States. Despite roughly 23,000 impounds, they finished the year with a 91 percent save rate for dogs and cats, a monumental achievement and a beacon of hope for advocates in other parts of the country. The claim that this level of lifesaving could not be achieved in a large, urban center was proven false. But while the vast majority of dogs and cats are being saved, Austin is still killing healthy and treatable animals.

Even while we celebrate Austin and other communities which are saving better than 90 percent of dogs and cats, we must urge them to climb higher still, to work diligently and

We must have a language for progress and we should celebrate the many communities nationwide saving all healthy and treatable dogs and cats. But the No Kill journey remains as much a journey in those communities (albeit a shorter one), and not a destination to be used to excuse the killing of those who are not yet being caught by the safety net they've established.

quickly to save not just a greater percentage of dogs and cats, but to ensure that the safety net extends to all animals entering shelters—to rabbits, guinea pigs, mice, hamsters, rats, birds, reptiles and also injured wild animals who often enter these shelters in need of veterinary attention, such as pigeons, crows, opossums, skunks and raccoons.

As success spreads to more and more places, the No Kill movement must not simply sit back and wait for the others to catch up. It must upgrade to No Kill 2.0 with open and loving arms. The animals who are currently falling through the cracks are just as entitled to their lives as dogs and cats and their killing is no less tragic. They also deserve a protective embrace.

A CALL FOR THE WILD

Given that most shelters in the U.S. value animals so little, it should come as no surprise that other "rescue" agencies in other fields do, too. Tragically, many wildlife rehabilitators use variants of the same excuses that rationalize the killing of animals in shelters to rationalize the killing of wild animals. Species bias— that movement's equivalent of sheltering's breed bias—is endemic to wildlife rescue. Rehabilitators who subscribe to this view refuse to treat those animals who do not fall within their limited scope of compassion, either because the animals in question are individuals from a numerous and thriving species, such as rats, pigeons or crows, or because they are cruelly and erroneously perceived as "invasive" (see pages 200-202). The only attention such

rehabilitators are often willing to give these animals is to kill them. Indeed, No Kill shelters which partner with wildlife "rehabbers" should ensure that such groups or individuals do not favor convenience killing over rehabilitation, do not favor death over sanctuary care or adoption for those animals who cannot be returned safety to the wild (a legal option for some species) and do not operate from a self-serving philosophy that equates killing with kindness when the animal in question is not mortally suffering. Ensuring that every animal entering a shelter—whether classified as "domestic" or "wild"—is treated fairly, compassionately and as an individual whose right to life is paramount is, after all, what the No Kill movement is all about.

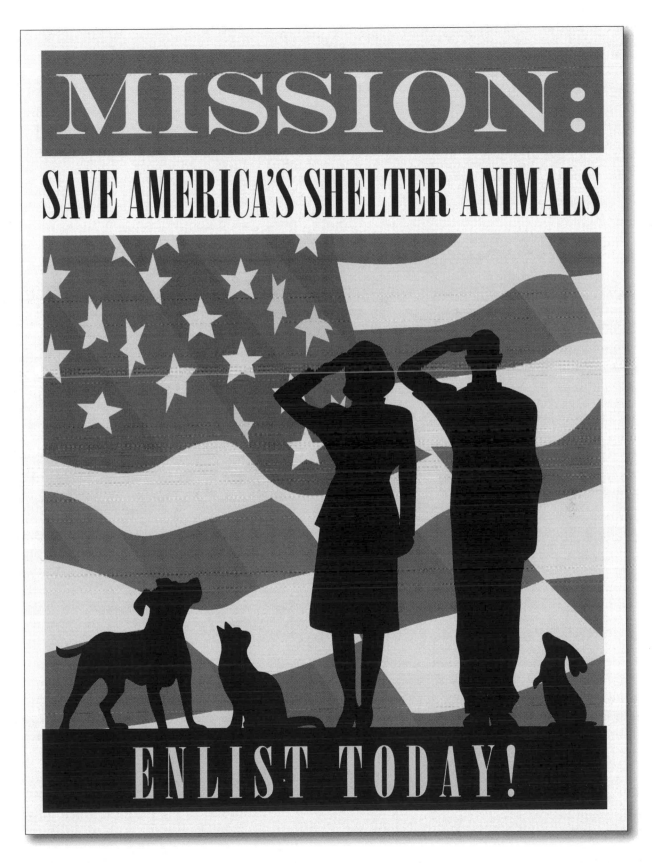

What Would Happen to Animal Shelters If the Large National "Animal Protection" Groups Did Not Exist?

WE WOULD REFORM THEM

In 2010, the Governor of Delaware introduced a bill called the Delaware Companion Animal Protection Act. The proposed law included a rescue rights provision. It made foster care official state policy, required posting "all stray animals on the Internet with sufficient detail to allow them to be recognized and claimed by their owners" and more. Like all legislation, it involved compromise. But it was a fairly strong, comprehensive bill mandating progressive protocols statewide. It was the kind of bill the national animal protection organizations bitterly oppose and are currently fighting elsewhere. And yet, the Delaware law not only passed, it passed *unanimously* in both houses of the state legislature and was signed into law by

the Governor—all without a single voice or vote in opposition.

To legislators, to the Delaware animal-loving public, to the rescue groups which participated in the passing of this bill, there was nothing controversial about it. At hearings and in the media, there was no fear mongering about hoarders, no fear mongering about dog fighting, no fear mongering about overcrowding, no fear mongering about costs, no fear mongering about anything. The bill outlawed some of the most egregious sheltering practices that cause animals to be killed and it mandated common sense procedures that gave them every opportunity for life. And no one thought doing either of those things would be a bad or controversial idea. Why? Because there was no one to confuse them into thinking it was. The large national animal protection groups had no idea this legislation had been introduced.

Wisely, activists who worked with the legislators to draft the language did not publicize their efforts, knowing that to do so would be to invite opposition. And not being informed, the opposition never materialized and the bill sailed through the Delaware legislature effortlessly.

What could we, the American public, accomplish for animals in shelters if the large national animal protection groups didn't continually stop us from doing so? We could protect animals. We could reform shelters. We could orient our nation toward lifesaving.

The Governor of Delaware signs the Companion Animal Protection Act into law. The bill passed the Delaware legislature unanimously and there was no official opposition. Why? None of the national animal protection groups knew about it.

What Would Their Sincerity Look Like?

What does the American public—which funds our national animal protections groups through their philanthropic dollars—have a right to expect? What would the large national groups be doing differently if they truly embraced the goal of an end to shelter killing?

In 2001, Nathan began his job as Executive Director of the Tompkins County SPCA in Ithaca, New York. At the time, the SPCA in Tompkins County was typical of most shelters in the country: it had a poor public image, it killed a lot of animals and it blamed the community for doing so. Once there, however, Nathan announced his lifesaving initiative and asked the community for help. The response was overwhelming. People from all walks of life volunteered, inspired by the goal and eager to assist. Some walked dogs. Others socialized cats. Many people fostered or adopted animals. Veterinarians offered their services at reduced rates or free of charge. Business owners donated products as incentives to adopt. Nathan was not timid about asking for help and most people were incredibly generous and eager to assist. The goal of ending the killing of animals in the shelter became a communitywide effort. And overnight, by harnessing the public's compassion and changing the way the shelter operated, Tompkins County, New York, became the first No Kill community in U.S. history.

Nathan didn't have to convince anyone that this was a good idea or a worthy goal. The people of Tompkins County were ready and willing to make it a reality as soon as he got there. They just needed someone to tell them it was possible and to show them how to do it. And the achievement became a source of community pride, with bumper stickers throughout the county proclaiming, "The Safest Community for Homeless Animals in the U.S." That is the same story in the dozens of communities across the country which have followed the lead of Tompkins County and ended the killing of savable animals in their shelters, too.

The battle to save the lives of shelter animals is not against a callous public indifferent to the plight of animals as we have been told for the past 50 years. The battle is within. The battle is against the cowards of the animal protection movement who refuse to stand up to their colleagues and friends running shelters that are mired in the failed and defunct philosophies that allow—indeed *cause*—killing. The battle is against those who claim to be part of the animal protection movement but fail to recognize the yearly killing of millions of animals as the unnecessary and cruel slaughter it is. It is against those who will not change themselves and to demand that their colleagues change when that is what ethics compel.

Americans have become accustomed to accepting little from the nation's animal protection groups. For decades, HSUS and the ASPCA have not offered much beyond an annual fundraising calendar with pictures of kittens and puppies and platitudes about the human-animal bond. And with no alternative vision to support, the American public has been

> **The more Americans hinge their donations on an organization's sincerity, integrity and performance rather than its superficial label, the sooner our nation's large animal protection groups will be forced to start building, rather than blocking, the road to a brighter future for America's animals.**

donating generously to these organizations, making them rich and powerful while demanding nothing in terms of concrete results in return. Today, many within the animal protection movement have moved beyond the superficial and defeatist hand-wringing of these groups to recognizing that shelter killing is not an inevitability imposed onto helpless shelters, but a problem with a real solution. In light of this good news, what do we—the people who fund these organizations with our philanthropic dollars—have a right to expect? How high should we set the bar? What would the large national groups be doing differently if they truly embraced the goal of an end to shelter killing?

They would report to the public and shelter administrators that No Kill has been achieved, require full implementation of the No Kill Equation and demand the removal of shelter managers who refuse to do so. They would celebrate the communities that have achieved No Kill success so that others could emulate their achievements. They would argue in all publications, advocacy efforts, educational materials, media interactions and conferences that No Kill is the only legitimate standard for

animal sheltering—and must be immediately embraced by all shelters. They would assist activists trying to reform their shelters rather than fighting them—even when doing so means confronting a fractious shelter director. They would stop rewarding failing shelter directors with speaking engagements, with features in their magazines, with national awards, or with hundreds of thousands of dollars to be squandered. And they would invest their huge resources in lobbying for codification of No Kill into law.

With a group like HSUS or the ASPCA leading the charge, communities could very easily outlaw the shelter killing of companion animals. If one of these organizations were to champion such a law in any given community, who would dare oppose? What animal control director could stand up against HSUS or ASPCA political muscle, since that strength is backed by the will of their community? Who would be left to legitimize their refusal to change or to parrot their diversionary platitudes about public irresponsibility, pet overpopulation and the need to kill?

Only time will tell how long allegiance to their kill-oriented colleagues, to their antiquated philosophies and to their failed models will hold them back from the success they and this movement can achieve the moment they decide to embrace it. But of this much we can be certain: it is a generous and animal-loving American public that pays their salaries. And the more Americans hinge their donations on an organization's sincerity, integrity and performance rather than its superficial label, the sooner our nation's large animal protection groups will be forced—by sheer necessity—to start building, rather than blocking, the road to a brighter future for America's animals.

PARDON OUR DUST

FOR THOSE ON THE OUTSIDE LOOKING IN—for a legislator who wants to get support for a bill to save lives, but finds himself battling against the very organizations that should be his most passionate supporters; for a reporter who is featuring a local shelter's high rates of neglect and killing and wants reaction from the large national organizations, but finds herself hearing those organizations deflect criticism; for the public at large which sees a heart-wrenching commercial and wants to help, only to read an article online critical of that organization—the divided nature of the animal protection movement can be frustrating. "Why can't they put aside their differences and get along?" they ask. Indeed, it is tempting to dismiss these conflicts as nothing more than bickering or battles of ego. But they are nothing of the kind. There is a deep and truly contentious dichotomy within the movement today, a difference of philosophy, a clash of values that is considered and conscientious and reflects an irreconcilable divide in who we are and what we believe.

Right now, the animal protection movement is in the throes of an important evolution. What might seem like self-destructive behavior is actually evidence of progress. For the first time in more than a century, some in the animal protection movement have recognized that we have a serious crisis in our nation's shelters—rampant neglect, cruelty and unnecessary killing—which others have chosen to ignore, downplay, excuse and obfuscate. More importantly, we have recognized that there is a solution. The animal protection movement is awaking from a long slumber, and the old-guard animal protection groups which grew very wealthy and powerful in spite of delivering very little progress for shelter animals, are deeply threatened and fighting back. As history shows, this is what happens in every social justice movement and the animal protection movement is no exception.

Social progress is rarely made in a steady, linear fashion. Often, it proceeds in fits and starts, depending on leadership. When a movement is founded by strong, sincere and determined leaders with a clear vision, measurable goals and the will to achieve them, people become inspired and motivated, the movement grows and change ensues. Over time, however, the organizations these leaders founded can become bureaucratic, with none of the zeal that once characterized them. Instead, they become complacent, content to bemoan the sad state of affairs, raise money doing so, but not seek the substantive change that might solve the problem upon which they fundraise.

Since 2001 when the nation's first No Kill community proved that a better, kinder and gentler form of animal sheltering is possible—where shelters are temporary way stations to a better life, rather than death camps—that success has grown into a nascent revolution, one that offers a solution to shelter killing that the large national organizations, for all their decades of existence and all the millions in their bank accounts, never have. Rather, they have assured us that such a

> **We are fighting the same fight as other social reformers in history who, likewise, had to start their work by first cleaning house.**

notion—a No Kill nation—was so impossible, even the act of considering it was of no value; or, in their own words, "not worthy of a passing daydream." As No Kill advocates struggle to bring change to a stagnant movement plagued by calcified, harmful and disproven dogma that, quite literally, kills, we are fighting the same battle as other successful reformers in history who, likewise, had to start their work by first cleaning house.

> **The battle now raging within the animal protection movement is a battle not of degree, but of *kind*—evidence of hopelessly irreconcilable contradictions within the movement itself, one championing death, and the other, life.**

It is the battle William Lloyd Garrison, the founder of the movement to abolish slavery and grant equal rights in the United States, had to fight when he called for immediate emancipation in spite of powerful so-called "anti-slavery" societies that in reality preached racism and condoned the status-quo. It is the same battle faced by the suffragist Alice Paul when she was condemned by the leaders of her movement for the "indecency" of protesting in front of the White House, action which, after years of capitulation to politicians by suffrage leaders, finally ended with the 19th Amendment. And it is the same struggle faced by Martin Luther King, Jr., whose "Letter From Birmingham Jail" to his fellow clergymen revealed his own struggles with the leadership of the civil rights movement, powerful people who were threatened by the urgency and immediacy of his calls for equality and his bold actions to achieve it,

people who had become power brokers selling an agenda for the future, and not today. And so it is with the No Kill cause as well.

When the early founders of the animal protection movement died and their organizations took over the job of killing those they had been formed to protect, a fiery zeal was replaced with a smoldering ember that gave little light or warmth and the humane movement went to sleep. People like the tirelessly devoted ASPCA founder, Henry Bergh, were replaced with individuals who care so little for animals as to allow tremendous cruelty and killing to continue unabated, even when they could use the power their positions afford to stop it. After over 100 years of this antiquated and deadly paradigm, the grassroots of the animal protection movement is finally waking up.

Today, we are a movement in transition, struggling to reach our fullest potential by overcoming internal forces that for years have prevented progress and substantive action behind what until now has been mere empty rhetoric. The battle now raging within the animal protection movement is a battle not of degree, but of *kind*—evidence of hopelessly incompatible contradictions within the movement itself: one championing death, and the other, life. This tension is vital to help the movement reclaim the determination, spirit and goals of its early founders. And it will end only when the need to distinguish between "No Kill" and "the animal protection movement" no longer exists, because both sides will have finally become what they should have been all along: one and the same.

What Can You Do?
FIGHT BACK!
HELP RECLAIM OUR NATION'S SHELTERS & ANIMAL PROTECTION ORGANIZATIONS

THE LARGE ANIMAL PROTECTION GROUPS have never created a single No Kill community in the U.S. because that has never been their goal. But smaller organizations have. Individuals have. If you want to help animals, do it yourself: like the activist who started a No Kill movement in his community where he took on not only an entrenched shelter director, but also the mighty ASPCA—and won. Or the animal lover who became informed about the No Kill movement and immediately walked into his local shelter, announced, "There will be no more killing in the shelter," and then proceeded to make it come true. Or the animal rescuer who singlehandedly created the infrastructure necessary for her local shelter to go No Kill. Or the husband-and-wife team that began marketing shelter animals, resulting in adoption rates of over 95 percent. Or the long-time animal welfare professional who took over a shelter known for cruel treatment of animals and high rates of killing and overnight turned it one of the safest communities for homeless animals in America.

No Kill advocates come from all walks of life. In one Kentucky community, a critical care nurse spearheaded the effort. In a Texas community, a police officer led the charge. In California, it's a college professor. In Nevada, it's a marine working with a corporate retail buyer. Though they have different backgrounds, different skills and a different focus, these activists shared a commitment to end the killing in their community and the determination to see it through. Their story can be your story. You'll be amazed at what you can accomplish if you grant yourself the authority to try.

DO IT YOURSELF

There are many ways to join the No Kill revolution: you can lobby for reform and legislation, you can help elect pro-No Kill candidates to local office, you can start a blog and much more. To download the following free guides that empower YOU to stop the killing, visit nokilladvocacycenter.org.

How Does Your Community's Shelter Measure Up?

How to Determine If Your Shelter Is Doing a Good Job and What To Do If It's Not

The No Kill Revolution Starts with You:

Reforming Animal Control In Your Community Through Effective Political Advocacy

There Ought to Be a Shelter Reform Law:

An Activist's Guide to Passing Humane Legislation

The Companion Animal Protection Act:
Model Legislation to Improve the Performance and Life-Saving of Animal Shelters

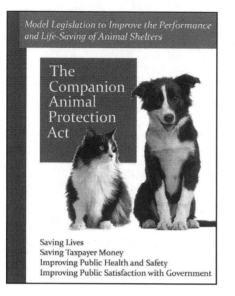

You Can Do It:
Adopt Your Way Out of Killing

Dollars & Sense:
The Economic Benefits of No Kill Animal Control

No Kill 101:
A Primer on No Kill Animal Control Sheltering for Public Officials

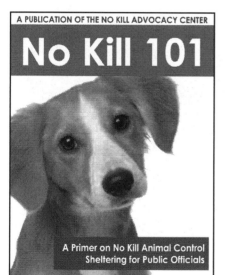

and more at:
nokilladvocacycenter.org

STOP FUNDING THE OPPOSITION

Stop donating to organizations that kill animals and fight No Kill reform efforts. Encourage others to do the same. When donors start giving less and demanding more, change will follow.

LEARN MORE & STAY INFORMED

Knowledge is an essential tool of effective advocacy. For more information, read Nathan's books *Redemption* and *Irreconcilable Differences*. And stay up on the latest No Kill news by following Nathan through his blog (nathanwinograd.com) and on Facebook (facebook.com/nathanwinograd).

JOIN THE REVOLUTION

If every animal shelter in the United States embraced the No Kill philosophy and the programs and services that make it possible, we would save nearly four million animals who are scheduled to die in shelters this year, and the year after that. It is not an impossible dream.

No Kill Advocacy Center

A No Kill nation is within our reach...

nokilladvocacycenter.org

ACKNOWLEDGMENTS
THANK YOU

Thank you to the following people for exposing many of the tragedies highlighted in this book: Shirley Thistlethwaite, John Sibley, Kerry Clair, Bett Sundermeyer, Doug Rae, Mike Fry, Michelle Williamson, P.J. McKosky, Larry Tucker, Ryan Clinton, Valerie Hayes, Amanda St. John and others. Thank you to the following for additional support: Orly Degani, Barbara Saunders and Michael Baus. Any errors are the authors.

ABOUT THE AUTHORS

NATHAN

Nathan is the director of the national No Kill Advocacy Center. He is a graduate of Stanford Law School, and a former criminal prosecutor as well as corporate attorney. He has written animal protection legislation at the state and national levels, has spoken nationally and internationally on animal issues and has created successful No Kill programs in both urban and rural communities. Under his leadership, Tompkins County, New York, became the first No Kill community in the United States. Nathan is the author of *Redemption*, which won five national book awards and is the most acclaimed book on animal shelters ever written. This is his fourth book.

JENNIFER

Jennifer has worked in the animal rights movement for over 20 years. She is a graduate of the University of San Francisco and has a master's degree in the Humanities from Dominican University. She is the co-author (with Nathan) of *All American Vegan*, winner of USA Book News' Best Cookbook in its class for 2011. Jennifer is a founding Board Member of the No Kill Advocacy Center and divides her time between promoting the No Kill philosophy and vegan advocacy. This is her second book.

The Winograds live in the San Francisco Bay Area with their two children, shelter dog, formerly feral cats and rescued pigeons.

Learn more and stay connected with the authors at nathanwinograd.com.

Made in the USA
San Bernardino, CA
12 February 2017